The Collapse of North Korea

Tara O

The Collapse of North Korea

Challenges, Planning and Geopolitics of Unification

Tara O
Pacific Forum Center for Strategic and
International Studies
Honolulu, USA

ISBN 978-1-137-59800-4   ISBN 978-1-137-59801-1 (eBook)
DOI 10.1057/978-1-137-59801-1

Library of Congress Control Number: 2016941865

© The Editor(s) (if applicable) and The Author(s) 2016
The author(s) has/have asserted their right(s) to be identified as the author(s) of this work in accordance with the Copyright, Designs and Patents Act 1988.
This work is subject to copyright. All rights are solely and exclusively licensed by the Publisher, whether the whole or part of the material is concerned, specifically the rights of translation, reprinting, reuse of illustrations, recitation, broadcasting, reproduction on microfilms or in any other physical way, and transmission or information storage and retrieval, electronic adaptation, computer software, or by similar or dissimilar methodology now known or hereafter developed.
The use of general descriptive names, registered names, trademarks, service marks, etc. in this publication does not imply, even in the absence of a specific statement, that such names are exempt from the relevant protective laws and regulations and therefore free for general use.
The publisher, the authors and the editors are safe to assume that the advice and information in this book are believed to be true and accurate at the date of publication. Neither the publisher nor the authors or the editors give a warranty, express or implied, with respect to the material contained herein or for any errors or omissions that may have been made.

Cover illustration: © Melisa Hasan

Printed on acid-free paper

This Palgrave Macmillan imprint is published by Springer Nature
The registered company is Macmillan Publishers Ltd. London

*To my grandmother and my parents
and all those hoping for Korean unification*

Acknowledgments

I am grateful to numerous friends and colleagues. In particular, Bruce Bechtol gave me the encouragement I needed to take this work to the publishing stage. Kongdan "Katy" Oh has for many years been a mentor and a friend. James K. Galbraith has been instrumental in helping me develop this work, as well as Bobby Inman and James Steinberg. I also owe a debt to those among Korea and Asia specialists, officials, and friends, who have been supportive: Chan-il An, Guy Arrigoni, John Burzynski, Robert Collins, Ralph Cossa, Robert Dujarric, L. Gordon Flake, Brad Glosserman, Mike Green, Steve Herman, Peter Humphrey, Mike Green, Mike Keefe, Hugo Wheegook Kim, Jae-bum Kim, Suk-woo Kim, Andre Lankov, David Maxwell, Derek Mitchell, Brian Myers, Chris Nelson, William Newcomb, Sang-woo Rhee, Kihl-jae Ryoo, Greg Scarlatoiu, Daniel Shearf, LJ Singleton, Scott Snyder, Steve Tharp, and Jacco Zwetsloot. If I have left anyone out, it is due to my oversight, as so many people have provided support through this project. Lastly, to my family who has always been there for me, especially my husband Jonathan Mueller, who has consistently provided me with love and moral support.

The views expressed in this work are solely my own. It does not reflect the policy or position of any U.S. government entity or other organizations with which I have been affiliated.

Additionally, the views expressed by the interviewees in this work are their own and do not reflect the policy or position of the organizations with which they are affiliated.

Contents

1	**Introduction**	1
	1 Purpose of the Book	2
	2 North Korea's Class System of Songbun	3
	3 North Korea's Paradox	5
	4 Structure of the Book	8
2	**The Unification Scenarios and Cost**	9
	1 Gradual and Peaceful (Confederation) Unification	10
	1.1 Analysis: Gradual and Peaceful Process	11
	2 Unification Through War	14
	2.1 Analysis: War	15
	3 Collapse and Absorption	17
	3.1 Analysis: Collapse and Absorption	17
	4 Unification Cost	19
	5 Summary	21
3	**Thinking About Collapse: Indicators and Triggers**	25
	1 Indicators of Collapse	26
	1.1 Economic System and the Provision for Basic Needs	26
	1.2 External Assistance	29
	1.3 Information Control	31
	1.4 Leadership Succession and Power Consolidation	33
	1.5 Elites	34
	1.6 Defectors	35

		2	Triggers	36
			2.1 Elite Disaffection and Factionalism	36
			2.2 Famine and Mass Migration	38
			2.3 Mass Opposition	38

4 Geopolitical Landscape and Regional Bilateral Issues — 45
   1 Geopolitical Landscape — 47
   2 Deepening Economic Relations — 50
   3 Regional Powers' National Interests — 54
     3.1 United States — 54
     3.2 China — 56
     3.3 Japan — 60
     3.4 Russia — 64
     3.5 South Korea — 66
   4 Bilateral Issues — 68
     4.1 United States–South Korea — 68
     4.2 China–South Korea — 72
     4.3 Japan–South Korea — 75
   5 Areas for Future Cooperation — 77
     5.1 Pre-collapse: Plan and Coordinate — 77
     5.2 North Korea's Nuclear Weapons Program — 79
     5.3 Stability and Economic Development — 82
   6 Summary — 84

5 Preparing for and Responding to Collapse — 93
   1 Control of Nuclear Weapons — 95
     1.1 Nuclear Weapons Accountability — 96
     1.2 Nunn-Lugar Act (Cooperative Threat Reduction Program) — 97
   2 Disorder in the Immediate Aftermath of Collapse — 97
     2.1 System of Control — 97
     2.2 Stability Operations — 99
     2.3 Rescue Operation: Political Camp Prisoners — 100
   3 Providing for Basic Needs — 100
     3.1 Lack of Basic Goods and Services — 100
     3.2 Basic Services Provision — 100

	4	Migration	102
		4.1 Short-term Migration	103
		4.2 Medium- to Long-Term Migration	104
		4.3 Education and Retraining	105
	5	Elites	105
	6	Infrastructure	106
	7	Unemployment (Medium- to Long-Term)	107
	8	Social Integration	108
		8.1 Defectors in South Korea	108
		8.2 Education	110
	9	Military Integration	110
	10	Economic Development	112
		10.1 Unification Cost and Financing	112
		10.2 North's Labor	114
		10.3 North's Mineral Wealth	114
	11	Reforestation and Flood Mitigation	115
	12	Developing the DMZ	116

6 Summary   123
1 Unification Scenarios   124
2 Collapse Indicators and Triggers   125
   2.1 Economic System   125
   2.2 External Assistance for Sustenance   125
   2.3 Information Control   126
   2.4 Leadership Succession and Power Consolidation   126
   2.5 Elite Disaffection and Factionalism   126
   2.6 Defectors   126
3 The Roles of the Regional Powers   127
   3.1 National Interests   127
   3.2 Regional Cooperation   128
   3.3 Nuclear Weapons and Regional Relations   129
4 Preparing for and Responding to Collapse   129
   4.1 Control of Nuclear Weapons   130
   4.2 Disorder in the Immediate Aftermath of Collapse   130
   4.3 Providing for Basic Needs   130
   4.4 Migration   130
   4.5 Elites   131
   4.6 Infrastructure   131

  4.7 *Unemployment*   131
  4.8 *Social Integration*   132
  4.9 *Military Integration*   132
  4.10 *Economic Development*   132
  4.11 *Other Efforts*   133
 5 *Conclusion*   133

Appendix 1   135
 Unification and South Korea   135
 Unification and Reunification   135
 Korean Names and Spelling   135
 Various Ways to Express "Korea"   136

Bibliography   137

Index   159

List of Abbreviations and Acronyms

ADB	Asian Development Bank
ADIZ	air defense identification zone
ARF	ASEAN Regional Forum
ASEAN	Association of Southeast Asian Nations
CFC	Combined Forces Command
CTR	Cooperative Threat Reduction
DMZ	demilitarized zone
DOD	Department of Defense
DOE	Department of Energy
DPRK	Democratic People's Republic of Korea (North Korea)
DVD	digital video disc
FTA	Free Trade Agreement
FY	Fiscal Year
GATT	General Agreement on Tariffs and Trade
GDP	Gross Domestic Product
GIC	Gaesong Industrial Complex
GNI	Gross National Income
IAEA	International Atomic Energy Agency
IFI	International Financial Institution
IMF	International Monetary Fund
IMS	Interagency Management System
JCS	Joint Chiefs of Staff
KORCOM	Korea Command
KORUS	Korea–U.S.
KPA	Korean People's Army
KWP	Korean Workers' Party
MPS	Ministry of People's Security

MSC	Military Security Command
MSS	Ministry of State Security
NATO	North Atlantic Treaty Organization
NGO	nongovernmental organization
NVA	National People's Army
OPCON	Operational Control
PAP	People's Armed Police
PDS	Public Distribution System
PLA	People's Liberation Army
POSCO	Pohang Steel Company
ROK	Republic of Korea (South Korea)
S/CRS	U.S. State Department's Office of the Coordinator for Reconstruction and Stabilization
SAR	Special Administrative Region
SOE	state-owned enterprise
SOF	Special Operations Forces
TAP	Transition Assistance Program
TKR	Trans-Korea Railway
TSR	Trans-Siberian Railway
UNCMAC	UN Command Military Armistice Commission
UNHCR	UN High Commissioner for Refugees
USFK	U.S. Forces Korea
WMD	weapons of mass destruction
WTO	World Trade Organization

List of Figures

Fig. 4.1 Map of Northeast Asia 46
Fig. 5.1 Korea at Night: Dark North Korea, Bright South Korea (Satellite imagery of Korea at night, Image Caption ISS038-E-038300 (January 30, 2014). Image courtesy of the Earth Science and Remote Sensing Unit, NASA Johnson Space Center, http://eol.jsc.nasa.gov/SearchPhotos/photo.pl?mission=ISS038&roll=E&frame=38300 (accessed December 11, 2014) 101

List of Tables

Table 2.1	South–North Gap (2014) and West–East Gap (1989)	19
Table 3.1	North Korea's top trade partners (2014, estimated)	30
Table 3.2	North Korean defectors to South Korea	35
Table 4.1	Population (2014 estimate)	48
Table 4.2	Gross Domestic Product (GDP 2014)	48
Table 4.3	Military (active duty) (2014)	49
Table 4.4	Military expenditure (2014)	50
Table 4.5	South Korea's top trading partners (2014 estimate)	51
Table 4.6	China's top trading partners (2014 estimate)	52
Table 4.7	Japan's top trading partners (2014 estimate)	52
Table 4.8	U.S. trade balance, by partner country (2014)	55
Table 4.9	Major foreign holders of U.S. Treasury securities (April 2015)	55

CHAPTER 1

Introduction

Abstract A collapsed North Korea would be a watershed event, unleashing dynamics that would redefine the geopolitical landscape and test the future of the region. The regional powers—South Korea, China, Japan, Russia, and the United States—are ill prepared to handle short-and long-term challenges to their vital national interests emerging from a collapsed North Korea. If Pyongyang collapses, the result could be mass migration, mass suffering due to political, institutional, and economic instability, and uncontrolled nuclear weapons. The regional powers should anticipate several possible scenarios and develop plans to mitigate negative consequences.

Following the fall of the Berlin Wall in 1989 and the subsequent German unification in 1990, the conventional wisdom was that North Korea or the Democratic People's Republic of Korea (DPRK) would also fall shortly and Korea would be unified. Two and a half decades later, North Korea still stands, with the third-generation Kim succession, nuclear weapons program, and a dysfunctional economy. Despite defying experts' predictions of its collapse for so long, specialists continue to question how long the regime can last. North Korea's economy is in shambles. Its central planning and distribution system has failed to provide the basic needs of its people. Necessity gave rise to black markets, but the regime is not prepared to fully embrace the markets. To remedy its economic problems, North Korea must reform and open up its economy; yet to do so could invite external information that might compete with the official narrative.

© The Editor(s) (if applicable) and The Author(s) 2016
Tara O, *The Collapse of North Korea*,
DOI 10.1057/978-1-137-59801-1_1

The resulting loss of faith among the population would challenge the regime's legitimacy and its firm grip on power.

A collapsed North Korea would be a watershed event, unleashing dynamics that would redefine the geopolitical landscape and test the future of the region. The regional powers—South Korea, China, Japan, Russia, and the U.S.—are ill prepared to handle short- and long-term challenges to their vital national interests emerging from a collapsed North Korea. If Pyongyang collapses, the result could be mass migration, mass suffering due to instability, and uncontrolled nuclear weapons. Such a volatile situation could halt or even reverse the progress of this dynamic and prosperous region, with widespread international implications. However, the regional powers are ill prepared for such a contingency. Each is focused on a different aspect of the potential disaster. China is concerned about the mass refugee flow from North Korea and the loss of a buffer state, and it therefore continues to support the North Korean regime. Despite Pyongyang's continued irritation, including nuclear and missile tests, Beijing provides aid, trade, and political support to sustain the Kim regime. South Korea or the Republic of Korea (ROK) fears the high unification cost as well as the influx of North Koreans, and so desires slow integration with North Korea. South Korea under presidents Park Geun-hye and Lee Myung-bak has begun to address the issue, which was a taboo under the two previous presidents. Meanwhile, the U.S. is focused on the control of nuclear weapons and materials.

The long-term development of North Korea will also require regional and international coordination. The regional powers should anticipate several possible scenarios and develop plans to mitigate negative consequences. Such a forward-looking approach would help establish a solid foundation to manage the challenges of the most likely contingencies and set the stage for a more stable and prosperous future for the region.

1   Purpose of the Book

The purpose of this book is to highlight the rising risk of North Korea's collapse and to urge the neighboring countries to plan and prepare for such a cataclysmic event. It begins by describing various unification scenarios, of which collapse is one. The study explains the conditions affecting the stability of North Korea's regime, identifies the regional issues that could affect cooperation, and explores ways to respond to the challenges of collapse.

The majority of the unification literature focuses on unification scenarios and costs. Due to the political sensitivities of the regional powers and

North Korean regime's longevity compared to the former Soviet Union and Central and East European states, a regime collapse has not been a main focus of literature for some time. Recently, there has been a greater number of collapse or contingency studies. This book addresses various challenges of unification in detail, with an emphasis on planning and preparing. It also describes regional powers' bilateral concerns because their potential impacts on the strategic calculations regarding unification.

The North Korean regime is a system of government that controls all aspects of public and private life, including people's thoughts and attitudes. The leader has the absolute power and dedication to him is all-important. Due to a strong cult of personality propagated by the state's myth-making machine and enforced by the state security apparatus, the leader is elevated to a godlike status of a theocratic state.[1] The Korean Workers' Party transmits ruler Kim's ambitions and will to the entire society, and the people are expected not only to adhere to them, but also to support them enthusiastically. The regime forces people to understand their own life experience by conforming to the official doctrine. The regime limits people's self-realization and autonomy. This effort for total control by repressing the population is a crucial flaw of the system and it is unsustainable.

2   NORTH KOREA'S CLASS SYSTEM OF *SONGBUN*

The North Korean regime created a class system to control every aspect of human life to further the political objectives of the ruling elites. North Korea's current structure is not so much a Marxist-socialist system as a system consisting of three classes based on *Songbun*, which is determined by heredity and loyalty. The *Songbun* classification system is a state-sanctioned discriminatory system that categorizes every North Korean based on the position, status, and occupation of not only the person in question but also those of his/her parents and extended family.

> Everyone in North Korea seems to know pretty much what his songbun is, although there are no precise gradations and no official notice is ever given. At every important juncture in life—at the end of middle school and high school, with admission or nonadmissions to college, entry or nonentry into the army, admission or nonadmission to the party, approval or nonapproval for marriage, assignment to a job, or transfer into or out of the city or into or out of a collective farm—it is fairly obvious whether one's songbun is good or bad.[39]

Every North Korean is investigated and classified into one of three broad groups of loyalty—the core class, the wavering class, and the hostile class—which are further divided into 51 subgroups.[40] The system "creates a form of slave labor for a third of North Korea's population of 23 million citizens and loyalty-bound servants out of the remainder."[41]

The core group consists of those most loyal to the Kim regime, including those who were factory workers, poor farmers, office clerks, soldiers, and revolutionaries (anti-Japanese) in the pre-liberation period, as well as the families of those who were killed during the Korean War.[42] The core class comprises about 20–25% of the population, of which about two million are estimated to be the top cadre serving in key positions that sustain and protect the regime.[43] In return for loyalty, the core receives the best housing, food, jobs, education, medical care, and other perquisites.

The ordinary or wavering-class members are those whose loyalty is questionable, but can potentially be won over by constant ideological indoctrination. This class of people comprises 45–55% of North Korea's population and includes merchants, farmers, and service workers. The ordinary citizens live on luck, effort, and bribery. They may get extra food or gifts on special days, such as Kim Jong-un's birthday. The regime is aware that this class of ordinary citizens should not become discontented to the point of opposing the regime, as it comprises the majority of the public.

The hostile group, about 20–25%, is considered "suspicious" and includes those whose family members were wealthy landlords, merchants, and religious leaders, and are therefore considered counter to the socialist revolution and disloyal to the regime. Seen as the class enemy by the Kim regime, they are subjected to close scrutiny by the regime's extensive security apparatus and heavily discriminated against regarding food, housing, medical care, education, employment, military service, and marriage. Members of the hostile group fend for themselves in the countryside.

Outside the three main groups are some 200,000 people in concentration camps, whose existence North Korea denies.[44] Thomas Hobbes' portrayal of life as "poor, nasty, brutish, and short" describes this class rather accurately. The existence of political prison camps and the atrocities committed there by the regime are highlighted in the Kirby Report, the investigative work of the UN Human Rights Council's Commission of Inquiry on Human Rights in the DPRK, published in February 2014. Among various disturbing findings in the report are the standing orders to kill those held in the camps in the event of an armed conflict or revolution to eliminate the evidence of the camps' existence.[45]

Party cadre and security officials keep detailed records of everyone and continually update the records.⁴⁶ Although it is easy for one's *songbun* to be downgraded, it is much more difficult to improve one's *songbun*. Downgrading occurs for lack of ideological fervor, marrying someone with bad *songbun*, or even for being related to someone who commits a crime. Crimes include leaving North Korea or not revering the Kim family enough.

Initially, it was possible to hide one's *songbun* by concealing that the grandfather or an uncle was a doctor, Christian minister, or landowner. However, the North Korean regime conducted full-scale secret background investigations in the late 1960s, with repeated probes to weed out any substantial opposition to the Kim rule.⁴⁷ The regime implements the social stratification through various security organizations. The Ministry of Public Security (MPS)'s *Resident Registration Project Reference Manual* describes how to investigate North Koreans' *songbun*, with each section beginning with Kim Il-sung's and Kim Jong-il's personal instructions on the significance of differentiating people on the basis of loyalty.⁴⁸ The ordinary class, armed with information, could pose a potent challenge to the current regime if they are able to organize and demand changes. The regime will need to continue to co-opt the core class for support. To extract loyalty, Kim Jong-un needs resources to continuously provide perquisites to this group. The core group members are probably better informed about the outside world than the ordinary class because they have access to more goods and information; at the same time, the core benefits most from the current system. If the benefits stop, then this class could also present a challenge to the current regime, especially if their personal security concerns are not addressed.

3 NORTH KOREA'S PARADOX

The regime enforces the totalitarian, autocratic, and theocratic state through fear and monopoly of information. It employs a secret police apparatus and a network of informants to constantly surveil the population, violate human rights, and control the flow of information.² The state-sanctioned discrimination system of *Songbun* also extends the state's control by classifying the population by loyalty level, which is based on family background. The artificial division creates a small group of people whose loyalty is bought with privileges. The regime, with information monopoly, creates official stories and blocks outside information which competes with the official versions. Propaganda portrays the Kims, whether it is Kim Il-sung, Kim Jong-il, or Kim Jong-un, as nurturing leaders who protect and provide for the people.[3] Such unchecked propaganda provides legitimacy and engenders strong faith in the leader and the system, one of the critical components for regime survival. Total control of the society is one of the reasons the regime can maintain political continuity, despite economic hardship.[4] However, information is seeping into North Korea because of markets.

Markets emerged in the mid-1990s to cope with famine. The state no longer had enough food to distribute through its Public Distribution System (PDS). Hungry, people turned elsewhere for food. Markets emerged. Most of the small-scale private economic activities are illegal or unofficial, but they have grown and spread to various places in North Korea. In addition to food, portable media players, South Korean drama DVDs, and tunable radios are also found on the market, bringing in additional information.[5]

Outside information broadens people's perspectives and can change people's hearts and minds regarding the leader and the system. It provides a window to alternate lives. While such changes may or may not lead to mass insurrection or a *coup d'état*, the regime fears such possibilities.

North Korea shows increasing signs of systemic weaknesses. North Korea is plagued by floods and famine, faces chronic food shortages, and has a bleak economy. The regime continues to prioritize weapons and the extravagant lifestyle of the leaders over meeting the basic needs of its people. Its nuclear weapons program and repressive system have isolated the regime in an increasingly globalized world. If the government refuses to open up and reform, its inability weakens its legitimacy and the system could collapse and precipitate the regime's demise.

On the other hand, the openness and reform necessary to fix these problems would allow people access to outside information and greater self-sufficiency, both of which are threats to the regime. The outside information would compete with the regime's version of the truth, leading to questions about the regime itself, leaving skeptic, rather than loyal and submissive, subjects. Greater self-sufficiency would reduce reliance on the state, which would also degrade the regime's control over the population. Together, they would undermine domestic support and shake the foundation of the DPRK regime.

The North Korean predicament can be summarized as a tension between the need to reform its unsuccessful economic system and the fear that the mechanism for reform, greater openness, would sow seeds of discontent and create domestic political instability.

Instead of implementing genuine reform to fix its economy, the North Korean regime relies on *Juche* (self-sufficiency), taking an isolationist stance in the age of globalism, and the policy of *Songun* (military first), directing a significant part of the country's resources to guns and lavish leadership lifestyle rather than rice. The Party Central Committee in 2013 adopted a new political and economic policy of *Byungjin* of simultaneously developing nuclear weapons and the economy, which harkens back to 1962 when Kim Il-sung's *Byungjin* line touted the simultaneous development of the economy and national defense. In reality, Kim Il-sung's *Byungjin* leaned heavily toward the military and Kim Jong-un's *Byungjin* focused more on nuclear weapons development, rather than the economy, which has already isolated the country.[6] With greater international pressure for interconnectivity, operating in a relatively isolated manner is harmful to the economy.[7] Despite *Juche*, North Korea has been dependent on outside help for decades, from the former Soviet Union in earlier days, the U.S. and South Korea during the Sunshine Policy era, and China more recently.

As part of *Songun*, North Korea has pursued a nuclear weapons and missile program. North Korea is trying to win concessions from the international community, including monetary and food aid and a security guarantee, a major step that would boost the regime's domestic legitimacy. Pyongyang's nuclear weapons program and delivery system are used to gain leverage for this purpose.

North Korea's best course of action, if it is to preserve its current regime, as Marcus Noland notes, is to muddle along,[8] attempting to balance the benefits of openness and reform with the costs of such actions while simultaneously trying to extract concessions from foreign powers. Because the broken system's fundamental problems have not been addressed, it is unclear how long the Pyongyang regime can muddle through. At some point, the cracks in this brittle system may prove too many and too deep, precipitating a collapse and a nightmare scenario for the region.

In the international community, discussions of North Korea's possible collapse are fueled by its continued weak economy, information seeping into the country, chronic inability to feed its population, and concerns over Kim Jong-un's hold on power. If North Korea collapses, it would destabilize the region and fundamentally affect the surrounding powers. It would likely lead to a reunification of the two Koreas and extensively alter the strategic landscape of Northeast Asia.

Whatever the probability of regime collapse, the potential for such large-scale disruption is too serious to ignore. This author, therefore, argues that the regional powers—South Korea, the U.S., and China especially, and also Japan and Russia—prepare for managing the aftermath of North Korea's collapse because their security and prosperity would be significantly affected by the collapse.

4   Structure of the Book

After reviewing various unification scenarios and costs in Chap. 2, Chap. 3 further examines and analyzes indicators and triggers of North Korea's potential collapse. Chapter 4 focuses on the regional powers of the U.S., China, Japan, Russia, and South Korea, studying their national interests, issues to be resolved with Korea, areas of cooperation, and key challenges. In Chap. 5, the author considers numerous challenges posed by a collapse and explores potential mitigating responses. High-priority issues include nuclear weapons loss, disorder, and mass migration. In the long run, economic development would be crucial. To set the foundation for long-term regional stability and prosperity, the regional powers should cooperate on planning and execution of stability and development efforts.

Notes

1. Sang-woo Rhee, *Bukhan Jeongchi Byeoncheon Shinjeongchejeui Jinhwa gwajeong (Evolution of North Korean Theocracy)*, Doseo Chulpan Oreum: Seoul, 2014, 109.
2. For details on how North Korea controls people through a system of fear, see Ken E. Gause. *Coercion, Control, Surveillance and Punishment: An Examination of the North Korean Police State*, Washington, DC: Committee for Human Rights in North Korea, 2012.
3. B.R. Myers, *The Cleanest Race*. (New York: Melville House, 2010), 34–36.
4. Ken E. Gause. *Coercion, Control, Surveillance and Punishment*, 10.
5. Lucy Craft, "TV dramas from South saturates black market in North Korea, bringing hope, and risk," *CBS News*, December 10, 2013, http://www.cbsnews.com/news/north-koreas-dangerous-addiction-to-daytime-tv/.
6. So Yeol Kim, "Byungjin Lives a Kim Seeks Guns and Butter" *DailyNK*, 1 April 2013, http://www.dailynk.com/english/read.php?cataId=nk01700&num=10453.
7. Stephen Bradner, "North Korea's Strategy," in *Competitive Strategies*, Arlington, Virginia, NPEC/Institute for National Security Studies, Army War College, June 12–14, 2000, 4.
8. Marcus Noland, *Avoiding the Apocalypse* (Washington, DC: Institute for International Economics, 2000), 333.

CHAPTER 2

The Unification Scenarios and Cost

Abstract A review of various unification scenarios provides a broader context for analysis. The three most common types of scenarios are peaceful and gradual unification, war leading to unification, and the collapse of North Korea and unification by default. Some scenarios such as war might be combined with the collapse case, which makes understanding the other scenarios pertinent. There are costs associated with these scenarios. And since these costs and the means to meet these expenses are major parts of unification planning, this chapter will also review various unification cost estimates.

The unification of the Korean Peninsula is inevitably linked to North Korea's demise, and numerous experts have presented alternative unification scenarios. The three most common types of scenarios are peaceful and gradual unification, war leading to unification, and the collapse of North Korea and unification by default. These scenarios are known by other names, and there are other scenarios in addition to these three common ones. The gradual long-term approach envisions the two Koreas starting with greater exchanges. They might then form a confederation in which the two systems peacefully coexist. The third stage is unification, but some see confederation as the final stage. The war scenario could occur with or without DPRK's collapse. In war scenarios, North Korea initiates the attack, and the victor is usually seen as the combined ROK–U.S. forces. The collapse scenario centers on the concept of North Korea's collapse and its subsequent absorption by South Korea.

Costs vary by different scenarios and methods. Some unification costs are estimated based on the German case. Since these costs and the means to meet such expenses are major parts of unification planning, this chapter will also review various unification cost estimates.

While this study focuses on the collapse of North Korea, a review of various unification scenarios could provide a broader context for analysis. Some scenarios such as war might be combined with the collapse case, which makes understanding other scenarios pertinent. The collapse scenario has been less frequently discussed until recently as the Pyongyang regime has shown resilience over time. Accordingly, several unification scenarios are examined in this chapter.

1 Gradual and Peaceful (Confederation) Unification

Gradual unification refers to a peaceful integration of South Korea and North Korea and is sometimes referred to as the "soft landing" scenario. This scenario anticipates a lengthy period of peaceful coexistence, greater inter-Korean interaction, and slow structural changes along the lines of one state, but two systems and two governments.[1]

This scenario is based on both Seoul and Pyongyang undergoing philosophical changes in attitudes and assumptions about each other and both instituting a series of interim steps needed for larger-scale changes necessary for unification.[2] The interim steps include both parties accepting each other as equal and legal entities, and negotiating a mutually acceptable and binding political settlement.

The main driver for such an outcome would be economic activities, such as trade, investment, and joint ventures, to create functional interaction among individuals, firms, and various other entities in order to provide the foundation for political and social unity.[3] This gradual and peaceful view is similar to the confederation scenario.

The assumption for confederation is not a sudden collapse of North Korea, but rather gradual leadership and systemic changes, which would reduce inter-Korean tensions. The concept of confederation has evolved over time as well. Initially, the North's idea of confederation was more like the "federation" of a unitary, centralized system. South Korea considered a much looser structure. In fact, the Rho Tae-woo administration in the late 1980s used the term "commonwealth" rather than confederation.[4]

North Korea, with greater uncertainties and economic difficulties, saw confederation as the final stage, with separate regimes existing peacefully for an indefinite period.[5]

1.1   Analysis: Gradual and Peaceful Process

The first scenario is the longer-term outcome favored by South Korea, especially during Kim Dae-jung's Sunshine Policy period, because it is deemed the least destabilizing. Other scenarios have more uncertainties and conjure up the daunting nature and exorbitant costs of unification. Norman Levin and Yong-Sup Han in *Sunshine in Korea* describe the Sunshine Policy of engaging North Korea based on the premise that North Korea will not collapse, this engagement being the only viable alternative to high tensions and conflict on the Korean Peninsula.[6] To facilitate greater interaction, Kim Dae-jung's administration encouraged economic exchanges and cooperation. Kim also hoped to create an environment for North Korea to reform on its own. During this period, many South Koreans no longer talked of unification, but rather of exchanges and cooperation.[7] The policy focused on interactions, rather than merger or unification. Exchanges and cooperation were the initial steps toward confederation.

Pyongyang also supported the idea of confederation. In the *Confederation as an Approach to the Unification of the Motherland*, a collection of Kim Il-sung's speeches and thoughts on the topic, Kim acknowledges the practical nature of confederation as a step toward unification. In his speech to the Supreme People's Council in 1962, Kim Il-sung suggested a confederation in which South Korea's current system would be left intact and each side remains independent of each other, with no interference in internal politics.[8] Thus, North Korea under Kim Jong-il responded positively when Kim Dae-jung announced his intention of peaceful coexistence in his March 1990 Berlin Declaration.[9] In 2000, Kim Dae-jung and Kim Jong-il met for the first ever summit between the two Koreas to sign the June 15 Joint Declaration to improve inter-Korean relations. They agreed to start exchanges of separated family members, to promote balanced economic development through economic cooperation, to encourage exchanges and cooperation in society, culture, sports, health, and the environment, and to establish a dialogue between the two governments.[10]

The governments held talks on ministerial, military, economic, and social issues accompanied by exchanges in the media, arts and culture, sports, education, and religion. Of note is the resumption of family reunions (held only once previously in 1985) that reunited over 1,000 families separated by war and partition.[11] Economic cooperation entailed reconnecting the railroad and roads along the eastern and western corridors through the demilitarized zone (DMZ). The roads on both coasts have been connected, but North Korea refuses to connect the east coast rail road. Other pillars of economic cooperation are the promotion of Mount Geumgang tourism and the establishment of the Gaesong Industrial Complex (GIC), both in North Korea. Mount Geumgang is famous for its scenic beauty and has a deep psychological symbolism for Koreans. Gaesong, a once ancient capital, also has military importance; a North Korean military unit moved to the rear of Gaesong to accommodate the building of the business complex. Gaesong is conveniently located near the DMZ and the South Korean cities of Seoul (the source of capital) and Incheon (international shipping). In addition to military talks, the road connection required the removal of mines in parts of the DMZ, which was completed in 2002.[12] South Korea provided significant amounts of food, fertilizer, and other aid to North Korea, including millions of dollars for the Mount Geumgang tourism project and the GIC.[13] The problem, however, was reciprocity and further hostilities.

South Korea's actions were not matched by North Korea. Thousands of South Korean tourists and business workers went to North Korea, but contact with average North Koreans was prohibited, and while some separated families meet in family reunions, North Korea does not allow home visits or mail exchanges. The killing of a South Korean tourist by a North Korean soldier in 2008 put a halt on Mount Geumgang tourism. In March 2010, the relations took a further nosedive when North Korea sank South Korean corvette *Cheonan*, which killed 46 South Korean sailors. In November of the same year, DPRK shelled *Yeonpyeong Island*, an island in the West Sea, which killed four South Koreans including two civilians and destroyed property. Korea specialist Andrei Lankov doubts the effectiveness of the South Korean approach under the Sunshine Policy, arguing that South Korea seemed to be avoiding the cost of unification by keeping the North Korean regime afloat through large amounts of aid while trying to encourage North Korea to reform.[14] South Korea's engagement policy was unsuccessful at building trust, and North Korea continues to deny recognition of South Korea. Another Korea specialist notes that the Ministry of Unification during the Sunshine period should have been nicknamed the "Ministry of Division," as its education efforts centered on making the South Korean public fear the social and economic costs of unification.[15] According to senior-ranking North Korean defector Hwang Jang-yup, the North's confederation plan is a political cover to keep the international community off guard while sowing chaos in order to lead South Korea to a revolution and a new socialist government, which would then cooperate with the Pyongyang regime to unify the country.[16]

Aid without reciprocity has been halted since the installation of South Korea's president Lee Myung-bak. With his emphasis on reciprocity and transparency as well as resolving the nuclear issue first, the inter-Korea exchanges have come to a virtual standstill. Mount Geumgang tourism was scotched after a North Korean soldier shot and killed a female tourist in July 2008 and Gaesong's business operations were halted by South Korea in response to North Korea's missile test in February 2016. Gaesong Industrial Park was shut down in the past by North Korean government. The activities at Gaesong significantly decreased after North Korea expelled South Korean officials from the complex in 2010 and blocked the commuter road. Lee conditioned considerable economic, humanitarian, and political benefits on denuclearization and the opening of North Korea, promising to boost the per capita income of North Koreans to $3,000 in 10 years.[17] Numerous inter-Korean activities and assistance to the North slowed down or came to a standstill after North Korea's attacks on *Yeonpyeong* Island.

Soon after Park Geun-hye became South Korea's president in 2013, the activities at *Gaesong* complex ground to a halt after North Korea yet again expelled South Korean officials and blocked the road in addition to removing all 53,000 North Korean workers from the complex. The annual wage of $90 million was paid directly to the North Korean government, rather than to the workers.[18] While the North Korean government was benefitting from the arrangement, it expressed anger at the South Korean media's depiction of the complex as a cash cow for the North Korean regime. Although Gaesong Industrial Park reopened in September of the same year, it challenged the new president, who pledged to enhance inter-Korean relations. Park's North Korean policy pursues a trust-building process and the Dresden Initiative. They both focus on a step-by-step, principled approach toward inter-Korean cooperation, while maintaining strong deterrence. Her policy is similar to that of her predecessor Lee Myong-bak in that it focuses on principles and strong deterrence, but it differs in that it focuses on small and specific projects that are more manageable to build trust.[19] Pyongyang has criticized her policy as well as previous ones, including the Sunshine Policy, as one that attempts to unify Korea through absorption. The Park administration replies that a South Korea–led absorption of North Korea is undesirable due to high costs and side effects, and that "the unification that we pursue is a peaceful one, mutually agreed upon by both South and North Korea."[20]

South Korean leaders have discussed gradual peaceful unification. This approach may prove more difficult than anticipated, especially since North Korea is unwilling to cooperate. Additionally, due to its long time horizon of several decades or more, it is possible that other events could lead to unification faster, as described in the war and collapse scenarios below.

2 Unification Through War

In the conflict scenario, DPRK's military attacks the combined ROK and U.S. forces. The current strategic context is dramatically different than the one that allowed North Korea to attack South Korea in 1950. South Korea is no longer weak, the Soviet Union and China are unlikely to support North Korean aggression, and the commitment from the U.S. is strong and unambiguous. However, DPRK still has a formidable destructive capability and its basic military objectives have not changed. Its objectives are to maintain military capabilities for wartime strategic and operational surprise and successful breakthrough operations before U.S. reinforcements arrive. It focuses on using massive firepower, including artillery, multiple rocket launchers, and missiles that it has placed near the DMZ. Its possession of weapons of mass destruction (WMD) complicates the matter. The war scenario is one which the U.S.–ROK Combined Forces Command (CFC) prepares for, but is less likely as the war might end the Kim regime. This scenario might be expected to develop if the North Korean regime becomes desperate or minor conflict between the DPRK and ROK escalates.

Nevertheless, given high tensions and room for miscalculation, the war scenario is still plausible. The defining characteristics of the war outcome are mass civilian casualties, large-scale industrial devastation in Seoul and other urban metropolitan areas, and the desolation of North Korea. Japan would also see mass destruction, as North Korea would likely launch missiles to prevent U.S. and Japanese intervention. The scenario assumes that while North Korea would inflict tremendous damage on South Korea, Pyongyang would lose the war, and South Korea and the U.S., as victorious powers, would administer and occupy the northern half of the peninsula.[21]

2.1 Analysis: War

The war scenario describes a desperate outgoing North Korean regime deciding it has nothing to lose, attacking South Korea, and then suffering defeat in war. Another possibility is that Kim Jong-un decides to reunify by attacking South Korea.[22] War could also result from escalation of a minor skirmish, such as a border clash. Analysts anticipate that such a war would cause severe damage, but the combined U.S. and ROK forces would win the conflict, and South Korea would absorb North Korea. The U.S., China, and international entities would play greater roles in stability and development in the war scenario, and the infusion of funds would be quicker due to the pressing need to restore stability.

The war scenario demands careful consideration because North Korea continues to conduct military provocations, develop its military capability, and maintain its intention of reunifying Korea under DPRK rule. As recently as June 2015, North Korea attacked a South Korean border town with a rocket in response to South Korea broadcasting loud speakers along the DMZ, which was also in response to the mine explosion in the DMZ that maimed two ROK soldiers. The investigation revealed that DPRK had placed those mines. In 2010, North Korea sank a South Korean naval vessel *Cheonan* and shelled the South Korean island of *Yeonpyeong*. On October 12, 2009, North Korea test-fired five short-range missiles toward the sea from its east coast.[23] By testing its most advanced short-range missile, the KN-02,[24] North Korea displayed its continued efforts to develop missiles as well as its military capability.

North Korea has not changed its strategy. With 1.2 million troops, North Korea has the world's fourth largest military. Pyongyang spends about a third of its gross national income (GNI) on the military, according to Korea Institute for Defense Analyses.[25] Since the 1990s, North Korea has been assessed to deploy 70% of its military within 40–60 miles of the DMZ.[26] The forward deployment of such a large force means that the ROK–U.S. military has less warning time of aggression from DPRK. Numerous artillery and tanks are poised to attack Seoul metropolitan area, 30 miles south of the DMZ, South Korea's political, economic, and cultural center with 25 million inhabitants.[27] North Korea's strategy of unification includes fomenting a revolution within South Korea, which leads to unification, with force if necessary, under the North Korean regime.[28] According to Hwang Jang-yup, Kim Jong-il has declared that should North Korea implode, "we'll take the rest of the world with us."[29] This declaration suggests that a collapsing North Korea could start a war out of desperation, even under the new leadership of Kim Jong-un.

No doubt the devastation would be colossal and swift if Pyongyang were to attack. However, the prediction is that the CFC would ultimately defeat North Korean aggression. An ROK–U.S. victory would spell the demise of the North Korean regime and the beginning of the absorption process. This scenario would allow the U.S. and South Korea to rapidly establish control over North Korea's nuclear weapons and facilities. Stability operations would quickly follow. The common interest in rapidly establishing stability could lead to multilateral cooperation. There would be less ambiguity about the presence of the ROK and U.S. military forces in the northern half of the peninsula since the conflict would bring the military forces there and the victorious parties would then need to stay in the immediate aftermath to provide stability. Multilateral entities, such as the UN, might also help with stability operations and building local capacity to provide for the people.

The scenario is complicated by China's role. To what extent would China go in order to prevent the North Korean regime from falling, either with or without requests for assistance? Out of concern for North Korea's stability, Beijing has provided assistance, especially grains and crude oil, to Pyongyang since the mid-1990s.[30] China may send its forces along or beyond its borders to avert or manage instability in North Korea.[31] China's entrance into the conflict could complicate the situation, especially if it were to establish a buffer zone with Chinese troops inside northern Korea.

Although the North Korean military capability is formidable, this scenario is less likely given the credible deterrence of the U.S.–ROK alliance, less enthusiastic support for a North Korean military adventure by China and Russia, and the North Korean awareness of the high probability that its regime would not survive the war.

3   Collapse and Absorption

The collapse and absorption scenario assumes the collapse of North Korea followed by an absorption by South Korea. The outcome would be less benign than peaceful integration, and was described as a "hard landing" by the Kim Yong-sam administration in South Korea in 1990s.[32] The "hard landing" would be caused by the inability of the North Korean regime to maintain effective control over its political, economic, social, and military systems, causing the dissolution of the regime and ultimately the state. This scenario, popular immediately after the Soviet Union's collapse, is regaining momentum as North Korea's dire economic conditions persist and outside information penetrates North Korea, creating a challenge for the regime to maintain control. The traits of the default outcome assume a trigger precipitating regime collapse that leads to a sudden unification. The scenario requires external interventions to restore order in North Korea.[33] The initial focus would be on managing mass migration, as well as on political, social, and economic integration, all of which are anticipated to present even more acute problems than in the war scenario.[34]

3.1   *Analysis: Collapse and Absorption*

In this scenario, North Korea collapses due to its unsustainable system, and South Korea absorbs North Korea. Interest in the collapse scenario surged after German unification, the fall of the communist regimes in Eastern and Central Europe, and the disintegration of the Soviet Union.[35] The North Korean government's inability to provide for its people with its failed economic system, however, has not led to its collapse. Nonetheless, the North Korean regime is acutely aware of the possibility. In the treatise *On the Fundamentals of Revolutionary Party Building*, Kim Jong-il writes:

> The setback faced by socialism in a number of countries is a serious lesson for us.... The collapse of parties which had been building socialism was an abnormal occurrence.... If its organizational and ideological bases are solid, the socialist ruling party can thwart all the schemes of the imperialists and class enemies to undermine the party.... Renegade socialists and reactionaries, talking about "democracy" and "glasnost", used the shortcomings revealed in the socialist ruling parties as a means of misleading the public opinion.... The historical lesson from the collapse of the socialist ruling parties and of the socialist systems in many countries is that the purity of the socialist idea must be maintained firmly if the cause of the socialism is to be completed.[36]

Kim Jong-il further states that *Juche*, or self-reliance, ideology is fundamental to a more revolutionary and militant party to continually promote the cause of socialism.[37] Although far from self-reliant in practice, Kim's promotion of *Juche* and *Songun* were attempts to strengthen the ideological foundation of the people in order to prevent the discontent that may cause regime collapse. The North Korean regime chose to promote *Juche* and *Songun* policies to reinforce the ideological basis for supporting the regime, instead of instituting real reforms focused on systemic change. Kim Jong-un has continued this tradition, taking drastic measures to limit personal-level economic exchanges with China and conducting North Korea's fourth nuclear test in January 2016. Even with Kim Jong-un's *Byungjin* policy, the priority is to develop nuclear weapons. North Korea seeks more international food donations in light of a severe drought, but shows no sign of scaling back on its nuclear weapons program. Consequently, North Korea has suffered chronic food shortages and continued weakness in its economy, which may prove to be difficult to sustain. In other words, North Korea may indeed implode and unification could occur as South Korea absorbs a collapsed North Korea.

A variation is the collapse scenario combined with an armed conflict, if a border skirmish escalates into war or a designated successor is unable to maintain power, extract loyalty, and assert internal control.[38] With the loss of central control, factional power struggles could involve violence, leading to civil war.[39] Another possibility is ROK–U.S. forces facing insurgency in North Korea after North Korea's defeat. Any violence could make post-collapse management dramatically more difficult since humanitarian operations must occur concurrently with counterinsurgency or war.

From the above unification scenarios, three general categories emerge: gradual and peaceful unification, war, and collapse and absorption. The gradual approach, considered the least disruptive, may not necessarily lead to unification and it could be overcome by other events leading to unification. War is possible but not likely in the current context, although some sort of armed conflict may result from the desperation of an outgoing regime or a border skirmish spiraling out of control. Although North Korea has defied predictions of its collapse since the early 1990s, its precarious circumstances may yet lead to collapse and absorption by South Korea.

4   Unification Cost

South Koreans question the desirability of sudden unification even without a war because of the likelihood of mass migration, economic cost, and social problems. They often cite Germany, which had a long period of east–west exchanges and cooperation through *Ostpolitik* before unification in 1990 but still faces numerous difficulties.

The gap between the Koreas is much greater than that of the former West Germany and East Germany. For instance, the South Korean economy was almost 44 times larger than North Korea's in 2014, while West Germany's economy was only 12 times larger than East Germany's when the Berlin Wall fell.[40] The per capita income ratio for Germany was 3:1, while for Korea, it is 21:1, a significant gap. One indicator of development is the infant mortality rate. As depicted in Table 2.1, infant mortality for West Germany and East Germany were almost identical, but for South Korea, it is 4 per 1000 live births and for North Korea, it is 25 per 1000—again a huge gap.

Table 2.1   South–North Gap (2014) and West–East Gap (1989)[a]

	South Korea (S)	North Korea (N)	Ratio (S:N)	West Germany (W)	East Germany (E)	Ratio (W:E)
Population (thousands)	50,424	24,662	2.0:1	62.1	16.6	3.7:1
GNI/GDP[b] ($ billions)	1420.43	32.5	43.8:1	1197.5	96.9	12.4:1
GNI/GDP[b] per capita ($)	28,169	1319	21.4:1	19,283	5840	3.3:1
Infant mortality (per 1000 births)	3.93	24.50	0.16:1	7.4	7.5	0.99:1

Sources: *Bank of Korea, CIA World Factbook, The Economist*

[a]"Nam Bookhan-ui Jooyo Geongje Jipyo Bigyo (Comparison of Key Economic Indicators between South Korea and North Korea)," Bank of Korea, http://www.bok.or.kr/broadcast.action?menuNaviId=2236, (figures are converted to U.S. dollars using $1:KRW 1053.63, an average for 2014), (accessed October 6, 2015), *CIA World Factbook, 2013–14* (for infant mortality rates, 2014 estimate), https://www.cia.gov/library/publications/the-world-factbook/rankorder/2091rank.html, accessed June 2, 2015), *The Economist*, May 10, 1997, 78 for German statistics

[b]Gross National Income (GNI) for South Korea and North Korea; Gross National Product (GDP) for West Germany and East Germany

When the 1997 Asian Financial Crisis hit, with capital flight, plunging exchange rates, and social despair, South Korea suffered a severe economic setback. Bankruptcies and massive layoffs, unheard of in the past, were common. People lost homes. Suicide rates skyrocketed. The exchange rate plummeted. The International Monetary Fund (IMF) infused billions of dollars in capital in one of the largest bailouts in its history. With this experience and with some feeling little or no emotional ties with North Korea, South Koreans are reluctant to experience the inevitable hardship and costs associated with unification.[41] With the younger generation, however, this negative attitude toward unification is changing.

Although estimating the cost of unification is difficult, various calculations do exist. In *Avoiding the Apocalypse*, Marcus Noland reviews various studies that estimate Korean unification costs. Cost estimates vary widely from $3.1 trillion, $1.2 trillion, $600 billion, $200 billion, to minus $541 billion.[42] Noland points out that most studies use the German experience and measure the costs in terms of budgetary expenditures; benefits are viewed as offsetting possibilities, primarily military demobilization. The problem with such calculation is that the North Korean military, like the majority of the South Korean military, consists of conscripts, who are paid less. Thus the savings from demobilization would not be as great. On the other hand, conscripts would presumably switch from low-productivity military activities to higher-productivity activities, creating a larger tax base, thereby reducing the unification cost.[43] Most of these figures have unification dates of 2006 or earlier. Given inflation and the widening gap between the two Koreas, future figures would be higher.

Other studies widen the unification cost estimate range even further. Charles Wolf and Kamil Akarmov give estimates of $50 billion to $667 billion,[44] while Peter Beck provides an estimate of $2 trillion to $5 trillion over 30 years.[45] In 2013, South Korea's Ministry of Finance announced that South Korea would pay up to 7% of its annual Gross Domestic Product (GDP) for 10 years, or roughly $1 trillion, if it were to reunite with North Korea in the next eight years.[46]

Whether the cost is hundreds of billions of dollars or trillions of dollars, it will be large. Former West Germany transferred $1.4 trillion to the East during 1991–2004, about 5–6% of the cumulative GDP.[47] The income gap is greater in Korea than in Germany, leading to the conclusion that the unification cost for Korea would be much higher. The cost frightens South Koreans; however, as South Korea's economy continues to grow at a faster rate than North Korea's, the gap will likely continue to widen at an increasing rate, making longer-term unification even more costly. The anticipated costs are estimates only and would vary depending on a variety of factors including the nature and timing of the collapse.

5   Summary

The unification scenarios focus primarily on three different possibilities: gradual and peaceful unification between North and South Korea, unification as a result of war, and collapse of the North and absorption into the South. The gradual approach is a peaceful reconciliation between South Korea and North Korea, which eventually may lead to unification, or may stop at the confederation phase, where both systems peacefully coexist. The key is for North Korea to be willing to reform and open its system for slow integration. The North Korean regime seems to be unwilling or incapable of such a change. On the other end of the spectrum is war and unification as a by-product of war. It assumes full-scale attack on South Korea by North Korea. A conflict may also arise from limited North Korean violence and brinkmanship that spirals out of control. The war scenario is deemed least likely, both because of the credibility of U.S.–ROK deterrence and because North Korean leaders are not likely to choose a path leading to the regime's downfall. The third scenario is collapse and absorption. The North Korean regime dissolves because it cannot maintain effective control over its political, economic, social, and military systems, and the regime and ultimately the state collapse. The unification expenses associated with various scenarios are costly, and gradual unification is not necessarily the least costly due to the increasing gap between South Korea and North Korea with time. While the gradual approach—absence of war and chaos—may be desired by many, the collapse scenario is not implausible, especially given North Korea's economic problems, inability to feed its own population, and unstable system. The next chapter examines and analyzes indicators and triggers of North Korea's potential collapse.

Notes

1. Mitchell, 3.
2. Pollack and Lee, 49–50.
3. Mitchell, 4.
4. Interview with Park Young-ho, Korea Institute for National Unification (KINU), Seoul, June 27, 2006.

5. Harrison, *Korean Endgame: A Strategy for Reunification and U.S. Disengagement*, 75–76.
6. Norman D. Levin and Yong-Sup Han, *Sunshine in Korea: The South Korean Debate over Policies Toward North Korea* (Santa Monica: RAND, 2002), 31.
7. Interview with Kihl-jae Ryoo, Dean of Academic Affairs, Associate Professor of Political Science, University of North Korean Studies, Seoul, June 22, 2006.
8. Kim Il Sung, "Chosun Minju ju-ui Inmin Gonghwaguk Jeongbu-ui Dangmyun Gwaeob-e Daehayeo (Regarding the Tasks Facing the Government of Democratic People's Republic of Korea); a speech at the Supreme People's Council on 23 October 1962," in *Ryunbangje Joguk Tongil Bangahm-e (Confederation as an Approach to the Unification of the Motherland)* (Pyongyang: Chosun Rodongdang Chulpahnsah (North Korean Workers' Party Publisher), 1996), 13. It is important to note that Kim's official statements, however, did not always match with his deeds. He may have supported the confederation approach, but not necessarily without interference in internal politics.
9. Republic of Korea Ministry of Unification, "Peace and Cooperation: White Paper on Korean Unification 2001," 2001, 28.
10. For details, see Governments of South Korea and North Korea, "June 15 South–North Joint Declaration," 2000.
11. Republic of Korea Ministry of Unification, "North Korea Facts and Figures," Seoul, 2006.
12. Republic of Korea Ministry of Unification, "Promoting Peace and Cooperation: Five Years of the Kim Dae-jung Administration," 2003, 131.
13. Interview with Park Young-ho.
14. Interview with Andrei Lankov, North Korea specialist and professor, Seoul, June 20, 2006.
15. Interview with Brian Myers, North Korea specialist and professor, Seoul, June 26, 2006.
16. Hwang Jang Yup, "North Korea's Southern Policy and Inter-Korean Relations," in *Testimonies of North Korean Defectors*, fas.org, January 1999, http://www.fas.org/irp/world/rok/nis-docs/.
17. Jae-Jean Suh, "The Lee Myung-bak Government's North Korea Policy: A Study on Its Historical and Theoretical Foundation," *Korea Institute for National Unification*, May 2009, 3.
18. Alastair Gale, "Pyongyang Threatens to End Venture," *The Wall Street Journal*, April 8, 2013 (accessed June 20, 2015).

19. "The Road to a Happy Unification," *Korea Institute for National Unification*, (brochure), circa 2014, file: http://www.kinu.or.kr/eng/pub/pub_02_01.jsp?page=1&num=190&mode=view&field=&text=&order=&dir=&bid=DATA05&ses=, 10 (accessed June 30, 2015).
20. Ibid.
21. Mitchell, 8.
22. Peter Humphrey, "Korean Reunification: How It Will Happen," *American Intelligence Journal* 26, no. 2 (Winter 2008/2009): 71.
23. Sam Kim, "N. Korea test-fires missiles, draws line ahead of talks: analysts" *Yonhap News Agency*, October 12, 2009, http://english.yonhapnews.co.kr/national/2009/10/12/23/0301000000AEN20091012007100315F.HTML.
24. KN-02 Short-Range Ballistic Missile is a variant of Soviet-built SS-21 missile. North Korea test-fired the missile in the East Sea toward Japan, and the range appears to be 100–120 kilometers. For further information, see "Weapons of Mass Destruction: KN-02 Short Range Ballistic Missile" in Global Security, http://www.globalsecurity.org/wmd/world/dprk/kn-2.htm, accessed May 31, 2011.
25. "North Korea spends about a third of income on military: group," *Reuters Canada*, January 18, 2011, http://ca.reuters.com/article/topNews/idCATRE70H1BW20110118 (accessed July 5, 2015).
26. Bechtol, Bruce E. Jr., "Understanding the North Korea Threat to the Security of the Korean Peninsula and East Asia: Declined or Evolved?," in *Korea at the Crossroads: Challenges and Prospects; IKS International Conference*, Seoul, The Institute of Korean Studies, November 17, 2008, 6.
27. "Sudogwon Ingu Jibjoong Hyunhwang (Current Population of Metropolitan Capital Area)," Narajipyo, 2009.
28. Hwang, "North Korea's Southern Policy and Inter-Korean Relations."
29. Hwang Jang Yup, "Preparations for War in North Korea," in *Testimonies of North Korean Defectors*, fas.org, January 1999.
30. Pollack and Lee, *Preparing for Korean Unification: Scenarios & Implications*, 14.
31. Scott Snyder and Joel Wit, "China Views: Breaking the Stalemate on the Korean Peninsula," in *USIP Special Report No. 183*, Washington, DC, U.S. Institute of Peace, February 2007, 7.
32. Mitchell, 5.
33. Derek Mitchell, "A Blueprint for U.S. Policy toward a Unified Korea," *The Washington Quarterly* 26, no. 1 (2002–03): 6.

34. Ibid. Mitchell, 6.
35. Mitchell, "A Blueprint for U.S. Policy toward a Unified Korea," 5.
36. Jong Il Kim, *On the Fundamentals of Revolutionary Party Building: A Treatise Written on the Occasion of the 47th Anniversary of the Foundation of the Workers' Party of Korea, 10 October 1992* (Pyongyang: Foreign Language Publishing House, 1992), 2–10.
37. Kim, 11.
38. Pollack and Lee, *Preparing for Korean Unification: Scenarios & Implications*, 64.
39. Maxwell, "Catastrophic Collapse of North Korea: Implications for the United States Military," 18.
40. "National Accounts Main Aggregates Database," United Nations Statistics Division, September 2008.
41. "South Koreans Grow Wary of Unification," *Washington Post*, October 17, 2011, http://www.washingtonpost.com/world/south-korean-youth-grow-wary-of-unification/2011/10/14/gIQA3ujmqL_story.html (accessed October 28, 2014).
42. See the estimates chart in Noland, *Avoiding the Apocalypse*, 308.
43. Noland, 308.
44. Charles Wolf Jr. and Kamil Akramov, *North Korean Paradoxes: Circumstances, Costs, and Consequences of Korean Unification* (Santa Monica: RAND, 2005), 39.
45. Peter Beck, "Contemplating Korean Reunification," *The Wall Street Journal*, January 4, 2010, http://online.wsj.com/article/SB10001424052748704340304574635180086832934.html.
46. Kim, Christine, "Korean unification may cost South 7% of GDP: ministry," *Reuters*, January 1, 2013, http://www.reuters.com/article/2013/01/01/us-korea-north-unification-idUSBRE90004F20130101 and Shearf, Daniel, "South Korea Committee to Prepare for Reunification with North," *Voice of America*, February 25, 2014, http://www.voanews.com/content/south-korea-forming-committee-to-prepare-for-reunifcation-with-north-korea/1858571.html (accessed November 1, 2014).
47. Wolf and Akramov, *North Korean Paradoxes*, 28.

CHAPTER 3

Thinking About Collapse: Indicators and Triggers

Abstract This chapter examines indicators and triggers of a collapse. Various indicators, such as the deteriorating economic conditions, external assistance, and information penetration, provide clues to a possible collapse in North Korea. These indicators, along with a triggering event such as another famine, leadership disaffection, or mass migration, should be monitored closely to assess whether and when North Korea might collapse so that preparations can be made by the international community to meet this contingency with appropriate responses.

The complete collapse of a nuclear-armed hermit kingdom would be an unprecedented event. Forecasting a collapse is perilous, yet past experiences provide guidelines to what to look for. This chapter explores and summarizes what we expect might be the major triggers of a collapse, and the major underlying indicators.

Various indicators provide clues to a possible collapse in North Korea. These indicators, along with a triggering event such as another famine, should be monitored closely to assess whether and when North Korea might collapse so that the international community can deal with this contingency with appropriate responses. The surprising longevity of the North Korean regime should not lead to complacency. As discussed in prior chapters, and at greater length later in this study, it is in the interest of the regional powers to insure that the many challenges likely to arise from the collapse of North Korea are handled appropriately to minimize suffering and hasten stabilization of the region.

© The Editor(s) (if applicable) and The Author(s) 2016
Tara O, *The Collapse of North Korea*,
DOI 10.1057/978-1-137-59801-1_3

North Korea's system, some argue, has already failed. Scobell defines a failed regime as "one that is extremely disorganized and in many respects has ceased to function even though significant institutions still exist."[1] He conceptualizes collapse as a process, not an outcome, arguing that the process of regime collapse in North Korea has already begun.[2] North Korea also appears to have reached Phase 4, suppression, of Robert Collins' Seven Phases of Collapse.[3] Since Kim Jong-un took power, he replaced 40% of the top military and 20–30% of senior party officials, and executed 70 officials in the first half of 2015.[4] Phase 4 follows Phase 3, the rise of local independence via the black market and widespread corruption to circumvent a failing central government.[5] Unofficial and illegal market activities are increasing, with the help of corruption. According to Collins' phases, North Korea seems to have moved to the next phase toward a collapse.

Using analysis of historical and contemporary data, this chapter explores the indicators that North Korea may be on the verge of collapse or is already in the process of collapsing. The chapter also describes the most likely triggers for North Korea's collapse.

1   Indicators of Collapse

The most important indicators of collapse include North Korea's deteriorating economic conditions, its reliance on external assistance, the degree of information penetration, leadership succession and power struggle, the role of elites, and the number and rate of changes in defections.

1.1   Economic System and the Provision for Basic Needs

North Korea has not adopted the reforms necessary to resolve the dire problems of its economy. Continued severe economic problems could eventually erode support for the Pyongyang regime.

In a socialist system, the state owns and administers the means of production and distribution of goods, including food. A government that cannot provide food to its own population, especially when food is available globally, has a significant weakness in its system. North Korea's Public Distribution System (PDS), DPRK's central allocation system for food distribution, has failed to meet the population demand for food since the early 1990s. As a result, one million people, about 5% of North Korea's population, perished during the great famine of 1995–1997.[6] Some organizations estimate the deaths from famine to be as high as 3.5 million, with an additional 300,000 people escaping from North Korea in search of food.[7]

The North Korean government attributes the famine and chronic food shortages to floods and drought, and indirectly to the demise of preferential trade relations with Russia and China. Haggard and Noland assert that the official explanation blaming only external factors is misleading.[8] North Korea has long depended on outside assistance, first from the Soviet Union, later from China, then from South Korea (especially during the Sunshine Policy period), and again from China. North Korea experienced a fundamental economic shock when the Soviet Union cut aid and demanded hard currency, rather than barter, in exchange for its support. The North Korean government began to decrease food rations in 1987 when the Soviet Union cut food assistance.[9] Despite warning signs prior to the famine, the North Korean government was slow to implement measures to ensure adequate food supply. Instead in 1991, it emphasized reducing demand by exhorting North Koreans to eat less with the "let's eat two meals a day" campaign.[10]

North Korea did request and receive humanitarian food aid during the height of the famine, but instead of using it to increase the overall food supply, it offset the aid by reducing commercial food imports and using the savings for other purposes.[11] During the famine of the 1990s, Kim Jong-il spent $100 million to renovate his father's former palace, Kumsusan, into a mausoleum.[12] Other priorities included, for instance, the purchase of 40 MiG-21 fighters and eight military helicopters from Kazakhstan in 1991.[13] Furthermore, since the famine, and while it was receiving food, energy, and other aid, North Korea conducted four nuclear tests (2006, 2009, 2013, and 2016) and numerous missile tests. The North Korean focus on *Songun* rather than food shows that the regime attempts to garner public support by emphasizing ideology rather than by providing basic needs.

Faced with food shortages, the North Korean population resorted to scrounging for food in the woods. Local markets to buy and sell food emerged spontaneously, a practice unheard of and unauthorized prior to the famine. Severe famine led to some marketization of the economy, which provided some relief. However, official and unofficial mechanisms for dealing with food shortages compete with the state control, which keeps the regime in power.

In July 2002, North Korea implemented economic reforms focused on market and foreign investment, a surprising measure given the rather far-reaching effort. Marketization, although illegal, had been occurring for years. The policy change in 2002 in effect decriminalized the market, allowing grains and certain goods to be traded. The reforms included dramatic increases in prices and wages, endorsement of private enterprises, drastic currency devaluation, and changes in foreign investment laws. The price increases reflected emerging market prices that were much higher than the official ones, and wages rose to offset the price increases. These increases, however, were not accompanied by the revival of industrial sector production. Furthermore, the government decided to monetize the subsidy costs to loss-generating state-owned industrial enterprises, creating a situation with an increased money supply and not enough products to purchase. The results were severe inflation and growing social disparity. Inflation ensued at an estimated annual rate of over 100% since August 2002 for some time.[14]

Because the market system tends to produce winners and losers, another unintended consequence of the economic reforms was an increase in social inequality, along with new and more individualist ways of thinking and independent behavior. Alarmed, in October 2005, the government reversed its earlier decisions, banning the private sale of grain, limiting trading, and reverting to the regime-controlled Public Distribution System (PDS). This policy reversion may have been an effort to mollify a population affected by high food prices, which were about eight times as high in 2004 as in mid-2002 when the reform began, but also to regain control over its populace.[15] Despite the reversion to PDS, the distribution system never recovered because it could not deliver food and other basic provisions that people needed.

In 2009, the government took further measures, suddenly introducing new currency at a 100:1 ratio, which expropriated the savings of the newly emerging middle class.[16] The North Koreans could exchange up to 100,000 won (or about $35–40), enough to feed a family for two months. Any additional amount had to be deposited at a bank, but only up to 300,000 won. In effect, the state confiscated any savings over the maximum deposit amount allowed. Such action angered those affected. Many of the market traders were women in their 40s and 50s. Despite threats of arrest, they openly expressed their bitterness at the currency reform by protesting against the leadership.[17] Ordinary citizens reportedly had sympathy for the protesters. The circumstances and the scale of the protest were such that the authorities summarily executed 12 "masterminds," increased the alert for mass defections across the border with China, and took measures to placate the public, such as increasing the ceiling of the amount that could be exchanged to 500,000 won.[18] Kim Young-il, North Korea's Premier, offered a rare apology to the public and Park Nam-ki, the head of the Party's finance planning division and the alleged architect of the failed reform, was dismissed and executed.[19]

Rare are the reports of riots and large-scale discontent, but such signs of defiance indicate some loss of state control. As North Korea's fragile economy weakens and widespread food shortages continue, perhaps the regime's monopoly on control is diminishing as well. Discontent with the economic situation could trigger further organized opposition movements, challenging the regime and possibly leading to its collapse.

Widespread food shortages continue to this day. While food shortages are key concerns, the system also fails to address other needs of the population, such as medical care and energy. The state continues to try to centrally control the distribution of food and goods; however, the task has become too complex, with tragic consequences.

1.2 External Assistance

The regime's foremost interest is survival, which requires reform and an open economy, given its economic difficulties. Opening, however, can create a new set of actors, thoughts, and behaviors that could challenge the regime's legitimacy. As such, North Korea refuses to undertake serious reform. Its alternative is to rely on assistance from outside. Foreign assistance plays an essential role in the North Korean regime's survival.

In the early 2000s, about one-third of North Korea's revenue came from aid, about one-third from conventional sources, and the remainder from unconventional sources, primarily illicit activities.[20] Pyongyang's continued focus on nuclear and missile tests prompted UN sanctions, which further limits North Korea's trade options with the world. As shown in Table 3.1, China and South Korea provided the majority of North Korea's "imports," 73% and 19%, respectively, in 2012.[21] The definition of imports is unclear, as aid is also included in this figure. While it is difficult to obtain data, and the classification of aid versus imports is ambiguous, the transfers from China and South Korea to North Korea are clearly significant.

The threat of instability in North Korea is enough to extract assistance from China. China provides the majority of North Korea's imports. The figure has risen dramatically from 46% in 2008 to 79% in 2014.[22] This trend is likely to continue, especially given the chilled inter-Korean

Table 3.1 North Korea's top trade partners (2014, estimated)[a]

Rank	Export	Import
1	China (54.9%)	China (79%)
2	Algeria (30%)	South Korea (11%)
3	South Korea (16%)	Republic of Congo (4.5%)

Source: *CIA World Factbook*

[a]*CIA*. https://www.cia.gov/library/publications/the-world-factbook/fields/2050.html and https://www.cia.gov/library/publications/the-world-factbook/fields/2061.html (accessed July 3, 2015)

relationship and China's concern for stability across its border. While it is difficult to assess the magnitude of Beijing's support to Pyongyang, Haggard and Noland estimated in 2007 that support amounts to $7 billion cumulatively since the mid-1980s, which includes aid, foreign direct investment (FDI), and border trade.[23] China supplies a substantial portion of North Korea's food and energy, and apparently provides most of its oil requirements. During Chinese Premier Wen Jiabao's visit to Pyongyang in October 2009, substantial aid was promised. A Chinese Foreign Ministry official stated that China provides assistance to North Korea within China's capacity to improve North Korean people's lives and assist their economic development, hinting that enough assistance would be given to impact people's lives and development.[24] North Korea's continued focus on its nuclear weapons program, however, complicates Chinese support. North Korea's third nuclear test in February 2013 and subsequent "satellite" launch two months later irritated its big neighbor, as did Pyongyang's fourth nuclear test in January 2016 and another rocket launch a month later. In response to North Korea's April 2013 "satellite" launch, a blatant use of ballistic missile technology, the UN Security Council openly condemned the launch, stating that it has caused a grave security concern in the region.[25] The UN again "strongly condemned" the launch in 2016. The condemnation would not have been possible without the support of China. Chinese policy specialists discuss recalibrating China–North Korea bilateral relations.

South Korean aid has also been crucial for North Korea. The Sunshine Policy begun in 1998 under President Kim Dae-jung was continued by his successor Rho Moo-hyun. Seoul's ten-year unconditional assistance was important for the survival of the Pyongyang regime. During the five years of Kim Dae-jung's administration, annual government and private aid from Seoul to Pyongyang averaged $92.56 million. This was about one-third of South Korea's $266 million official development assistance for loans and grants to developing countries.[26] During Rho Moo-hyun's five-year tenure, government and private humanitarian aid from South to North Korea doubled, to $1.835 billion.[27] For cash-strapped North Korea, the South Korean aid was significant.

Despite these gestures, the inter-Korean exchanges slowed dramatically. South Korean aid to North Korea and investment in inter-Korean projects dropped to its lowest level since the South–North Summit and the start of the Seoul's generous aid package in 2000. During the first 11 months of 2009, the South Korean government dispensed $54 million (68.3 billion won), 6.1% of the nearly $885 million (1.12 trillion won) allocated, toward aid and investment in North Korea.[28] In 2008, the respective figure was $215 million (231.2 billion won), which represents 18.1% of the allocated $1.18 billion (1.275 trillion won).[29] The steep cuts occurred after North Korea's first nuclear test and the cuts continued with North Korea's latest nuclear tests and provocations. The South Korean government suspended transfers of rice, fertilizer, and other aid, and the private sector followed suit by reducing indirect aid.[30] The assistance gap may cause further deterioration of North Korea's situation, or may be filled by the Chinese aid.

1.3   Information Control

North Korea watched the collapse of the former Soviet Union and East and Central European countries with horror.[31] These centralized economies collapsed partly because they could not provide for the needs of their citizens and lost legitimacy.

The Pyongyang regime needs domestic legitimacy to stay in power, which requires persuading the populace that the regime is looking out for their interests and providing for them. It needs to appear strong. The regime reinforces that image by its *Songun* and now *Byungjin* policy, and by displaying and occasionally demonstrating its military prowess through nuclear and missile tests and other armed provocations. The regime's legitimacy is based on myths of its leader's stature and lies that the system provides for the people well. The Kim regime also portrays South Korea as a poor country, far worse off than North Korea, with a government that is a puppet of the U.S. To get people to believe these fabrications, the Kim regime must prevent access to competing information. This explains North Korea's paranoia and strict control of information.

The North Korean government follows strict, harsh information and movement control measures. It controls the media and institutions, and relies on a system of watchers. In observing the failure of the communist bloc, the government was amazed at how quickly the people rejected the systems that they had outwardly embraced. The problem faced by the North Korean government is that the greater openness and reform necessary to correct the country's systemic failures could also shake the regime's foundation by bringing in competing information.

Despite strict information control, there are indications that outside information is increasingly reaching North Korea. Since the mid-1990s, North Koreans who crossed the border into China initially in search of food and later as unskilled workers help channel information back into North Korea. Some 500,000 North Korean border crossers have become aware of the wealth of China and South Korea, and some return to North Korea carrying this information with them.[32]

Cross-border traffic also brings in products that convey information. For example, tunable radios, illegal in North Korea, are smuggled in at an increasing rate.[33] External radio stations such as Free North Korea Radio and Radio Free Asia broadcast outside news to North Korea.[34] Despite the risk of getting caught, North Koreans reportedly watch South Korean TV dramas, also illegal in North Korea. Defectors report that *Hallyu* (Korean Wave), the term for South Korean soap operas, music, and movies, which have become increasingly popular in East Asian countries, is sweeping into North Korea as well.[35] Anyone seeing these South Korean cultural artifacts would find it difficult not to notice the prosperity that the South Koreans routinely enjoy—plentiful food, ubiquitous mobile phones, and nice cars. This show of wealth contradicts the official line that South Koreans live in poverty. Although the extent of information penetration is unclear, this "demonstration effect" could affect the general population in North Korea. As more North Koreans become aware of an alternate system, especially across the border to the south, they may demand change eventually.

The special economic zones of the Gaesong Industrial Complex (GIC) and the Geumgang Mountain tourist area, currently defunct, were additional sources of information about the outside world for North Koreans.

These sites brought South Koreans into North Korea and provide rare opportunities for interactions. As of November 2015, 54,763 North Korean employees and 803 South Korean managers worked at the complex.[36] North Korean officials wanted to rotate the North Korean workers annually, fearing that the workers would be exposed to too much outside information. However, annual rotation of workers also allowed a greater number of North Koreans to come into contact with South Korean managers and some of the business practices of South Korea. The annual rotation was infeasible in practice due to the learning curve required for business operations, but this policy highlighted the regime's fear of information. In addition, over 128,000 tourists had visited Gaesong, including the GIC, in 2015 alone.[37] Their ability to interact with the local population was limited, but their presence and behaviors undoubtedly made an impression on North Koreans, belying the government claim that South Korea was poor and backward.

Nearly 1.95 million South Korean tourists visited Mount Geumgang between late 1998 and 2008.[38] While there are fewer North Koreans working in the Geumgang tourism zone, and they have limited freedom to speak and act, they did see a continuous stream of middle-class, wealthy South Koreans. Pyongyang takes extreme measures to shield its people from the influence of South Korean managers and tourists, but even limited contact allows North Koreans a glimpse of South Korea and the larger world.

1.4 Leadership Succession and Power Consolidation

Whether Kim Jong-un can consolidate his power or not received heated debate after Kim Jong-il's death in December 2011, partly because Kim Jong-un barely had three years as an heir-designate, unlike his father, who had 20 years of grooming. In June 2008, the South Korean National Intelligence Service reported to the National Assembly that Kim Jong-il has designated his third son, Kim Jong-un, as his heir.[49] According to *Mainich Daily News*, official North Korean documents confirm that Kim Jong-un is the designated successor. New North Korean textbooks, such as *Educational Resources on the Greatness of our Revered General Kim Jong-un*, apparently educate the Ministry of People's Armed Forces and the national police on how to admire Kim Jong-un, while other documents urge prompt preparation of leadership succession.[50] These activities occurred around the time of speculations about Kim Jong-il's ill health in August 2008. He was conspicuously absent from the September

2008 military parade staged for North Korea's 60th anniversary (he had appeared in the ten previous anniversary parades).[51] North Korea released photos of Kim Jong-il's public appearances in early November. Experts suggest that the images were altered, noting, for instance, that the shadow of Kim Jong-il's leg was not aligned with the shadows of the soldiers on either side of him.[52] The suspect photos, rather than dampening speculation, raised greater concerns about Kim Jong-il's health. Since then, more photos of Kim Jong-il have appeared, but gone was the man of embonpoint; rather, these photos showed a thinner "Dear Leader."

After Kim Jong-il's death, regional leaders watched the succession process closely because a failed leadership succession could lead to the loss of control, which could then lead to a collapse. Some analysts believed that Jang Song-taek, Kim Jong-il's brother-in-law, would play a powerful behind-the-scenes role, while others believed that some military generals would be waiting to assert their power.[53] Still others presumed that collective leadership, consisting of officials from the party, the military, and the National Defense Commission, would emerge to fill the power vacuum until a new leader arose.[54]

Kim Jong-il's mythical stature and grip on power were such that the continuity of power and system was questionable and the outcome of a succession scenario was unpredictable.

Almost five years after his father's death, Kim Jong-un remains in power as do Kim Jong-il's various policies, including nuclear weapons development. Is Kim Jong-un fully in charge? Does he exert full authority over the state apparatus and, if so, what policies will he pursue? Answers to these questions may be linked to the potential contingency in North Korea. Monitoring Kim Jong-un's status could provide warning and the timing of a potential collapse.

1.5 Elites

Intra-elite schisms contributed to the regime collapses in Romania in 1989 and the Soviet Union in 1991.[55] The elites are the top tier within the core social class described in the *Songbun* section.[56] In North Korea, the core is loyal to Kim Jong-un in return for privileges. The elites are those within the core with even higher status and perquisites with greater authority and control. Using information about elites in North Korea as an indicator of North Korea's chances of collapsing would require more research on the nature of the elite system in the country. For example, it would be important to identify the elites and determine what proportion are military, party bureaucrats, and economic specialists. One way to identify members of the elites might be to examine those allowed to leave the country officially, as these people must have obtained a certain level of trust and privilege. Members of the elites who defect might indicate disaffection in that small circle. The number of defectors has increased significantly; however, most are low-level officials or ordinary people.

Where do these groups of elites stand on policy matters? Which group is likely to prevail? Their positions on succession could provide a glimpse into whether there might be a power struggle or a coup, which could then lead to a collapse, including perhaps civil war. In case of a collapse, focusing on this indicator could help identify those who might cooperate on matters such as nuclear weapons control and economic reform.

1.6 Defectors

Another sign of state failure is the dramatic increase in the number of defectors from North Korea. In the early 1990s, defectors numbered less than ten per year. As Table 3.2 shows, the numbers started to climb into the hundreds starting in 1999, and since 2002, the figures have jumped to several thousands per year.[57] Over 28,000 North Korean defectors had been resettled in South Korea by 2015.[58]

Table 3.2 North Korean defectors to South Korea[a]

Year	Prior to 1990	1990	1991	1992	1993	1994	1995	1996	1997	1998
Number	607	9	9	8	8	52	41	56	85	72

Year	1999	2000	2001	2002	2003	2004	2005	2006	2007
Number	148	312	583	1139	1281	1894	1387	2018	2544

Year	2008	2009	2010	2011	2012	2013	2014	2015	Total
Number	2809	2929	2402	2706	1509	1516	1397	1276	28,795

Source: ROK Ministry of Unification

[a]ROK Ministry of Unification, *Tongil Baekseo 2005 (Unification White Paper 2005)*; "Bukhan Ital Joomin Jeongchaek" (North Korean Defectors Policy), Ministry of Unification, http://www.unikorea.go.kr/content.do?cmsid=1518 (accessed September 9, 2015)

Defectors to South Korea risk their lives crossing the border from North Korea into China, face the perils of forced deportation back to North Korea or human trafficking in China, and then, with assistance and luck, make a dangerous journey to a third country before reaching South Korea. Many more remain in China. Nongovernmental organizations (NGOs) estimate that 100,000–300,000 North Korean refugees live in China.[59]

Despite the hardship and danger, North Koreans are leaving their homes at an increasing rate.[60] This trend could indicate that growing numbers of North Koreans want a different system than the one provided by the current regime.

2 Triggers

While indicators are measures of trends that may reveal the stability or instability of the North Korean regime, the concept of triggers refers to specific events that might precipitate a crisis and lead to collapse. Three possible triggers are elite disaffection, famine and ensuing mass migration, and mass opposition to government policies or social conditions in the North.

2.1 *Elite Disaffection and Factionalism*

So far Kim Jong-un remains in power. Purges and shifting of power bases have marked the power consolidation process. Jang Song-taek, Kim Jong-un's uncle and widely viewed as number two in North Korea, was accused of being a counterrevolutionary, stripped of all his titles, and executed in 2013. Also purged were Ri Yong-ho, the former Chief of the General Staff of the Korean People's Army, and U Dong-Cheuk, the Minister of the Ministry of State Security (formerly State Security Department) in 2012.[61] Thus, the heads of the three pillars of the power structure—the party, the military, and the state security—have completely been purged. The purges in the military were especially frequent. The Chief of the General Staff has been replaced three times and the Minister of the People's Armed Forces has been replaced five times in a little over three years of Kim Jong-un's reign.[62] By comparison, Kim Il-sung changed his defense chief five times in 46 years of his rule and Kim Jong-il, three times in 17 years.[63] The relatively recent high-level purge involved Hyon Yong Chul, the

Minister of People's Armed Forces, who faced a sensational execution by antiaircraft gun in 2015.[64] Fearing for their lives, a dozen senior North Korean party and military officials reportedly defected to South Korea or are seeking asylum in third countries.[65] The purges apparently continue to this date. It is uncertain whether the power consolidation process is stabilizing. Kim's brutality, however, could be undermining, rather than consolidating, his power base. There could be further power struggles. In contested succession, factions compete for power. If there are factions and personal rivalries, then the succession process could become messy as factions and individuals vie for power.[66] The succession struggle could be divisive, prolonged, and even violent. The support of the military and the intelligence agency would be crucial. The military itself could be a contestant for leadership, which may explain the frequent purges of the top military leadership. A new regime, rather than a continuation of the Kim regime, could emerge under this scenario. Contested succession could ultimately produce a regime change in North Korea; however, it would be difficult for a non-Kim family member to obtain legitimacy, because the basis of North Korea's leadership legitimacy revolves around the Kim family's godlike status. On the other hand, if a contestant could consolidate power, the new regime may be able to break away from past policies and adopt reforms, because it would not derive its legitimacy from the Kim family and hence not be bound by its policies.

The failed succession of a collapsed government may produce no clear leader capable of overseeing a functioning state, which leads to its demise.[67] A self-declared government may not be able to control the entire country. Add the chronic problems of food shortages, floods, and dilapidated roads, and the new government may be unable to maintain North Korea as a functioning state. If the new government's authority breaks down, the regime would enter a terminal phase and become ripe for absorption by South Korea. This situation would be similar to the German experience. When German unification looked inevitable, the East German leaders, in a desperate attempt to retain some control, reached out and worked with the West German government to manage the situation. Further, it could be the hard-landing case of collapse, disintegration, and chaos or the ousting of Kim Jong-un with factions competing for power, resulting in a civil war.[68]

No matter what regime emerges, however, it will be vulnerable to internal pressure if it fails to reform North Korea's systemic weaknesses.

2.2 Famine and Mass Migration

Another trigger to consider is famine and a repeat of North Koreans crossing the border into China for food, but on a much larger scale. After experiencing the famine in the mid-1990s, people facing another starvation may decide to leave North Korea sooner. The 1990s famine killed about one million North Koreans. With food shortages and the broken PDS, people relied on markets that emerged spontaneously, where they could find food at a market price. What amplified the importance of this coping mechanism is that the alternative—demanding that the government provide for the people—was probably unthinkable as the consequences of such a protest would be too severe. Any criticism of the leader or the system is met with harsh punishment, including execution. If the market is not robust enough to supply adequate food, there could be mass migration. This time, the people may leave en masse early enough to avoid devastating starvation. Food shortage, famine, and mass migration could trigger a crisis by taxing the regime's authority to control the population.

2.3 Mass Opposition

Opposition, demonstrations, or criticisms of the Kim regime are rare. However, there are reports of such activities. On December 1, 2009, North Korea suddenly announced that it was replacing its old currency with new notes at a 100:1 ratio, to be implemented within five days, with a limit of 100,000 won (about $35 to $40, enough to feed a family for two months).[69] Amounts over that had to be put into a bank with a maximum deposit up to 300,000 won allowed. Any savings over that amount, in effect, would be confiscated by the state.

This currency reform angered many North Koreans. Market traders are primarily women in their 40s and 50s, and it is reported that they openly expressed their anger at the currency move by protesting against the leadership, defying threats of arrest.[70] It is reported that rioters gained the sympathy of ordinary citizens and assumed a scale such that the authorities summarily executed 12 "masterminds" and ordered a heightened alert for mass defections. The government also reportedly took measures to placate the public, including increasing the amount that could be exchanged to 500,000 won.[71] While reported riots are rare, at some point, organized opposition could trigger a greater movement, weakening the regime.

On June 26, 2015, a tussle among a group of merchants and security personnel reportedly occurred at a market in Musan-gun, Hamgyeong Bukdo, when the latter confiscated the goods belonging to the merchants.[72] Armed security guards were deployed, the market was shut down, and the people involved in the scuffle were taken to unknown locations. This incident occurred during the potato crop failure in the same month and the months-long drought, which even the North Korean authorities dubbed "the worst drought in 100 year[s]."[73] People's discontent surfaced when the officials took away the means of livelihood for people eking out a meager living, especially during difficult times of drought and expected severe food shortage.[74]

Fearing an organized opposition, the North Korean regime prohibits the freedom of expression and assembly and strictly controls information. However, outside information has been seeping into North Korea through markets—DVDs, tunable radios, and merchants with information from China, for instance. According to Nat Kretchum and Jane Kim's report, a substantial number of North Koreans, especially those living along the border with China and the elites, have access to outside media, including foreign radio broadcasts and South Korean DVDs, which provide information previously unknown or contradicting the official version.[75] In the long run, the continued exposure to outside information could produce more North Koreans questioning the regime and its policies.

A trigger starts a process. Possible triggers for the collapse of North Korea include succession, famine and migration, and mass opposition. While this list is not exhaustive, these triggers, combined with the indicators of trends showing the vulnerability and decline of the North Korean system, could prompt one of the main contingency scenarios that would require a response from the regional powers.

Notes

1. Scobell, "Projecting Pyongyang: The Future of North Korea's Kim Jong Il Regime," ix.
2. Scobell, xiii.
3. Robert D. Kaplan, "When North Korea Falls," *The Atlantic*, October 2006, http://www.theatlantic.com/magazine/archive/2006/10/when-north-korea-falls/305228/.
4. "Over 40% of N. Korean Brass Replaced by Purges," *The Chosun Ilbo*, July 15, 2015, http://english.chosun.com/site/data/html_dir/2015/07/15/2015071500951.html.

5. Kaplan.
6. Stephan Haggard and Marcus Noland, *Famine in North Korea: Markets, Aid, and Reform* (New York: Columbia University Press, 2007), 1.
7. "Alternative NGO Report on the Committee on Economic, Social and Cultural Rights of the Second Periodic Report of Democratic People's Republic of Korea," Seoul, The Good Friends, November 2003, 4.
8. Haggard and Noland, *Famine in North Korea: Markets, Aid, and Reform*, 9.
9. "North Korea Hunger," in *AlertNet*, Thomson Reuters Foundation, October 7, 2008, http://www.alertnet.org/db/crisisprofiles/KP_FAM.htm?v=timeline.
10. "North Korea Hunger."
11. Haggard and Noland, *Famine in North Korea: Markets, Aid, and Reform*, 10.
12. Sung Hui Moon, "Forced to Build Kim Monuments," *Radio Free Asia*, October 12, 2012, http://www.rfa.org/english/news/korea/monuments-10122012153828.html.
13. "Hunger and Human Rights: The Politics of Famine," Washington, DC, U.S. Committee for Human Rights in North Korea, November 2, 2007, http://www.hrnk.org/hunger/origins.html.
14. Haggard, Stephen, and Marcus Noland, 21.
15. Beck, Lindsay, "N. Korea Korea's market reform hard to see," *Reuters*, October 31, 2005, 3, http://today.reuters.com/news/newsArticle.aspx?type=lifeAndLeisureNews&storyID=2005-10-31T153442Z_01_RID155815_RTRUKOC_0_US-KOREA-NORTH-REFORMS.xml.
16. Sung Hwee Moon, "Public Currency Announcement Broadcast," *DailyNK*, December 1, 2009, http://wwwldailynk.com/english/read.php?cataId=nk01500&num=5722 (accessed November 1, 2014).
17. "'Women Power' Gathers Against N. Korean Currency Shock," *Chosun Ilbo*, December 8, 2009. http://english.chosun.com/site/data/html_dir/2009/12/08/2009120800307.html (accessed June 10, 2009).
18. "N. Korea Backtracks as Currency Reform Sparks Riots," *Chosun Ilbo*, December 15, 2009, http://enlish.chosun.com/site/data/html_dir/209/12/15/2009121500361.html (accessed June 10, 2009).
19. Scott Snyder, "North Korea Currency Reform: What Happened and What Will Happen to Its Economy?" Paper presented at *2010 Global Forum on North Korea Economy*, Korea Economic Daily and Hyundai Research Institute, Seoul, Korea, March 31, 2010, 4.
20. Marcus Noland, "North Korea in Transition," *The Korean Journal of Defense Analysis* XVII, no. 1 (Spring 2005): 11.
21. *CIA World Factbook*, Central Intelligence Agency, 2014.
22. *CIA*.

23. Stephan Haggard and Marcus Noland, "North Korea's External Economic Relations," in *Working Paper Series*, Washington, DC, Peterson Institute for International Economics, 2007, 13.
24. "China Hints at Substantial Economic Aid to N. Korea," *Chosun Ilbo*, September 30, 2009. http://english.chosun.com/site/data/html_dir/2009/09/30/2009093000295.html.
25. "Security Council strongly condemns DPR Korea's satellite launch attempt," *UN News Centre*, April 16, 2012. http://www.un.org/apps/news/story.asp?NewsID=41784&Cr=Democratic&Cr1=Korea&Kw1=#.VG0JdPnF98Y (accessed November 5, 2014).
26. Republic of Korea Ministry of Unification, "Promoting Peace and Cooperation: Five Years of the Kim Dae-jung Administration," 154.
27. Sabine Burghart and Rudiger Frank, "Inter-Korean Cooperation 2000–2008: Commercial and Non-Commercial Transactions and Human Exchanges," in *Vienna Working Papers on East Asian Economy and Society*, ed. Rudiger Frank, Vienna, University of Vienna, Vol. 1, No. 1, 2008, 18.
28. "Inter-Korean Investment Lowest Since 2000," in *NK Brief*, Seoul, The Institute for Far Eastern Studies, December 9, 2009, http://ifes.kyungnam.ac.kr/eng/m05/s10/content.asp?nkbriefNO=328&GoP=1. The 2009 average exchange rate of 1 South Korean won to 0.00079 U.S. dollars is used, from OANDA, http://www.oanda.com/currency/historical-rates.
29. "Inter-Korean Investment."
30. "Inter-Korean Investment."
31. Kim, *On the Fundamentals of Revolutionary Party Building: A Treatise written on the Occasion of the 47th Anniversary of the Foundation of the Workers' Party of Korea, 10 October 1992*, 2.
32. Andrei Lankov, "Changes in View of Outside World by North Koreans," *Yonhap News*, November 5, 2009, http://english.yonhapnews.co.kr/northkorea/2009/10/29/66/0401000000AEN20091029008200325F.HTML.
33. Lankov.
34. Susan Chun, "Radio gives hope to North and South Koreans," in *CNN*, February 27, 2008, http://edition.cnn.com/2008/WORLD/asiapcf/02/27/cho.dissidentradio/. *Mission Statement* (Radio Free Asia, 1998–2009, December 17, 2009); available from http://www.rfa.org/english/about/mission.html.
35. Chang-Kyun Lee, Jinhee Bonny, and Young Yoon Choi, "North Korea Cracks Down on Korean Wave of Illicit TV," Washington, DC, Radio Free Asia, July 17, 2007, http://www.rfa.org/english/news/in_depth/korea_wave-20070717.html.

36. "Gaesong Gongdan Saengsanaek Mit Bukhan Geunroja Hyeonghwang" (Gaesong Industrial Complex Production and North Korean Workers' Current Status), Ministry of Unification, data as of November 2015, http://www.unikorea.go.kr/content.do?cmsid=3099 (accessed February 6, 2016).
37. "Gaesong Gongdan."
38. The tourism was halted in July 2008 when a South Korean tourist was shot and killed by a North Korean soldier. For figures on tourists and other visitors, see InSung Ki and Karin Lee, "Mt. Kumgang and Inter-Korean Relations," *National Committee on North Korea*, Washington, DC, November 10, 2009, 2.
39. Hunter, Helen-Louise. *Kim Il-song's North Korea*. (Westport: Praeger, 1999), 6.
40. Oh, Kongdan and Hassig, Ralph C. *North Korea Through the Looking Glass*. (Washington, DC: Brookings Institution Press, 2000), 133.
41. Collins, 1.
42. Oh and Hassig, 133 and Collins, Robert. *Marked for Life: Songbun, North Korea's Social Classification System*. (Washington, DC: The Committee for Human Rights in North Korea, 2012), 39.
43. Kongdan Oh, "North Korea: The Nadir of Freedom," in *Living without Freedom: A History Institute for Teachers*, Philadelphia, Foreign Policy Research Institute, 2007. Collins, I.
44. Oh, 134.
45. *Report of the Detailed Findings of the Commission of Inquiry on Human Rights in the DPRK*, the UN Human Rights Council, February 7, 2014, 221.
46. Hunter, Helen-Louise. *Kim Il-song's North Korea*. (Westport: Praeger, 1999), 3.
47. Hunter, 4.
48. Collins, 3.
49. Blaine Harden, "North Korea's Kim Jong Il Chooses Youngest Son as Heir," *The Washington Post*, June 3, 2009, http://www.washingtonpost.com/wp-dyn/content/article/2009/06/01/AR2009060103750.html.
50. "Official documents confirm Kim Jong Un as next ruler of North Korea," *The Mainichi Daily News*, September 8, 2009, http://74.125.47.32/search?q=cache:VSCQGQFW6ssJ:mdn.mainichi.jp/mdnnews/international/archive/news/2009/09/08/20090908p2g00m0in028000c.html+kim+jung+un+mainichi+shimbun&cd=5&hl=en&ct=clnk&gl=us&client=firefox-a.
51. Mark Mazzetti and Sang-hun Choe, "North Korea's Leader Is Seriously Ill, U.S. Intelligence Officials Say," *The New York Times*, September 9, 2008.
52. 'Fake photo' revives Kim rumours (November 15, 2008), http://news.bbc.co.uk/2/hi/asia-pacific/7715458.stm, (accessed September 23, 2009).

53. Donald Kirk, "Kim Jong Un: North Korea's next leader?" *The Christian Science Monitor*, June 2, 2009, http://www.csmonitor.com/2009/0602/p06s04-woap.html.
54. Bong-geun Jun, "Scenarios of North Korea's Power Shift: After Kim Jong-il's 'Reported Illness'," in *Policy Brief No. 2008–7*, Seoul, Institute of Foreign Affairs and National Security, November 2008, 11.
55. Scobell, "Projecting Pyongyang: The Future of North Korea's Kim Jong Il Regime," 30.
56. Oh, "North Korea."
57. "Tongil Baekseo 2005 (Unification White Paper 2005)," 171. "Over 2,800 N. Korean defectors come to South in 2008," *Yonhap News Agency*, September 27, 2009, http://english.yonhapnews.co.kr/northkorea/2009/09/27/94/0401000000AEN20090927003800320F.HTML.
58. Bukhan Ital Joomin Jeongchaek (North Korean Defector Policy), Tongye Jaryo (Data & Statistics), Ministry of Unification, data as of October 2014, http://www.unikorea.go.kr/content.do?cmsid=1518.
59. Sung-ho Ko, Ki-seon Chung, and Yoo-seok Oh, "North Korean Defectors: Their Life and Well-Being after Defection," *Asian Perspective* 28, no. 2 (2004): 68.
60. Since Kim Jong-un came to power, the defector numbers declined dramatically, owing probably to his border tightening and harsh measures.
61. Eun Seo Shin, "'Eungoo 7 Inbang' Buk U Dong Cheuk Jinanhae Jasal (The Suicide of U Dong Cheuk, 1 of '7 Key Figures Surrounding the Funeral Car,' Last Year)," *TV Chosun*, December 6, 2013, http://news.chosun.com/site/data/html_dir/2013/12/06/2013120603492.html?Dep0=twitter&d=2013120603492.
62. "Bookhan Sookchung-ui Yeogsa (The History of North Korean Purges)," *Daehanmingook Geun Hyeondaisa Series* (Korea's Recent Events), December 29, 2013, http://koreastory.kr/bbs/board.php?bo_table=issue&wr_id=56&page=1 and "N. Korea names new defense chief," *Chosun Ilbo*, June 16, 2015, http://english.chosun.com/site/data/html_dir/2015/06/16/2015061601225.html.
63. "Bookhan Sookchung-ui Yeogsa."
64. "N. Korea Confirms Execution of Army Chief," *The Chosun Ilbo*, June 15, 2015, http://english.chosun.com/site/data/html_dir/2015/06/15/2015061501311.html.
65. "A Dozen Senior N. Korean Officials Defect," *The Chosun Ilbo*, July 2, 2015, http://english.chosun.com/site/data/html_dir/2015/07/02/2015070201795.html.
66. Stares and Wit, 12.
67. Stares and Wit, 14.
68. Maxwell, 16–17.

69. Sung Hwee Moon, *Public Currency Announcement Broadcast*, http://www.dailynk.com/english/read.php?cataId=nk01500&num=5722 (accessed December 28, 2009).
70. "'Women Power' Gathers against N. Korean Currency Shock," *Chosun Ilbo*, December 8, 2009, http://english.chosun.com/site/data/html_dir/2009/12/08/2009120800307.html.
71. "N. Korea Backtracks as Currency Reform Sparks Riots," *Chosun Ilbo*, December 15, 2009, http://english.chosun.com/site/data/html_dir/2009/12/15/2009121500361.html.
72. Song-Min Choi, "Buk Musanseo Boahnwon-Jangsakkeun Jipdan Nantoogeuk...Sasangja Sushipmyeong (Security Personnel–Merchants Groups Scuffle in Musan, North Korea), *DailyNK*, June 29, 2015, http://www.dailynk.com/korean/read.php?cataId=nk04500&num=106436 (accessed July 2, 2015).
73. "Severe Drought Hits DPRK," *Korean Central News Agency of DPRK*, June 16, 2015, http://www.kcna.co.jp/index-e.htm.
74. Song-Min Choi.
75. Kretchum, Nat and Kim, Jane, "A Quiet Opening: North Koreans in a Changing Media Environment," *Intermedia*, May 2012, 8.

CHAPTER 4

Geopolitical Landscape and Regional Bilateral Issues

Abstract A complex set of national interests of South Korea, North Korea, the United States, China, Japan, and Russia converge or clash on the Korean Peninsula, creating multifaceted international relations, including alliances, trade, investments, shared histories, and war. The collapse of North Korea and subsequent Korean unification would alter the geostrategic landscape and profoundly affect the national interests. Korea will need support from the international community in a collapse situation, especially from the regional powers, for stabilization and reconstruction. This chapter examines the national interests and concerns of each major player, ongoing bilateral issues, and areas for possible cooperation in the event of a North Korea's collapse.

The Korean Peninsula's long history shapes the geopolitical realities in Northeast Asia. It is here that the interests of some of the world's major powers intersect (See Figure 4.1). North Korean instability would impact all the regional powers, especially South Korea, China, and the U.S., but also Japan and Russia. South Korea and China would be most directly impacted by a collapse, especially by mass emigration from North Korea. The control of North Korean nuclear weapons would pose a serious problem, especially for the U.S., but also for China.

While the need to plan for managing the aftermath of North Korea's collapse is clear, China has been reluctant to do so, as this is politically sensitive for its relations with North Korea. South Korea, during the Sunshine Policy, also avoided planning for fear of angering North Korea

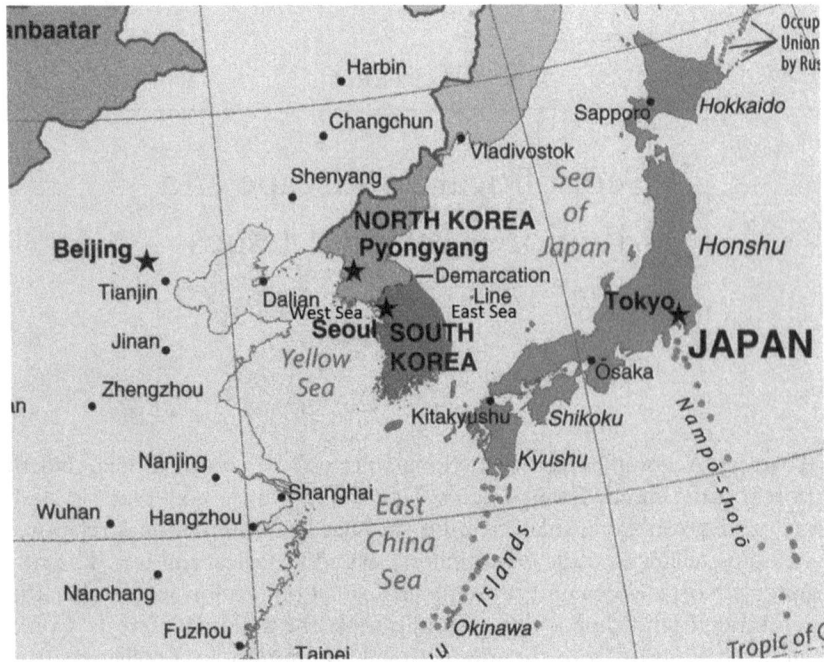

Fig. 4.1 Map of Northeast Asia (Source: CIA. Author modified. Courtesy of the University of Texas Libraries, The University of Texas at Austin)

and threatening the South–North rapprochement. The Lee Myong-bak administration was less reluctant and had reportedly discussed collapse contingency planning with the U.S.[1] Lee also proposed a unification tax in 2010, but the public gave a lukewarm response and it did not materialize. Under President Park Geun-hye, Seoul has become more active in recognizing the importance of unification planning, starting with an effort to change the perception that unification has downsides only because of its high financial and social costs. She described the Korean unification as a "jackpot" that will benefit the South Korean public as well as the neighboring countries with massive infrastructure and other investments that would revitalize growth in the region, including China and Russia.[2] She is on the right path to start addressing the need for planning. The danger of not planning is that if North Korea does collapse, neighboring states would be unprepared for possibly cataclysmic challenges.

The South Korean government, military, and civil society could heavily be involved in restoring order and economic development, paving the way for unification. Common language, ethnicity, culture, and shared history are important in this regard. A united Korea would reflect the South Korean system of democratic government and market economy. In a collapse situation involving war, the combined ROK–U.S. forces would repel the aggression. In the immediate conclusion of war, the combined forces would be present in North Korea as victors involved in stability operations. It is important to consult with China on the U.S. military's presence in the northern part of the peninsula. China would need to understand that the troops would be present to insure stability. If U.S. forces become involved in dealing with uncontrolled nuclear weapons, China should understand the benefit, as China also would be concerned about nuclear weapons and materials crossing its border. South Korea, China, and the U.S. have asymmetric roles and capabilities. They need to seek common and convergent interests and coordinate their responses for a potential collapse.

1   Geopolitical Landscape

After describing the geopolitical landscape and economic relations among the major powers in the region, this chapter examines the national interests and concerns of each major player, ongoing and unresolved bilateral issues, and areas for possible cooperation in the event of a North Korean collapse.

Four major world powers—China, Japan, Russia, and the United States—play an important role in the Korean Peninsula (Tables 4.1, 4.2, 4.3, and 4.4). China is the world's most populous country with the second largest economy and the world's largest active-duty military force. Japan, with the third largest economy, ranks ninth in defense expenditures and tenth in population size. Russia is ranked in the top ten in population size and economy, and has the fifth largest active-duty military and the third largest defense spending. The third most populous country, the U.S., is the sole superpower with the world's largest economy and defense spending. These powers' national interests sometimes converge and at other times do not.

The two Koreas have their own interests, and each has become a significant regional actor. South Korea has the world's thirteenth largest economy, tenth largest defense budget, and sixth largest active-duty military. Although its economy is in shambles, North Korea is believed to have nuclear weapons and the world's fourth largest military in terms of number of troops.

Table 4.1 Population (2014 estimate)[a]

Rank	Country	(million)
1	China	1355.7
2	India	1236.3
3	U.S.	318.9
4	Indonesia	253.7
5	Brazil	202.7
6	Pakistan	196.2
7	Nigeria	177.2
8	Bangladesh	166.3
9	Russia	142.5
10	Japan	127.1
26	South Korea	49.0
51	North Korea	24.9

Source: *CIA World Factbook*

[a]"Country Comparison: Population," *CIA World Factbook*, Central Intelligence Agency, https://www.cia.gov/library/publications/the-world-factbook/rankorder/2119rank.html (accessed July 3, 2015)

Table 4.2 Gross Domestic Product (GDP 2014)[a]

Rank	Country	($ billion)
1	U.S.	17,419
2	China	10,360
3	Japan	4601
4	Germany	3853
5	UK	2942
6	France	2829
7	Brazil	2346
8	Italy	2144
9	India	2067
10	Russia	1861
13	South Korea	1410
89	North Korea	34*

Sources: *World Bank*, *Bank of Korea*

[a]"Data: GDP Ranking," *The World Bank*, updated July 1, 2015, http://data.worldbank.org/data-catalog/GDP-ranking-table (accessed July 4, 2015), and for North Korea, "Gross Domestic Product Estimates for North Korea in 2013," Bank of Korea, June 28, 2014, 5, http://www.bok.or.kr/autonomy.search?home=eng, [Gross National Income (GNI) figures are converted to U.S. dollars using $1:KRW 1049, an average for the first six months of 2014]

Table 4.3 Military (active duty) (2014)[a]

Rank	Country	(1000)
1	China	2333
2	U.S.	1400
3	India	1325
4	North Korea	1200*
5	Russia	766
6	South Korea	669*
7	Pakistan	617
8	Iran	545
9	Algeria	512
10	Indonesia	476

Sources: Global Firepower; *ROK–U.S. Combined Forces Command/U.S. Forces Korea and U.S. Department of Defense

[a]"Active Military Manpower by Country," Global Firepower, http://www.globalfirepower.com/active-military-manpower.asp, (accessed July 4, 2015); *1.2 million is the number often estimated. See http://www.cfr.org/global/global-conflict-tracker/p32137#!/?marker=5. The ROK–U.S. Combined Forces Command/U.S. Forces Korea *Strategic Digest* Spring 2014, 11, shows the figure of around 1 million. See also "Military and Security Developments Involving the Democratic People's Republic of Korea," Office of the Secretary of Defense Annual Report to Congress, February 4, 2014, 16–18

A complex set of national interests converge or clash on the Korean Peninsula, creating multifaceted international relations. The interconnections among these six countries take a variety of forms, including alliances, trade, investments, shared histories, and war. The regional powers' strategic considerations include security, territorial sovereignty, and enhancing their own power and influence in the region. The collapse of North Korea and subsequent Korean unification would alter the geostrategic landscape and profoundly affect these national interests.

After the collapse, Korea will need support from the international community, especially the regional powers, for stabilization and reconstruction. The most desirable scenario for the post-unification Korean Peninsula includes a successfully developed and integrated nonnuclear Korea acting as a responsible regional and world stakeholder. Unified Korea would need to cooperate with the U.S., China, Japan, and Russia to enhance regional stability.

Table 4.4 Military expenditure (2014)[a]

Rank	Country	($ million)
1	U.S.	609,914
2	China	216,371
3	Russia	84,462
4	Saudi Arabia	80,762
5	France	62,289
6	UK	60,482
7	India	49,968
8	Germany	46,455
9	Japan	45,776
10	South Korea	36,677
29	North Korea	10,733**

Source: Stockholm International Research Institute

**Estimate based on one-third of North Korea's 2013 GNI

[a]"SIPRI Military Expenditure Database," Stockholm International Peace Research Institute, http://www.sipri.org/research/armaments/milex/milex_database (accessed July 3, 2015). For North Korean military spending estimate, refer to "North Korea spends about a third of income on military: group," *Reuters Canada*, January 18, 2011, http://ca.reuters.com/article/topNews/idCA-TRE70H1BW20110118 (accessed July 5, 2015).

2   Deepening Economic Relations

Northeast Asia accounts for a significant part of the world's trade and economy. Trade and investment among South Korea, China, and Japan have grown considerably. The trend will likely continue.

The three economies are each other's top trading partners (Tables 4.5, 4.6, and 4.7). However, these close economic ties are relatively recent. Trade linkages, especially with China, were rather weak until the 1990s. Japan and South Korea initially became major exporting nations within the framework of multilateral trading systems' General Agreement on Tariffs and Trade (GATT), later the World Trade Organization (WTO). In contrast, China remained an underdeveloped, centrally planned economy for most of the post–World War II period. Japan pursued export-led growth strategies post–World War II and South Korea started in the 1960s. Both countries rapidly increased trade, primarily with the U.S. in the earlier decades. In early 2000s or so, both countries' trade with China increased dramatically, overtaking the U.S. as their top trading partner, although significant ties with the U.S. remain.

Ideological, political, security, and historical differences have prevented deeper integration of the Northeast Asian countries. The communist regime in China blocked most cooperation with capitalistic societies until its own reforms began in the mid-1980s. The tension between Seoul and Pyongyang, and Beijing's support for Pyongyang, also limited contacts, as did historical animosity. The security threat and the ROK–U.S. and Japan–U.S. alliances reinforced close U.S. relations with South Korea and Japan, but not necessarily with each other or China until relatively recently. The U.S. has traditionally been the top trading partner with both South Korea and Japan. Although China has now become the top trading partner with these countries, the U.S. still remains their important trading partner.

The Chinese economy started to grow rapidly with economic reforms based on the export-led growth model that proved extremely successful for Japan and South Korea. China entered the WTO in December 2001 with the support of the U.S. after 15 years of arduous negotiation.[3] China's membership in the WTO was crucial for its economic growth. The U.S. is the top destination for Chinese exports, but China has also significantly deepened economic relations with Japan and South Korea. China and Japan's nongovernmental trade began in the 1950s, but it was not until 1972, when they normalized diplomatic relations, that their economic ties developed rapidly.

South Korea began indirect trade with China through Hong Kong and Singapore in 1983. With the establishment of diplomatic relations in 1992, direct bilateral trade developed rapidly. Their total trade increased

Table 4.5 South Korea's top trading partners (2014 estimate)[a]

Rank	Export (%)	Import (%)
1	China (25.4)	China (17.1)
2	U.S. (12.3)	Japan (10.2)
3	Japan (5.6)	U.S. (8.7)
4	Hong Kong (4.8)	Saudi Arabia (7.0)

Source: *CIA World Factbook*

[a]"Exports-Partners," *CIA World Factbook,* Central Intelligence Agency, https://www.cia.gov/library/publications/the-world-factbook/fields/2050.html and https://www.cia.gov/library/publications/the-world-factbook/fields/2061.html (accessed July 3, 2015)

Table 4.6 China's top trading partners (2014 estimate)[a]

Rank	Export (%)	Import (%)
1	U.S. (16.9)	South Korea (9.7)
2	Hong Kong (15.5)	Japan (8.3)
3	Japan (6.4)	U.S. (8.1)
4	South Korea (4.3)	Taiwan (7.8)

Source: *CIA World Factbook*
[a]"Exports-Patners"

Table 4.7 Japan's top trading partners (2014 estimate)[a]

Rank	Export (%)	Import (%)
1	U.S. (18.9)	China (22.3)
2	China (18.3)	U.S. (9.0)
3	South Korea (7.5)	Australia (5.9)
4	Hong Kong (5.5)	Saudi Arabia (5.9)

Source: *CIA World Factbook*
Note: South Korea is Japan's seventh largest source of imports
[a]"Exports-Patners"

from $5 billion in 1992 to $44 billion a decade later, almost a ninefold increase.[4] Trade totaled $227 billion in 2015.[5] As the data suggest, South Korea and China have robust trade relations.

For North Korea, China is an essential trading partner and aid provider. Beijing's economic relations with Pyongyang date to 1950, with exchanges mainly of fuel, raw materials, and manufacturing goods. Given North Korea's economic difficulties, China primarily transferred energy and food to North Korea. The total volume of Chinese–North Korean bilateral trade in 2014 was $6.9 billion, with North Korea importing $4.0 billion from and exporting $2.8 billion to China.[6] Despite North Korea's failed economy and its inability or refusal to pay hard currency, China has continued to provide economic assistance and increased trade. China is likely to continue such activities as Beijing emphasizes stability on its border as an overarching policy objective.

Inter-Korean economic relations are relatively small, but they are important for two reasons. First, the mere existence of any inter-Korean relations at all is significant, given decades of hostile posturing by both sides. The two main economic projects—the Gaesong Industrial Complex (GIC) and Mount Geumgang tourism projects, both in North Korea—are deeply symbolic. South Korea hoped the interactions would thaw the relations and convince North Korea to reform and move toward peaceful posture. Mount Geumgang tourism halted after a South Korean tourist was shot to death in 2008, but GIC business continued through various provocations by Pyongyang, until recently. North Korea conducted its fourth nuclear test in January 2016, followed by another missile test in February, prompting Seoul to halt the operations at GIC.[7] For North Korea, these projects bring in significant income for the regime. South Korea sent 616 billion won ($514.4 million) to GIC since its inception in 2004, in addition to 1,190 billion won ($993.7 million) spent on infrastructure, operations, and administration.[8] The project introduced capitalistic ideas of for-profit goods and services, and demonstrated the skills necessary for success, as well as facilitated some level of contact between South Koreans and North Koreans. While there were some benefits of limited interactions with North Koreans at the complex, the Park government probably felt that it could no longer support a regime that prioritizes resources toward nuclear weapons program.

Northeast Asia is an economically dynamic region with increasing interdependence among the member countries, which extends to the U.S. as a Pacific power. While the peace and stability they enjoy bring prosperity to the region, numerous unresolved issues could hinder further cooperation or become a trigger for instability. The two Koreas, China, Japan, and Russia have enduring and at times contentious historical and territorial issues with one another. South Korea and the U.S. are undergoing an alliance transformation and deepening economic ties, which can also be controversial at times. North Korea's nuclear weapons and its inability or refusal to reform are key concerns for all the surrounding countries.

The remainder of this chapter examines the regional powers' national interests and concerns and identifies potential areas of cooperation to build regional stability pre- and post-unification.

3   REGIONAL POWERS' NATIONAL INTERESTS

This section examines the national interests of the regional powers. Some of these interests have deep historical roots, which are appropriate to enable a clearer understanding of the current situation as seen by each country.

3.1   United States

Northeast Asia has been strategically and economically important to the U.S.. As a global superpower and a Pacific power, the U.S. has an interest in maintaining its influence in Northeast Asia. Its alliances with South Korea and Japan have provided a solid basis for promoting stability and economic growth in the region while extending its influence.

The U.S. also has strong economic ties, especially trade, with not only its allies South Korea and Japan, but also with China. These three countries accounted for about a quarter of the U.S. global trade in 2014 with China as the second largest trading partner at $591 billion, Japan as the fourth at $201 billion, and South Korea as the sixth at $114 billion (Table 4.8).[9] China, Japan, Russia, and South Korea accounted for holding 43% of U.S. Treasury Securities among foreign holders as of April 2015 (Table 4.9).[10]

Since the U.S.–ROK alliance focuses on deterring North Korea, once North Korea is no longer considered a threat, especially if it disappears as a state, it will be difficult to justify the alliance in its present form. If the U.S.–ROK alliance dissolves, the U.S.–Japan alliance, also partly focused on the North Korean threat, may be harder to maintain without other threats. These alliances have been useful for all parties involved and have provided an institutional basis for cooperation, which is also beneficial for the future. It would be in the interests of the U.S. and South Korea to maintain a transformed version of alliance to preserve the cooperation and influence. The alliance provides a solid and stable basis from which a key ally, Korea, a country initially caught in a vicious circle of poverty in the aftermath of the 1950–1953 Korean War, has transformed into one of the world's most economically and technologically advanced countries and a vibrant democracy—a tremendously successful foreign policy feat.

The alliance is already undergoing transformation. As discussed in greater detail later in this chapter, the two countries agreed to transfer wartime operational control from the U.S. to an ROK army general, initially based on a timeline, but recently based on conditions.[11] The two

Table 4.8   U.S. trade balance, by partner country (2014)[a]

Rank	Country	Imports ($ million)	Exports ($ million)	Total trade ($ million)
1	Canada	346,062.60	312,125.20	658,187.80
2	China	466,656.50	124,024.00	590,680.50
3	Mexico	294,157.50	240,326.20	534,483.70
4	Japan	133,938.70	66,964.10	200,902.80
5	Germany	123,181.00	49,442.60	172,623.60
6	South Korea	69,605.70	44,544.00	114,149.70
7	UK	54,048.50	53,865.10	107,913.60
8	France	47,015.10	31,197.50	78,212.60
9	Brazil	30,336.60	42,418.00	72,754.60
10	Taiwan	40,571.70	26,835.70	67,407.40
27	Russia	23,691.90	10,767.70	34,459.60

Source: U.S. International Trade Commission

[a]"U.S. Merchandise trade balance, by partner country 2014 in descending order of trade turnover (general imports plus total exports)," U.S. International Trade Commission, http://dataweb.usitc.gov/scripts/cy_m3_run.asp (accessed July 3, 2015)

Table 4.9   Major foreign holders of U.S. Treasury securities (April 2015)[a]

Rank	Country	U.S.$ (billion)	%
1	China	1263.4	20.59
2	Japan	1215.7	19.81
18	South Korea	71.8	1.17
20	Russia	66.5	1.08
	Subtotal	2617.4	42.65
	Grand total	6137.3	

Source: U.S. Treasury Department

[a]"Major Foreign Holders of Treasury Securities," U.S. Treasury Department, http://www.treasury.gov/resource-center/data-chart-center/tic/Documents/mfh.txt (accessed May 17, 2011)

sides have already agreed on the 2002 Land Partnership Program and the 2004 Yongsan Relocation Program designed to reduce the American military footprint in Korea.[12]

Alliance transformation is a natural outcome of Korea's success, the changed international security environment, and re-prioritized U.S. national security interests. As such, the transformation reflects more maturity, based on mutual respect and understanding. During President Park

Geun-hye's visit to the U.S. in May 2013 marking 60 years of bilateral partnership, President Barak Obama described the U.S.–ROK alliance as the linchpin of peace and security on the Korean Peninsula and the rest of the region, and added that both countries would strengthen and adapt the alliance to meet future security challenges.[13] Both leaders agreed to continue to implement the historic Korea–U.S. Free Trade Agreement (KORUS FTA), which boosts trade and provides jobs for both countries. The joint statement envisioned an increasing global role for South Korea and greater cooperation in a variety of issues:

> (T)he United States welcomes the Republic of Korea's leadership and active engagement on the world stage, including in international fora. We will strengthen our efforts to address global challenges such as climate change and to promote clean energy, energy security, human rights, humanitarian assistance, development assistance cooperation, counter-terrorism, peaceful uses of nuclear energy, nuclear safety, non-proliferation, cybersecurity, and counter-piracy. [14]

The partnership between the U.S. and South Korea is maturing beyond the narrow focus on North Korea and broadening into other global challenges declared in the joint statement.

3.2 *China*

China is an emerging great power, with a rapidly growing economy. With economic growth comes the financial capacity to build military power and extend political influence around the globe. China has come a long way from a per capita GDP of $33 when the People's Republic was established in 1949 to over $7594 in 2014.[15] In 2013, China overtook the U.S. as the world's biggest trading nation.[16] China has been the world's largest holder of dollar reserves since 2008, when it surpassed Japan. China became the third country in the world after the U.S. and the former Soviet Union to succeed in a spacewalk, when it launched the *Shenzhou* manned lunar spacecraft into orbit.[17] President Hu Jintao said that "[t]he forecast for China's development is infinitely optimistic," reflecting pride in the country's accomplishments and its positive outlook of its future.[18] This development occurred with Hu's policy of China's "peaceful rise," which implied that China was avoiding unnecessary international conflict.

In recent times, however, China under Xi Jinping has taken measures in the air and the sea to its east and south, which troubled its neighbors and awoke the U.S.. In November 2013, China abruptly declared air defense identification zone (ADIZ) over a large area of East China Sea, which overlaps with already established ADIZs of Japan, South Korea, and Taiwan. The new ADIZ covers Japanese-controlled Senkaku islets (Diaoyu in Chinese, and claimed by Japan, China, and Taiwan) and South Korean–claimed Ieodo (Suyan Jiao in Chinese, and disputed by South Korea and China). This declaration raised tension in the region and increased the risk of accidents, provocations, and miscommunications.[19] In the South China Sea, China embarked on a major land reclamation project, which included building an airfield and placing mobile artillery on the disputed Spratley Islands.[20] Robert Sutter of George Washington University explains that Beijing is shifting its foreign policy from reassuring its neighbors and the U.S. to an active and assertive one that is actually reducing China's influence in the region, despite significant economic ties.[21]

North Korea's provocations and continued pursuit of WMD could complicate the already complex situation in the region. North Korea's development of nuclear weapons could prompt a nuclear security dilemma, leading to a nuclear-armed Japan and South Korea, which would then directly affect China's security. The nuclear umbrella extended by the U.S. to its two allies and the prospect of denuclearizing North Korea keep the nuclear security dilemma in check. It is in China's interest to disarm North Korea of its nuclear weapons capability, which is also the goal of the Six-Party Talks that began in 2003. Although the talks were discontinued in 2009, the possibility of resuming discussions has resurfaced. China has been an active player as the chair of the Six-Party Talks and has worked to resolve the nuclear issue. In a collapse situation, it would also be in China's interest to ensure that North Korea's nuclear weapons and materials do not come across the border for further proliferation to other state or nonstate actors.

An even higher priority for China is the stability of North Korea.[22] A collapsed North Korea and the ensuing flood of refugees would affect China's economy and stability, especially in the northeastern provinces that border North Korea. China is also concerned that instability in North Korea may "irresistibly tempt" South Korea, an ally of the U.S., to reunify.[23]

Wu Baiyi of the Chinese Academy of Social Sciences describes China's interest in the Korean Peninsula thus:

> China has to compete with other major powers (i.e., the United States and Japan) over strategic superiority in any solution of the Korean issue....The renewal of the U.S.-Japanese alliance and the extension of its defense coverage deepened Chinese suspicions that the United States seeks regional hegemony and that the Japanese military might be revitalized. Korea is of practical importance to offset such possibilities. On the other hand, it is also in Beijing's vital interest to maintain a secure and friendly neighborhood in the sub-region.[24]

China does not want U.S. troops on its border during the unification process, and may send its troops to counter U.S. influence, reminiscent of when China sent "volunteer" troops to support North Korea against the U.S.-led UN forces during the Korean War.

Since Xi Jinping became the premier in China, Beijing's North Korea policy has been evolving. The debate between the traditionalists and strategists has increased. North Korea has become not so much a strategic asset but a strategic liability as it continues its nuclear weapons development, conducts military provocations, and refuses to reform, creating tension in the region. Peking University's Niu Jun provides an insightful analysis on China's shifting principles toward North Korea and the Korean Peninsula. The four traditional principles were: (1) preventing war on the Korean Peninsula, (2) preventing chaos in North Korea, (3) deterring South Korea–led unification, and (4) denuclearization.[25] Beijing has revised its official principles as follows: (1) denuclearization, (2) maintaining peace and stability, and (3) resolving the Korean Peninsula issue through dialogue, instead of the earlier four principles.[26] Denuclearization has been moved to the top, while deterring South Korea–led unification is deleted. It also does not specify North Korea, but refers to the entire Korean Peninsula, which implies dialogue with not only North Korea, but also South Korea. China's key concern is a unified Korea that may be strategically friendly, or at least not unfriendly, to China. To this end, relying solely on North Korea may not be the best option.

China has historically been a giant neighbor to Korea and has traditionally seen Korea as an integral part of its national security. It was through Korea that Japan invaded and controlled Manchuria in the late nineteenth century, unleashing a period of humiliation for a country that has historically considered itself the center of the world. China still views Japan with unease, especially since the historical issues are unresolved and Japan is a staunch ally of the U.S..

A report by the Asia Strategy Working Group states that China wants to be "flanked on all sides by nonthreatening, ideologically compatible regimes" to scotch subversive influences from outside its borders.[27] The U.S. is a strong supporter of Taiwan, which calls for democracy—a political system at odds with China's one-party system. As long as the Korean Peninsula is divided, North Korea acts as a buffer state against the U.S. and its influence. This buffer is becoming increasingly costly.

Unification would most likely leave South Korea, an ally of the U.S., in charge of the whole peninsula. Beijing would want to counter Washington and exert its own influence on the peninsula. For this reason, Chinese leaders liked Rho Moo-hyun's emphasis on peace and reconciliation with North Korea, regional cooperation and stability, and greater independence within the U.S.–ROK alliance relationship.[28] Rho's approach may have been seen as permitting the end of the U.S.–South Korean alliance after Korean unification, which would allow China to step in as South Korea's main strategic partner. Lee Myung-bak's election clouded this vision of Korea leaning away from the U.S. toward China. One of Lee's key early campaign pledges was to strengthen the U.S.–ROK alliance, especially after the trough in bilateral relations during the Rho administration. Perhaps concerned with Lee's emphasis on the alliance, the Chinese government sent a special envoy to Seoul to meet president-elect Lee even before Lee sent his special envoy to Beijing, reflecting eagerness by China to promote a higher-level relationship. During Lee Myung-bak's Beijing visit in May 2008, his first visit as the president, Lee and the Chinese president Hu Jintao elevated relations between the two countries to a "strategic cooperative partnership" level.[29] They reached extensive agreement, including stepping up exchanges and diplomatic and security cooperation resulting in intensified top-level meetings. The 2008 agreement also highlighted trade relations. China had overtaken the U.S. as South Korea's top trading partner, and bilateral trade was expected to increase dramatically. The Beijing–Seoul relations improved under President Park Geun-hye. Her first state visit to China in June 2013 was a "trip of heart and trust" and the two countries announced that they will reinforce their strategic cooperative partnership.[30] China will likely develop closer ties with South Korea while maintaining its relations with North Korea.

China is North Korea's closest supporter. During the Korean War, China sent "volunteers" to support North Korea at a significant human cost as well as forgoing its opportunity to unify with Taiwan by redirecting the use of forces on the Korean Peninsula. Throughout the Cold War, although North Korea played China against the Soviet Union, Beijing and Pyongyang forged closer relations. Recently, Chinese assistance has become even more crucial. In 2008, China provided 48% of North Korea's imports.[31] This was the year South Korea started to reduce or halt assistance to North Korea due to the latter's lack of reciprocity, the advent of the Lee Myong-bak administration, and the North Korean shooting of a South Korean tourist at Mount Geumgang. As of 2014, China accounted for over 79% of North Korea's imports, a significant portion.[32] Usually, imports signify goods traded with hard currency, but with North Korea's lack of hard currency and creative accounting, some of the "imports" can be viewed as aid. Because external assistance helps the broken North Korean economy limp along, if this support were halted, the regime could collapse. China, to prevent a North Korean collapse and in the absence of a better option, is likely to continue support for the Kim regime.

3.3 Japan

Japan has successfully pursued its national interests to ensure its security and prosperity. Its economy has grown to be the third largest in the world while its alliance with the U.S. has provided security guarantees. Ever since it began its modernization, Japan has been ambivalent about whether to strive to catch up with the West or to maintain an Asian identity.[33] However, Japan is tied to Asia not only geographically but also economically, politically, and culturally.

Economically, China and South Korea are Japan's significant trading partners. Cultural and educational exchanges have also increased. Japan's relations with its neighbors improved with normalization of diplomatic relations, with South Korea in 1965 and China in 1972. These ties have been strengthened since the 1980s, although frayed in recent years due to historical and territorial issues.

The security picture is more complex. Japan's 2014 defense white paper outlines its security concerns. They include Korean reunification, North Korea's nuclear and missile programs, North Korea's provocations, China's increased military assertiveness in and over the East China Sea, including the disputed Senkaku/Daioyutai Islands, and with Russia regarding the territorial claims over the Northern Territories/Kurile Islands as well as its annexation of Crimea.[34] The white paper mentions China's increased flying and maritime activities over or near the disputed territories, and expresses deep concern about China's establishment of the AIDZ as well as its aggressive measures, which may lead to unintended consequences.[35] It also highlights North Korea's WMD and missiles development, and states that its provocative words and actions "constitute[s] a serious destabilizing factor" for the security of Japan, the rest of the region, and the world.[36] The white paper notes Russia's increased naval and air activities in the region as well as the change in the status quo because of Russia's coercion of the Crimea, which heightens tension and impacts Asia.[37] Additionally, Japan sees secure sea lanes as essential to its survival, as the island nation relies heavily on imported oil and food, which transit through various waters of the world.

Japan's interest in the Korean Peninsula dates back prior to Korea's division. Japan has traditionally seen Korea as a dagger aimed at its heart.[38] It was through Korea that the Mongols tried to invade Japan. Resource-poor Japan also eyed the natural resources in northern Korea and Manchuria. Japan's determination that Korea not be dominated by powers hostile toward it prompted its competition with China and Russia starting in the late nineteenth century. Japan's victories in the Sino-Japanese War of 1895 and the Russo-Japanese War of 1904–1905 ensured its dominance over the Korean Peninsula and Manchuria. Japan solidified its control by annexing Korea in 1910 through to the end of World War II in 1945. Today, Japanese–Korean relations can be characterized as "near but far" due to their volatile history. South Koreans still recall when Hideyoshi of Japan invaded Korea in 1592, and the antagonistic feelings have not dissipated during the four centuries since.[39]

Tokyo and Seoul normalized relations in 1965 after a continuous strong push from Washington. Although normalization was highly unpopular in South Korea, it was vital to its economic development.[40] A key part of normalization negotiations was reparation to settle claims from the Japanese colonization of Korea. Normalization infused massive capital into the South Korean economy. The Japanese government provided $500 million in grants and loans and private firms invested $300 million at a time when South Korea's exports were only $200 million. South Korean president Park Chung-hee used the capital and Japanese technology to create a steel industry that set the course for South Korea's industrialization.[41]

The Pohang Steel Company (POSCO) is the world's fifth largest steel producer. The steel industry enabled South Korea to become the world's leading ship builder.[42] Since this beginning, Japan and South Korea have developed close economic ties.

On the security front, although there is no direct Japan–ROK alliance, they are allied *de facto* through their respective alliances with the U.S., an arrangement that has deterred threats to Japan that might come through the Korean Peninsula. The close U.S.–ROK security relationship, therefore, serves the interest of Japan.

Japan's relations with North Korea are rocky, and they have yet to normalize diplomatic relations. North Korea's nuclear weapons and missiles threaten Japan. Japan is well within the range of North Korea's missiles, and when North Korea tests its long-range missiles, some are aimed toward Japan. The abduction of Japanese citizens by North Korea remains a sticky point. Despite the unresolved abduction issue, the U.S. removed North Korea from the list of states sponsoring terrorism after the latter handed over documents on their nuclear program. While the U.S. supports Japan, making progress on North Korea's nuclear issue outweighed the abduction issue. Japan has no diplomatic leverage with South Korea, China, and Russia on resolving the abduction issue because Japan has historical and territorial disputes with each of these countries. As a result, Japan may feel isolated. Its public has become increasingly nationalistic and may call for a more independent security policy.[43] In fact, Prime Minister Abe's cabinet decided in 2014 to reinterpret Japan's constitution to ease the restrictions on its Self-Defense Force activities outside Japanese territory. Abe plans to take a step further by overhauling its national security laws in parliament.[44]

Korean reunification is a large and looming issue for Japan. The initial instability following a collapse of North Korea would affect Japan's stability and economy as well. While most of the expected mass movement of people would likely head for China and South Korea, Japan is another possible destination. Instability on the Korean Peninsula could also severely affect Japan's close economic ties with South Korea and China, impacting its domestic economy.

Any Japanese military participation in the peninsula, even under UN auspices, may be problematic and vigorously opposed by Korea given the history. However, Japan could play an important role in economic, humanitarian, and development realms.

Any rivalry that might emerge between the U.S. and China would concern Japan, as the U.S. is a key ally and China is a close trading partner and a major regional power. The rewriting of the geopolitical landscape is also a concern. Japan wants a friendly reunified Korea, not one tilted toward China or "aggressively nationalistic, anti-Japanese, and free of the restraint imposed by the DPRK menace and U.S. alliance."[45] Japan also would want Korea free of nuclear weapons. Tokyo's and Seoul's respective alliance with Washington and extended deterrence will continue to be useful in allaying the fear and promoting a more stable environment in the region.

Japan sees China as a rising power that will try to exert its influence in the region, eyeing China's 2.3 million forces and increasing military power with unease. China continues to modernize its military, expanding its air force, naval, and missile capabilities. China's defense budget for 2014 was $216 billion, reflecting double-digit growth since 1996.[46]

Japan's relationship with China is complicated. On the one hand, both have increased their trade and economic exchanges, becoming important trade partners. China is Japan's top trading partner while Japan is among China's top three trading partners.[47] On the other hand, there are major tensions. Japan has territorial and maritime disputes with China over the Senkaku/Diaoyu Islands in the East China Sea. China's aircraft and submarines have rapidly increased activities in and over the East China Sea and the Sea of Japan. The Japan Defense Agency reports that the number of scrambles against Chinese jet fighters increased by 35% to 415 in a 12-month period between 2013 and 2014.[48] On January 7, 2007, Japan upgraded its military agency from the Japan Defense Agency to the Ministry of Defense, a cabinet-level organization, signifying the growing importance of its defense apparatus. Japan worries about China's rapid rise in military capability and its intensified military activities in the waters and airspace around Japan. Japan emphasized the threat from China in its 2013 *National Security Strategy* as well as the *National Defense Program Guideline*, referring to China's military action as a regional and global concern.[49] Japan's 2013 *National Security Strategy* states that "gray zones"—neither pure peacetime nor contingencies—are especially serious in the Asia-Pacific region.[50] The 2013 *National Defense Program Guideline* calls for responding to situations, including "gray zones," to protect the integrity of Japan's territorial land, waters, and airspace.[51]

As the security environment evolves in Northeast Asia, Japan searches for a national strategy for the region's dynamic and enduring situations. Its alliance with the U.S. has served Japan well. While friendly relations with the U.S. are important, so are relations with its neighbors. Tokyo's economic ties with Beijing and Seoul have grown dramatically, but historical and territorial issues are stumbling blocks to further improvement of relations.

3.4 Russia

The former Soviet Union essentially created North Korea by moving into and occupying the northern half of the peninsula at the end of World War II and installing Kim Il-sung to lead that half. Moscow was instrumental in supporting Kim Il-sung, who adopted the Stalin-style totalitarian system that exists in North Korea today. In recent times, however, contemporary Russia does not appear to play a greater role in the great power politics on the Korean Peninsula compared to the U.S., China, and Japan. Historically, Russia has considered Korea important to its national interest, especially to the Russian Far East. The Russo-Japanese War of 1904–5 was a competition with Japan over Korea and Manchuria. During the Cold War, North Korea was at the forefront of the Soviet Union's ideological competition with the U.S., and the Soviet Union was involved in a hot war on the peninsula during the Korean War. After the collapse of the Soviet Union, Russia focused on pressing domestic problems, but it also established diplomatic relations with South Korea, hoping to capitalize on Northeast Asia's economic dynamism. Previously a superpower that rivaled the U.S., Russia is dismayed at the marginalization of its influence, and would likely seek to restore its role as a major world power.

Russia's involvement in the Korean Peninsula began in the 1860s when Czarist Russia gained the Maritime Territories from China, resulting in an 11-mile border with Korea. Initially, Russian interest focused on commercial extractions of gold and minerals. As China's Ching dynasty disintegrated and domestic strife made the Yi Dynasty in Seoul vulnerable, Japan moved to control the peninsula. For three decades, foreign powers competed for influence, culminating in the Russo-Japanese War. Japanese forces marched through Korea to Manchuria and the Russian border and overran Russian outposts in the Maritime Territories, delivering a humiliating defeat that is deeply embedded in Russian historical memory. Russia is acutely conscious of its vulnerability in Northeast Asia and the importance of denying Korea to hostile powers.

When Japan was about to surrender to the allies during World War II, the Soviet Union learned of it before the U.S. by intercepting a decoded diplomatic cable, and the Soviet Union quickly entered the Pacific War. With memories of the 1905 defeat, the Soviets demanded a role in accepting the Japanese surrender, quickly moving their forces to the northern Korean Peninsula and the Northern Territories/Kurile Islands while U.S. troops were still landing in the southern part of the peninsula. The Soviet Union had the clear intention to divide the peninsula, while the U.S. lacked a clear goal, allowing the Soviet Union to occupy northern Korea and solidifying its influence in the northern half, effectively setting in motion the division of the peninsula.[52] Moscow wanted a close military ally in Pyongyang and backed Kim Il-sung, installing "Soviet-Koreans" in key positions. The Soviet Union, however, lost further influence during the Korean War, when China sent its "volunteers" to aid North Korean war efforts. Moscow did not foresee its competition with China for influence in North Korea, as Pyongyang played Moscow and Beijing against each other. In the midst of the Cold War with the U.S. and as Sino-Soviet relations deteriorated, Moscow ended up providing $11.2 billion worth of Cold War military aid to Pyongyang, including advanced fighters, Scud missiles, and tanks.[53]

In the mid-1980s, Mikhail Gorbachev pursued *glasnost* and *perestroika* and moved the Soviet Union to a more balanced posture on the peninsula, establishing diplomatic relations with Seoul in 1990 and canceling the delivery of four nuclear reactors that had been promised to Pyongyang. The collapse of the Soviet Union in 1991 and the emergence of Boris Yeltsin cut off most assistance to North Korea, including military aid and oil. Yeltsin virtually wrote off Pyongyang, instead forging a new relationship with Seoul. The upsurge in nationalist and Communist forces in 1992 and subsequent years put pressure on Russia to reassess its Korea policy and reengage Pyongyang for strategic reasons.

The relationship between Moscow and Seoul began with high hopes. Gorbachev expected massive South Korean investment in the Russian Federation while Rho Tae-woo envisioned normalized relations with Moscow would facilitate improved relations with Pyongyang. These expectations were too high. South Korean investment in Russia was modest due to Russia's poor investment environment. Seoul agreed to provide $3 billion in loans to Moscow, but as Moscow was unable to make repayments, Seoul stopped disbursement after extending $1.47 billion.[54] Until the late 1990s, Seoul and Moscow explored a natural gas pipeline project capable of carrying up to 30 billion cubic meters of gas annually. The pipeline would have to go through North Korea. The pipeline was discussed between Seoul and Pyongyang in the Sunshine Policy era, but as with other inter-Korea projects, it proved difficult to get started and to maintain due to North Korean intransigence. While the pipeline through North Korea is on hold, the September 2008 meeting between Lee Myung-bak and his Russian counterpart, Dmitry Medvedev, picked up where the two countries left off in late 1990s. The meeting resulted in an agreement to install gas pipelines through Korea and Russia.[55] The agreement also included provisions for linking the inter-Korean railway to the Trans-Siberian Railway (TSR) and Rajin, a port near the North Korean–Russian border, which still have not been realized. At the summit between Park Geun-hye and Vladimir Putin in 2013, both sides signed a memorandum of understanding for South Korean companies to participate in the rail road project linking the North's port of Rajin to the Russian eastern town of Khasan, a pilot project to connect the TSR and Trans-Korean Railway (TKR), jointly led by Russia and North Korea.[56] The rail line would be an alternative to the maritime route currently used for international trade.

3.5 South Korea

The Republic of Korea is in search of its place in the world after spectacular successes in economic development and advances in politics, military, and technology. Its rankings in terms of its economy, military, and technology are envious by world standards—it has the thirteenth largest economy, the tenth largest military budget, and is the first in broadband access and tops in other technology areas. It has perhaps the world's most vibrant democracy. The country leads in shipbuilding, steel, and electronics. In the past decade, South Korea has been recognized for its soft power of "Hallyu," or Korean Wave, for the popularity of its dramas and music throughout East Asia.

These successes are only recent phenomena that belie Korea's shattered and turbulent past. In 1910, Korea lost centuries-old independence and became Japan's colony until 1945. Soon after came national partition, political turmoil, and a devastating war, which killed and dislocated millions, leaving the country and families divided and desperately poor. Six decades ago, South Korea was a war-ravaged, poor, agrarian society with little hope. The beginnings of industrialization a decade later led to rapid advances that served as a model for economic development around the world. Its achievements have made Korea more confident and increased its desire for a more independent Korean foreign policy. The younger generation especially wants Korea to assume a regional and global role commensurate with its hard and soft powers.

South Korea's major interests are tied closely to its relationships with the U.S.. The U.S.–ROK alliance has provided a firm foundation for peace and stability for over 60 years. The security relationship paved the way for linkages in trade, education, and technology transfer. This alliance would also provide stability during the early days of unification and help contain any pressures that might emerge from China or Russia in their efforts to extend their influence on the Korean Peninsula. The alliance relationship was a key factor when the U.S. decided with which country, among a list of countries, it would negotiate a free trade agreement since the North America Free Trade Agreement. The KORUS FTA is a historic agreement that deepens bilateral economic relations while strengthening long-standing relations in the security and political spheres.

The U.S. will be an important player in contingency and unification. If collapse is accompanied by war, U.S. military support will be crucial. Even without a war, U.S. assistance in tracking and controlling nuclear weapons would be important. The U.S. also has experience in stability and reconstruction operations, which would be monumental tasks in northern Korea. Washington's support would be needed to get funds from International Financial Institutions (IFIs) to a unified Korea for the development of northern Korea. Such support would also increase confidence for private financial institutions and countries such as Japan to invest in post-unification Korea. Foreign direct investment would impact a number of areas, including job creation, infrastructure development, and migration.

Bilateral relations between China and South Korea improved with normalization in 1992, and goodwill, trade, investment, and exchanges increased dramatically. Both consider stability a high priority and will want to take measures to quickly stabilize the peninsula after unification. The focus of development would be in northern Korea, which would also help develop the border area inside China. China's rapid development is not evenly distributed geographically, favoring the coastal areas. Northeast China is one of the neglected areas, and the Chinese government is concerned by the effects of uneven internal development. The prospect of further development in the region would serve China's interest as well as Korea's. However, South Korea would not welcome any significant Chinese military movement across the border on the Korean Peninsula during any contingencies. Equally, China may not welcome any U.S.

troop movement further north. This is one of the issues to be discussed among the regional actors.

In addition, any U.S.–China confrontation over Taiwan would put South Korea in an awkward situation, as it hosts U.S. military bases. Both South Korea and China are members of the Association of Southeast Asian Countries (ASEAN) Regional Forum (ARF), which consists of ASEAN countries plus China, South Korea, and Japan. China and South Korea agreed to a "strategic partnership," leading to more frequent high-level contacts.[57] These contacts and continued dialogue are crucial for cooperation not only on trade and financial matters, but also to manage contentious or latent issues.

The colonial legacy and unresolved historical issues have become major obstacles between Seoul and Tokyo, but closer cooperation could bring benefits to both sides. Despite cool emotional relations, economic ties between Japan and South Korea are quite strong. Japan provided not only massive capital investment after normalization, but also a development model for Korea. Both share the values of market economy and democracy.

Japan is an economic powerhouse with a strong interest in stabilizing the uncertain period following Korean unification. As such, Japan would be an important source of capital investment to develop northern Korea. Many pro–North Korea ethnic Koreans live in Japan, and they have sent remittances to relatives in North Korea. This group, after unification, could also be a source of support for northern Korea.

4 Bilateral Issues

The relations between the major regional powers and Korea, and among the regional powers, are complex. Some issues change rapidly, while others are relatively long term. This section identifies and explores the major issues likely to face each pair of bilateral actors relevant to the situation on the Korean Peninsula.

4.1 United States–South Korea

South Korea relies heavily on U.S. alliance for security. The alliance has served both countries well, allowing South Korea to focus on economic development with spectacular results, and giving the U.S. a foothold on the Asian mainland during the Cold War. However, with the changing global security environment, shifting U.S. threat priorities, and South Korea's growing power, Seoul and Washington both seek a broader alliance relationship.

In 2008, President Lee Myung-bak described the U.S.–ROK alliance as based on value, trust, and peace promotion. In choosing to make the U.S. his first foreign destination after assuming office as the president, Lee signaled the importance of repairing frayed relations under the previous administration. The Lee administration viewed the U.S.–ROK alliance not just in military terms, but also as a key to economic prosperity and Korea's medium- to long-term development strategy.[58] President Park Geun-hye has maintained the improved bilateral relations and developed robust ties with the Obama administration.

Since the attacks on the U.S. on September 11, 2001, the U.S. has been reexamining its global posture and the role of its allies and friends. Lee and U.S. President George W. Bush agreed to move the bilateral relationship toward a twenty-first-century strategic alliance, based on "freedom and democracy, human rights and the principle of market economy."[59] Former U.S. Ambassador to South Korea Alexander Vershbow stressed broadening the vision of the alliance beyond the military to a global agenda of environment, energy, antiproliferation, antiterrorism, peace promotion, postconflict reconstruction, natural disasters, human rights, and democracy.[60] The shared vision of expanding the bilateral relationship beyond security was reiterated during the June and November 2009 summits between presidents Obama and Lee, and again in May 2013 and November 2014 between presidents Obama and Park. At these summits, the leaders discussed cooperation on a variety of global challenges, including clean energy, peaceful use of nuclear energy, and human rights.[61] As the U.S. and South Korea search for a broader agenda, their alliance is undergoing transformation. One of the major issues confronting alliance transformation is the operational control (OPCON) transition from the U.S. to ROK.

Transition of Wartime Operational Control
After the end of the Cold War, some entities in the U.S. asked whether the Cold War structure of the alliances was necessary and the U.S. began raising the issue of burden-sharing with its allies, especially North Atlantic Treaty Organization (NATO) members. After the 9/11 attacks, the U.S. designated terrorism as its top threat and conducted a *Global Posture Review* to reassess its military presence around the world. Some in the U.S.,

recognizing South Korea's economic wealth, asked why the U.S. was responsible for the cost of South Korea's security. At the same time, some in South Korea saw the Yongsan Army Garrison in the middle of Seoul as symbolizing the perception of lack of full independence from a foreign power.

During the Rho Moo-hyun administration, the lowest point in the U.S.–ROK relations, the Korean defense minister asked his U.S. counterpart to transfer wartime operational control from a U.S. general to a Korean general—the so-called OPCON transfer.[62] Many in Korea seem to be unaware that Korea already has operational control during armistice (not "peace," since both Koreas are technically still at war). The ROK Joint Chiefs of Staff (JCS) is the top war-fighting command in Korea and it handles day-to-day defense operations, such as patrolling the DMZ, flying air patrols, and guarding the sea.[63] The ROK JCS is headed by a chairman, an ROK four-star general, who has operational control over all ROK forces. The OPCON transition then concerns the U.S.–ROK Combined Forces Command (CFC), which is a war-fighting command consisting of both ROK military and U.S. forces. This command is headed by a U.S. four-star general, with an ROK four-star general as deputy, and is responsible for military operations during war. Contrary to common belief, the U.S. commanding general does not automatically receive wartime operational control. Both the ROK and U.S. forces are provided to the U.S.–ROK CFC, and remain under the control of a bilateral committee system comprised of national authorities of both countries; therefore, neither the U.S. nor the ROK exercises unilateral control of the CFC at any time.[64] The ROK JCS then transitions into a headquarters that performs a similar role as a U.S. JCS in that it receives guidance from the president and the Minister of National Defense and passes it to the CFC.[65] While the CFC commanding general is responsible for theater military operations, his civilian bosses determine national-level policy. Thus the general is under civilian control. Civilian control is provided by the President and the Minister of Defense of the Republic of Korea and the President and the Secretary of Defense of the U.S.

Currently, a U.S. four-star general is the commander of the U.S.–ROK CFC. This command and control structure combines the two militaries for unity of command—a crucial principle of war, and interoperability— essential for operations. The organization is combined: the deputy commander is an ROK four-star general; the Assistant Chiefs of Staffs are headed alternately by U.S. and ROK personnel; the rest of the staff are integrated.[66] Such an interwoven arrangement is an ideal war-fighting command involving more than one country, a command structure to be emulated in multilateral operations. The U.S. provides forces to the U.S.–ROK CFC with U.S. Forces Korea (USFK), which is based in Korea. During war, the CFC would be reinforced by U.S. forces based elsewhere and the ROK would contribute most of its armed forces to the command. Separate rules govern the command of the designated forces depending on whether it is during armistice or hostility. In general, each nation commands its own forces on a day-to-day basis. During war, the commander of the CFC would exercise command. As mentioned, unity of command is crucial. The chaos on the battlefield demands a clear chain of command to reduce confusion, duplication, fratricide, and other fog and friction of war. Furthermore, the CFC is able to share resources and facilities. Co-location has tremendous positive impact on operations. Without the unity of command and co-location, any new arrangement would be inferior to the proven combined command.

The former United Nations Command/CFC Plans, Policy, and Strategy Director remarked that the issue is complicated because the vast majority of people who discuss the change lack a basic understanding of war fighting and the complexity of command and control during wartime.[67] Rho's key advisers probably did not understand what they were asking for; their credentials came from their activism in the height of the democracy movement as part of the "386 generation"—people in their 30s (at the time the term was coined in the 2000s) who attended colleges in the 1980s and were born in the 1960s.[68]

In the Unified Command Plan, the war-fighting command is the "supported" command and the other commands are "supporting" commands. In this case, the ROK entity, ROK JFC, would be the "supported" command and the U.S. entity, nominally called U.S. Korea Command (KORCOM), would be the "supporting" command.[69] The two sides agreed to OPCON transfer by April 2012, which was subsequently delayed to December 2015. At the 2014 U.S.–ROK Security Consultative Meeting, both sides agreed to a principle-based, rather than time-based, approach to OPCON transfer, effectively delaying the transfer further.[70]

Although South Korea asked for OPCON transfer, it is lukewarm about it. Rho Moo-hyun requested OPCON transfer during his administration in 2007 for reasons of national sovereignty and pride, and some have argued that he wanted to fundamentally change South Korea's relationship with the U.S..[71] When the idea was announced, it met harsh, widespread criticism in South Korea. All former South Korean ministers of defense and hundreds of retired generals accused Rho of sacrificing the country's security to pursue his ideological agenda of fundamentally changing the ROK–U.S. relations.[72] At one point, nearly 20 retired ROK generals summoned the then defense minister to demand an explanation and express their opposition. With the conservative administration of Lee Myung-bak, voices in favor of delaying the transfer were louder and it was delayed. Under Park, the transfer was further delayed, dispensing with the previously used time-based method.

The real test of OPCON transfer is whether the U.S. and ROK can maintain their combined capability and interoperability after the combined organization separates into two distinct organizations, and whether the U.S. would be able to summon support as quickly and credibly for a war-fighting command led by an ROK general as it could for a command led by a U.S. general. In a collapse scenario, ROK-led military operations could boost legitimacy for South Korea. An ROK-led military presence may also be more acceptable to China.

4.2   China–South Korea

China and South Korea have developed close ties. In 2003, China replaced the U.S. as South Korea's top trading partner. The South Korean view of China was largely positive between the establishment of diplomatic relations in 1992 and 2005. Since 2005, however, South Koreans have begun to mistrust China's outwardly benign face. In 2004, 53% of South Koreans viewed China as contributing to peace and 30% as increasing tensions and instability.[73] Four years later, in 2008, over 60% saw China as raising tensions and instability in the region and only 26% saw China as contributing to peace and stability.[74] Three-quarters of the South Korean public thought China's military power poses a threat to Korea's security, although only 15% see a "great deal" of threat.[75] While China–South Korea relations were at the lowest point during the Lee Myung-bak administration, relations improved significantly under Park Geun-hye. She emphasized improving Korea–China relations and the public is largely supportive of her efforts. At the same time, the Korean public is wary of China's growing hard power, according to a 2014 Asan report. While viewing China as a cooperative partner, 66% saw China's military rise as a threat to South Korea.[76] During the Lee administration, when Korea–China relations were relatively low, several specific issues changed South Koreans' perception of China. China's claims to the historical kingdom of Goguryeo (Gaogouli in Chinese) and the roughing up of Korean protesters by Chinese students in South Korea probably influenced public opinion in South Korea. China's increased military build-up and the establishment of ADIZ likely played a role in the perception of threat. Economic concerns are also important, especially as the technology gap narrows and South Korea becomes overdependent on China economically.

Koreans consider the ancient Goguryeo kingdom an essential part of Korea and its history. China's effort to incorporate Goguryeo into Chinese history has created a stir in Korea. The Goguryeo issue turned South Koreans' view of China from favorable to suspicious.

Koreans have long traced their history to the three historically contemporaneous kingdoms of Goguryeo, Baekje, and Shilla. The Goguryeo kingdom (37 BC to 668 AD) encompassed what is now part of South Korea, all of North Korea, and large portions of Northeast China, particularly Manchuria. China interprets Korea's historical claims to the region and cultural legacy as posing a threat of irredentism.[77] Several million ethnic Koreans live in China's northeastern provinces of Heilongjiang, Jilin, and Liaoning, a traditionally neglected area just north of the North Korean border. In 2002, the Chinese government funded the five-year Northeast Borderland History and Chain of Events Research Project, the "Northeast Project." The project claimed that Goguryeo was a subordinate state under the jurisdiction of the Chinese dynasties, and as such is part of Chinese history. This reinterpretation inflamed Koreans, whose identity is intrinsically linked to the three kingdoms. Korea traces its name from Goryeo (sometimes spelled Koryo), a kingdom that emerged from the unification of the three kingdoms, which was derived from Goguryeo. Beijing may not have expected such a strong backlash from the Korean public; the Chinese historical claim put brakes on the bilateral relationship. Realizing the deleterious effect of the history issue on the bilateral relations, Beijing dispatched senior diplomats to Seoul to ameliorate the situation.

North Korea's response to China's claim was less inflamed, but the issue angered both Koreas. North Korea initially did not protest China's claim to Goguryeo or its cultural legacy, probably due to its dependence on China. However, it did, actively seek to register the relics on its side of the border as a UNESCO World Heritage site in 2002, two years prior to China's request to register the relics on China's side of the border.[78] The general assembly of the World Heritage Committee in 2003 "deferred" the decision. China submitted its application for the next World Heritage Committee meeting in China in 2004, and both North Korea and China made the UNESCO World Heritage List.[79] The inscription on the UNESCO list of Goguryeo relics was one of the most sensitive and highly politicized processes the organization has confronted.[80]

While the controversy has died down, South Koreans are suspicious of China's motives because the history project lays the foundation for future claims should the situation in North Korea deteriorate. This history issue, unlike the one with Japan over its role during World War II, could have geopolitical implications on the Korean Peninsula after unification.

The negative feelings between the two countries escalated in April 2008, right before the Beijing Olympics. As the Olympic torch was passing through Korea, Chinese students in Seoul physically clashed with anti-China protesters rallying for Tibet and rights of North Korean refugees in China. The physical confrontation angered South Koreans. A false internet rumor that the Korean government had prosecuted and sentenced a Chinese protestor led to a backlash in China, including the Chinese crowd booing the Korean Olympic performers.

This low point in Beijing–Seoul relations turned around, marked by the summit between President Park Geun-hye and China's president Xi Jinping in 2013. Undergirded by a good personal relationship between the two leaders, the bilateral relations were enhanced appreciably. In a survey, 62% of the South Korean public had stated that relations have improved and 62.5% of South Koreans viewed China as a cooperative partner after the successful summit.[81] At the same time, 66% stated that China poses a military threat, although not as a direct threat to South Korea, but by making matters worse in an already complicated region.[82] China's declaration of the ADIZ over much of the East China Sea and the South China Sea did raise an alarm in South Korea and perhaps contributed to the rising threat perception. The pace and scope of China's reclamation project in the South China Sea in the disputed area also adds to the perception that China's activities are increasingly assertive.

Another area of concern is the economy. China's economic development has been rapid and was welcomed by South Korea who saw it as an opportunity for growth. This perception changed in 2012, when the majority of South Korean public started seeing China's economic rise as a threat. The survey conducted in May 2014 shows that 72% of the public views China as an economic threat.[83] As China enters the higher technology sectors, it could compete with South Korea. After unification, capital from South Korea would head toward northern Korea rather than to China, and some international investment will also be diverted to northern Korea. On the other hand, if this effort develops northern Korea and the adjacent area in China, China would also benefit because it would address China's regionally uneven development.

Potential Issues in Post-Unification Era
After unification, the large ethnic Korean population living in the area just north of North Korea may want to be part of Korea rather than of China. China fears irredentism, not only in this region, but also in other areas, such as Tibet. The impact of separation on Taiwan's demand for independence would be the ultimate nightmare for China. China, therefore, wants to maintain territorial integrity, and the Northeast project is an effort to bolster its goal.

China's historical relationship with Korea was based on a tributary system in which China was the suzerain. Ancient Korea maintained independence, accepted China's suzerainty, and paid tribute to China. Korea still recognizes China as a regional power, but it would not want to return to the past tributary arrangement; Korea wants to be recognized as having equal sovereignty. This is another issue to watch when China tries to exert its influence on a unified Korea. Some South Koreans are concerned that China may actually deploy troops within North Korea if it sees Pyongyang nearing a collapse. Some analysts, including Pollack and Lee, posit that if North Korea comes to the verge of collapse, Beijing may try to contain the risks within the territory of North Korea to secure its interests.[84]

China–South Korea relations have been marked by ups and downs, but it is currently on a positive trend, with a mixture of wariness. The trend is likely to continue, but in the long run, it will depend on whether the warming of relations with China continues or China's assertiveness sways the mood in the negative direction.

4.3 Japan–South Korea

Japan and Korea are in geographic proximity, but the feelings toward each other, both very nationalistic, remain distant. History and territory are two main areas of dispute. South Koreans still cite Hideyoshi's invasion of Korea in 1592 as well as Japan's harsh occupation of Korea from 1910 to 1945.[85] Although few living South Koreans experienced the occupation, the memory is kept alive through its education system and anecdotes.[86]

The Koreans are proud people who resent the colonial subjugation by a country Korea had historically considered inferior.

Historian Bruce Cumings writes: "Japanese imperialism stuck a knife in old Korea and twisted it, and that wound has gnawed at the Korean national identity ever since."[87] Japan has apologized, paid reparations to South Korea, and helped Korea develop through foreign direct investment. However, the apologies do not appear sincere to Koreans because Japanese prime ministers continue to visit the Yasukuni shrine, the burial site of some Class A war criminals, and because Japanese history textbooks misrepresent its role in World War II. This history issue has exacerbated with the administration of Abe, who not only visited the Yasukuni shrine, but is also making a concerted effort at rewriting history, including denying imperial Japan's officially sanctioned use of sex slaves for the imperial military. The history issue cannot be resolved by monetary contributions; it needs a commitment to deal seriously with wounded national pride. At the same time, it should be balanced with strategic considerations that benefit both countries.

The territorial dispute over Dokdo/Takeshima Island is yet another contentious point. Both South Korea and Japan claim this group of small islets in the East Sea/Sea of Japan. South Korea currently administers the islets and stations its Coast Guard there. Whenever the issue of the disputed island surfaces, it reaches a feverish pitch in Korea as it goes to the heart of identity and nationalism. The Korea.net web site managed by the Korean Culture and Information Service states that "[f]or Japan to insist on possession of Dokdo is *no different from denying Korea's history of liberation (sic)* from Japanese rule."[88] Both countries are attempting to gain international support for their positions. The Japan Ministry of Foreign Affairs web site explains Japan's position in ten different languages.[89] The Korea.net web site can be viewed in nine languages. The issue is not likely to be resolved soon. Fishing rights in the area exacerbates the problem. If other resources, such as oil reserves, are discovered in the island area, the contest for possession will become even fiercer.

Despite the historical problems and deteriorating relations in recent times, there is still room for cooperation. Seoul, Tokyo, and Washington agreed in the last days of 2014 on a trilateral intelligence-sharing pact, which allows the three countries to share intelligence to deal with North Korea's nuclear and missile programs.[90] This agreement, slated for signature in 2012, was canceled at the last minute due to South Korean public uproar during the increasing tension between South Korea and Japan.

Seoul and Tokyo also reached a breakthrough agreement in December 2015 on wartime sexual slavery, in which Japan admits wartime crime responsibility and plans to pay reparations to the victims.[91] Although relations still remain chilly, the fact that both Japan and Korea could sign such a pact shows that both countries can work together for a common purpose.

5 Areas for Future Cooperation

While regional conditions are potentially destabilizing, opportunities abound for cooperation and interdependence that could advance Northeast Asia's prosperity. Dealing with North Korea's nuclear weapons program, cooperating on a contingency scenario on the peninsula, and economic integration could yield positive results for the region. These areas of interdependence and cooperation are examined in the multilateral context.

5.1 Pre-collapse: Plan and Coordinate

Immediate chaos following a contingency must be managed. Depending on the scenario, South Korea, working with the Koreans in the north, could lead the efforts to manage the collapsed North Korea, toward unification. Cooperative relations among South Korea, China, and the U.S., particularly, but also Japan and Russia, would be essential to manage the challenges of collapse. Cooperation would also be necessary to provide the secure environment sought by investors, which helps to develop the northern half since hostile competition between the U.S. and China would drive away investments. China wants a friendly neighbor or one that accommodates its national interests. Too much U.S. influence, including American troops, would not be acceptable. Because of this concern, some in South Korea are concerned that China would move troops into North Korea if it collapses.[92] Washington would want to avoid instability and would support Seoul's effort to mitigate crisis. Seoul would need help from outside, but at the same time, it would want to limit the role of foreign powers on the peninsula. A Washington–Seoul–Beijing dialogue would be a key step in addressing the concerns of all parties.[93] This trilateral talk does not preclude other bilateral, trilateral, or multilateral talks, such as one with Tokyo. Japan is also concerned about its kidnapped citizens in North Korea, and would want their safe return.

The neighboring powers need a plan for a contingency, yet, these governments have had little or no substantive discussion to coordinate and manage instability in North Korea. It appears there were no serious discussions on a bilateral plan between South Korea and the U.S. until recently. Victor Cha, a senior Bush administration official, stated in 2008 that there was no agreed-upon mechanism for bilateral, trilateral, or other planning to deal with a collapsing North Korea.[94] A concept plan between Washington and Seoul existed, but all dialogue ceased under the Rho Moo-hyun government as his administration feared offending Pyongyang and giving the impression of U.S.–ROK conspiracy to collapse the DPRK regime.[95]

This situation changed under the Lee Myong-bak administration. At the ROK–U.S. Military Committee Meeting in October 2008, the U.S. proposed setting up a detailed plan in case North Korea collapses.[96] While Seoul still did not want to provoke North Korea unnecessarily, the two allies agreed on the basic principle of the need for a shared plan.[97] Although this recognition is a start, the upgrading of the concept plan to an operational plan would deal mainly with the military's role. The plan would need to embrace the roles of nonmilitary agencies, NGOs, international institutions, and the business community. The U.S. invited China in 2009 to discuss North Korea's future, but Beijing refused, emphasizing that it is unacceptable to allow North Korea to collapse.[98] Zhang Laingui, a North Korea expert in China, points out the difficulty of China holding such talks with the U.S., which might irritate Pyongyang; however, he acknowledges that discussing a contingency plan could reduce misunderstanding between China and the U.S. given the strategic demands of both sides.[99] Due to the political sensitivity, it may be prudent to have such discussions at the track II level, which involves collaboration among scholars and experts rather than direct government-to-government deliberations.

The UN headquarters in New York also does not have a plan in the event of Korean unification and any scenarios leading up to it.[100] To create a plan, the permanent members of the UN Security Council need to agree that it is necessary. The five permanent members are China, the U.S., the UK, France, and Russia. Both China and Russia have supported North Korea, and it may be too politically sensitive for them to discuss a plan. Additionally, the UN headquarters leaves the UN matters to the UN Command in Korea, and even if the UN Command did have a contingency plan, there seems to be no formal communications mechanism between the two.

When North Korea invaded South Korea in 1950, the UN responded swiftly, with the UN Security Council passing a resolution to condemn the attack and calling to protect South Korea. The UN Security Council Resolution created the UN Command comprised of 17 countries to repel North Korea's aggression. The UN gave the executive agent authority to the U.S.. The UN Command remains, led by a U.S. 4-star general who serves concurrently as commander of the U.S.–ROK CFC and the USFK.[101] The UN Command in Korea consists of 18 member states, including the ROK.[102] In addition, the UN Command Rear, located in Japan, is a major theater logistic enabler with seven bases in Japan where UNC Rear accredited members can sail or fly in under the UN Command flag per the UN–Government of Japan Status of Forces Agreement.[103] The UN Command Military Armistice Commission (UNCMAC), with a small staff, remains in Korea to supervise the implementation of the Armistice Agreement to settle through negotiations any violations of the agreement.[104] It is important to note that UNCMAC's authority and scope focus on the armistice, not unification. A lack of plan could lead to misunderstandings and chaos, which might result in other undesirable or dangerous scenarios.

Clearly, there is paucity of planning among major powers, who are key stakeholders on peninsular affairs. They need to collaborate and prepare for a potential collapse scenario.

5.2 North Korea's Nuclear Weapons Program

North Korea's nuclear weapons program is a concern for not only the U.S., but also China, Japan, and South Korea. Successfully denuclearizing North Korea would dispense with one of the major post-collapse problems, the control of North Korea's nuclear weapons. Thus, the nuclear issue is an area for cooperation.

Six-Party Talks
The Six-Party Talks include the five regional powers and North Korea. Washington proposed and Beijing hosted the first Six-Party Talks to address the North Korean nuclear weapons program in August 2003. The initial meeting included clearly stated positions from each government to create a solid baseline for negotiations.[105] Since then, six rounds of talks have been held with mixed results. The talks were discontinued in 2009 when North Korea pulled out and expelled nuclear inspectors in response to the UN's condemnation of North Korea's rocket launch in 2009.

The initial negotiations led to the September 2005 agreement that North Korea would eventually abandon its nuclear weapons program, readmit International Atomic Energy Agency (IAEA) inspectors, and rejoin the Nonproliferation Treaty.[106] In November 2005, the talks hit a stumbling block after the U.S. Treasury Department, enforcing Patriot Act provisions against dealing with illicit funds, placed restrictions on the Banco Delta Asia in Macau for laundering $25 million of North Korean funds. The Macau government froze some 50 North Korean accounts. Six-Party negotiations broke down, and Pyongyang increased its provocations, testing missiles in July 2006 and conducting a nuclear test in October 2006.[107]

China was able to get North Korea back to the talks and in February 2007 a denuclearization plan was negotiated. The U.S. tried to jump-start the 2005 agreement, promising to release the Banco Delta Asia funds and humanitarian and energy aid in exchange for which North Korea would have 60 days to shut down its main nuclear complex with verification by international inspectors and a complete declaration that the nuclear programs would be abandoned.[108]

North Korea partially disabled its nuclear reactor by shutting down its plutonium-producing nuclear plant at Yongbyon and in October 2007 agreed to end its nuclear program in exchange for economic and diplomatic concessions. A month later, Pyongyang started to disable three core facilities at Yongbyon in the presence of U.S. experts overseeing the disablement activities. North Korea provided 18,000 pages of documents on production records from its nuclear program to the U.S. in May 2008, followed by a declaration a month later as called for in the agreement. Although the declaration was late and incomplete, the U.S. responded by lifting the application of the Trading with the Enemy Act and removing North Korea from the list of State Sponsors of Terrorism.[109] In the same month, North Korea blew up the nuclear reactor cooling tower, an internationally televised but largely symbolic gesture.[110] Pyongyang also allowed the IAEA inspectors to return to North Korea.

The September 2008 talks came to a standstill as North Korea waited for the promised aid. It claimed that it fulfilled its side of the bargain by providing the declaration, while the U.S. delayed aid because the inventory was incomplete. As in the past, North Korea responded to the breakdown in talks by conducting more tests, this time a "satellite launch" on April 5, 2009. The UN Security Council unanimously condemned the launch. North Korea angrily declared that it will not take part in the talks, expelled the international nuclear inspectors, and informed the IAEA that it will resume its nuclear weapons program. Pyongyang then escalated the threat by detonating an underground nuclear device in May 2009. The UN responded with UN Security Council Resolution 1874, which called for increased sanctions and enforcement, including strengthening the arms embargo and inspections of suspicious vessels.[111]

The escalation continued with North Korea firing a series of missiles east from its launch site on the east coast. The situation has been spiraling downward. There was a hope that the nuclear standoff might turn around when the Chinese Premier Wen Jiabao visited Pyongyang in October 2009 with an offer of increased food, energy, and economic assistance in return for North Korea to rejoin the Six-Party Talks. Pyongyang indicated willingness to talk bilaterally with the U.S. and multilaterally in the Six-Party Talks. In December 2009, Ambassador Stephen Bosworth, U.S. Special Representative for North Korea Policy, went to Pyongyang to discuss resumption of the Six-Party Talks.[112] The possible resumption of talks did not resurface until February 2009, when the U.S. and North Korea announced a "leap day agreement" in which North Korea would agree to a moratorium on uranium enrichment and long-range missile and nuclear testing in return for substantial American food aid.[113] About a month later, North Korea launched a satellite, which failed to reach the orbit, but tested the missile technology, evaporating the possibility of resuming the Six-Party Talks.

The Nuclear Card
North Korea's nuclear weapons program has many dimensions. To be sure, it is a destructive weapon that threatens South Korea and the rest of the region. It is also a nuclear card in international negotiations. Internally, it is a powerful tool to placate and insure legitimacy and support from domestic constituents. It is also a symbol of international prestige against the backdrop of potential proliferation and the security dilemma facing the regional powers. North Korea is not likely to give up its nuclear weapons program. In a collapse situation, dealing with nuclear weapons and materials would emerge as an urgent matter.

Nuclear weapons lost during the chaos of collapse are major concerns not only for the U.S., but also for China and Russia, as these weapons could possibly cross borders into these countries. Accordingly, these countries need to collaborate with each other to ensure the security of the weapons. Because U.S. special operations forces may be tasked with locating and securing the weapons, prior consultation with China would alleviate potential misunderstanding of the presence of U.S. troops. If the nuclear weapons cross the border into China or Russia, then the parties involved will need to discuss the roles of their respective security entities in pursuing and securing these sensitive weapons and personnel. These countries, and especially China and the U.S., need to reach an understanding on this issue prior to collapse.

5.3 Stability and Economic Development

It is imperative for all the countries concerned to cooperate on stabilization and economic development of a reunified Korea. The efforts should be led by the Koreans—that is, Koreans in the South as well as the North—but the surrounding powers could provide support. One of the first measures would be the provision of basic services, such as food, water, and electricity. In the long term, they will need to focus on economic development to create a more stable environment.

Mass Refugee Flow

Given the porous border, China worries about mass refugee flow from North Korea. China would be sensitive to the large influx of refugees and may not want external influence. To manage the situation, however, prior coordination with South Korea, the U.S., and the UN High Commissioner for Refugees (UNHCR) could help. The UNHCR could manage a pre-designated area in northern China to handle North Korean refugees, with the understanding that international efforts to stabilize northern Korea would provide incentives for the refugees to return home. This option would be better than massing troops along or within the North Korean border, which could cause misunderstanding with the U.S.–ROK combined forces or ROK forces.

Assistance and Development

North Korea suffers chronic food and energy shortages. Initially, food aid may need to continue. North Korea's infrastructure is dilapidated and inadequate to provide basic services, much less economic development. Creating a nationwide infrastructure would be a massive project requiring huge investments. However, it would be a crucial step to providing water, electricity, transportation, and communications so that people can stay where they are instead of migrating, and to provide the basis for creating jobs, attract investments, and stimulate business activities.

Such infrastructure projects would benefit from international cooperation. IFIs, such as the World Bank and the Asian Development Bank (ADB), could extend grants and loans for infrastructure projects. The support of the U.S. would be important. Japan could also use its financial prowess to assist in infrastructure development. Other countries could also assist, either via direct government financing or by encouraging a consortium of private investors. Infrastructure development would not only establish the network needed to provide services to the public and businesses, but would also be important in the creation of jobs. A demobilized million-man military would pose a significant problem for the society if they were to sit idle, as their energy could be directed elsewhere. Infrastructure development is one of the largest sectors capable of absorbing the young and the restless.

In facing the challenges of a collapse scenario, various countries, especially China and the U.S., can help insure stability by engaging in dialogue prior to the reunification focused on transparency to minimize misunderstandings of each other's moves. A stable environment would be crucial to relieve public anxiety, attract investment to the region, and advance economic development.

Establishing Coordinating Mechanisms
To restore order, provide basic needs, reassure the public, and provide long-lasting stability after a collapse, coordination at the national and international levels is required. The efforts could be led by South Korea, actively engaging the UN and other international fora to forge an international consensus to alleviate humanitarian disaster. The U.S., as a major stakeholder in international organizations, could provide support in reaching consensus on development activities.

Coordination is also crucial at the local level. A coordination center, perhaps led by the South Korean government and engaging local populace, could integrate the efforts of NGOs and the government at the neighborhood, provincial, and national levels. The U.S. has experience in integration and coordination across agencies in Iraq and Afghanistan through the Interagency Management System (IMS), which uses the "whole of government" concept to address reconstruction and stabilization.[114] Developed by the U.S. State Department's Office of the Coordinator for Reconstruction and Stabilization (S/CRS), IMS is part of a framework for planning and coordinating U.S. reconstruction and stabilization operations.[115] The IMS brings together experts from the U.S. Departments of State, Defense, Homeland Security, Justice, Agriculture, Treasury, Transportation, Energy, Health and Human Services, and other agencies to provide unity of purpose through a wide-ranging planning and management process, and to pursue the goal in a unified effort through integrated operations in the field.[116] This "whole of government" concept could be a model for developing similar arrangements in a collapsed North Korea. It is important to develop a mechanism to coordinate efforts of the diverse entities and monitor those activities that will likely operate in a collapsed North Korea. At the same time, it is also imperative that China understand the U.S. and other presences as contributing to the stability of the region, rather than as threats. To enhance this understanding, China, the U.S., and South Korea would need to discuss their respective roles prior to collapse.

6 Summary

Korean unification would be a momentous event in the region, affecting not only Korea, but the interests and behaviors of the surrounding major powers. An examination of Korea's relations with its neighbors helps to illuminate the answers to these questions.

In describing Korea's relations with surrounding countries, the focus in this book is mainly on South Korea, not North Korea, although sometimes "Korea" is used to refer to both Koreas. Security concerns, unresolved historical issues, and territorial disputes are major features of bilateral relations. At the same time, growing economic ties link the economies of Korea and the regional powers, making their growth and prosperity more interdependent.

In summary, there are five major powers neighboring North Korea whose national interests and bilateral and multilateral relationships must be considered in any scenario for the future of the Korean Peninsula. The most important regional powers with the greatest stakes and responsibilities in a post-collapse scenario are South Korea, China, and the U.S., although Japan and Russia could play important roles. Understanding the geopolitical landscape and the major concerns of these countries helps to clarify areas for possible cooperation in the event of North Korea's collapse.

NOTES

1. Sung-ki Jung, "S. Korea, U.S. Chart Contingency Plans on N. Korea," *Korea Times*, April 22, 2009, http://www.koreatimes.co.kr/www/news/include/print.asp?newsIdx=43632.
2. Chang, Jae-soon and Joint Press Corps, "Park calls Korean unification 'jackpot' for neighbors too," *Yonhap News*, January 22, 2014, http://english.yonhapnews.co.kr/northkorea/2014/01/22/96/0401000000AEN20140122009200315F.html.
3. Claustre Bajona and Tianshu Chu, "China's WTO Accession and Its Effect on State-Owned Enterprises," in *East-West Center Working Papers*, Hawaii, April 2004, 1.
4. Chinese Ambassador to Finland Zhang Zhijian, *China's Economic and Commercial Relations with the Neighbouring Northeast Asian Countries* (People's Republic of China Embassy in Finland, May 14, 2004, http://www.fmprc.gov.cn/ce/cefi/eng/zfgx/dsjh/t106157.htm (accessed September 28, 2009).
5. "Import/Export by Country," *Korea Customs Service*, 2015, http://www.customs.go.kr/kcshome/trade/TradeCountryList.do?layoutMenuNo=21031, (accessed February 10, 2016).
6. "Jooyo Gookbyeol Soochool Ib-ag" (Import Export by Priority Trading Partners), *Korean Statistical Information Service*, December 15, 2014, http://kosis.kr/bukhan/statisticsList/statisticsList_01List.jsp#SubCont.
7. Shin, Hyon-hee, "Seoul to pull out of Gaesong Park," *The Korea Herald* February 10, 2016, http://m.koreaherald.com/view.php?ud=20160210000364&ntn=0#jyk.
8. Shin.
9. "Major Foreign Holders." The total U.S. trade in 2014 was $3,968,630.7 million. The portion for China, Japan, and South Korea was $905,733 million or 23% of U.S. trade.
10. "Major Foreign Holders."
11. *Joint Communiqué: The 46th ROK-U.S. Consultative Meeting* (United States–Republic of Korea, October 23, 2014), 5.
12. *Memorandum of Agreement between the Government of the Republic of Korea and the Government of the United States of America Regarding the Agreed Recommendation for Implementation of the Agreement between the Republic of Korea and the United States of America on the Relocation of the United States Forces from the Seoul Metropolitan Area (Yongsan Relocation Plan)*, ed. U.S.–ROK Status of Forces Agreement Joint Committee Ad Hoc Subcommittee for the Yongsan Relocation Plan (Seoul: Governments of the United States and the Republic of Korea, October 26, 2004), 4.

13. Slack, Megan, "President Obama Meets with President Park of South Korea," The White House Blog, May 7, 2013, http://www.whitehouse.gov/blog/2013/05/07/president-obama-meets-president-park-south-korea.
14. Barack Obama and Park Geun-hye, "Joint Declaration in Commemoration of the 60th Anniversary of the Alliance between the Republic of Korea and the United States of America," The White House, May 7, 2013.
15. "GDP Per Capita (Current U.S.$)," *The World Bank*, http://data.worldbank.org/indicator/NY.GDP.PCAP.CD (accessed July 6, 2015).
16. Monoghan, Angela, "China Surpasses U.S. as the world's largest trading nation," *The Guardian*, January 10, 2014, http://www.theguardian.com/business/2014/jan/10/china-surpasses-us-world-largest-trading-nation.
17. "Chinese President's Speech Celebrating First Spacewalk Published," *Sina English*, November 8, 2008.
18. "Is Korea Prepared for Superpower China?," *Chosun Ilbo*, October 3, 2009, http://english.chosun.com/site/data/html_dir/2009/10/02/2009100200297.html.
19. For further details, see Nicholas Szechenyi, Victor Cha, Bonny S. Glaser, Michael J. Green, and Christopher K. Johnson, "China's Air Defense Identification Zone: Impact on Regional Security," *Center for Strategic and International Studies*, November 26, 2013, http://csis.org/publication/chinas-air-defense-identification-zone-impact-regional-security.
20. David S. Cloud, "Defense Secretary Ashton Carter Warns Beijing on South China Sea Island-Building," *Los Angeles Times*, May 29, 2015, http://www.latimes.com/nation/la-na-ashton-carter-china-20150529-story.html (accessed July 9, 2015).
21. Robert Sutter, PacNet #38 "Xi Jinping's foreign policy: image versus reality – some adjustment required," *Pacific Forum CSIS*, July 7, 2015.
22. "Shades of Red: China's Debate over North Korea," 1.
23. Snyder and Wit, "China Views: Breaking the Stalemate on the Korean Peninsula," 7.
24. Wu Baiyi, "China on the Korean Peninsula: Interests and Roles," *The Korean Journal of Security Affairs* 11, no. 1 (2006): 67.
25. Heung-Kyu, Kim, "China's Position on Korean Unification and ROK-PRC Relations," *Korea Research Institute for Strategy*, no date (posted on January 1, 2014), 234, http://www.brookings.edu/~/media/events/2014/1/21-korean-peninsula-unification/kim-heung-kyu-paper.pdf.
26. Kim.
27. Dan Blumenthal and Aaron Friedberg, "An American Strategy for Asia," in *A Report of the Asia Strategy Working Group*, Washington, DC, American Enterprise Institute, 2009, 7.
28. Scott Snyder, "Lee Myung-bak's Foreign Policy: A 250-Day Assessment," in *Korea Institute for Defense Analyses*, Seoul, 2009, 11.

29. "China-ROK Joint Statement," Beijing, People's Republic of China Ministry of Foreign Affairs, May 28, 2008.
30. Hwang, Jaeho, "The ROK's China Policy Under Park Geun-hye: A New Model of ROK-PRC Relations," *International Journal of Korean Unification Studies*, Vol. 23, No. 1, June 2014, 104.
31. *CIA World Factbook*.
32. "North Korea Statistics: Export Import by Countries," (Jooyo Gookbyeol Soochool Ib Ak), *Korean Statistical Information Service*, http://kosis.kr/bukhan/statisticsList/statisticsList_01List.jsp#SubCont (accessed December 7, 2014).
33. Yutaka Kawashima, *Japanese Foreign Policy at the Crossroads: Challenges and Options for the Twenty-First Century* (Washington, DC: Brookings Institution Press, 2003), 4.
34. *Defense of Japan 2014*, Japan Ministry of Defense, 2014, 3–5.
35. Kawahima, 40–43.
36. Kawashima, 16.
37. Kawashima, 57–59.
38. Green, *Japan's Reluctant Realism: Foreign Policy Challenges in an Era of Uncertain Power*, 112.
39. Green.
40. Donald P. Gregg, "Park Chung Hee: Despite a dictatorial streak, South Korea's long-serving president converted an economic basket case into an industrial powerhouse," *Time* 154, no. 7/8 (August 23–30, 1999): http://www.time.com/time/asia/asia/magazine/1999/990823/park1.html.
41. Gregg.
42. "South Korea's POSCO expands energy work," *United Press International*, October 14, 2009, http://www.upi.com/Science_News/Resource-Wars/2009/10/14/South-Koreas-POSCO-expands-energy-work/UPI-13591255551644/. "Hyundai Heavy, South Korean shipyards plan debt sales," *Infomarine*, March 13, 2009, http://www.infomarine.gr/index.php?article=29659&cat=shipbuildingnews&mod=article.
43. Kenji Takita, "Japan's Response to the Peace Process on the Korean Peninsula," *The Korean Journal of Security Affairs* 11, no. 1 (June 26, 2006), 57.
44. Martin, Alexander, "Abe Re-elected Japan's Prime Minister," *The Wall Street Journal*, December 24, 2014, http://www.wsj.com/articles/abe-re-elected-japans-prime-minister-1419401541.
45. Dujarric, *Korean Unification and After: The Challenge for U.S. Strategy*, 27.
46. "Military Expenditure 1988–2013," Stockholm International Peace Research Institute (SIPRI), www.sipri.org (accessed on December 25,

2014), and "Annual Report to Congress: Military Power of the People's Republic of China 2006," ed. Office of the Secretary of Defense, Washington, DC, U.S. Department of Defense, 2006, 20.
47. See Tables 4.8 and 4.9.
48. Arrouas, Michelle, "Japanese Fighter Jet Scrambles against China Have Hit a Record High," *Time*, April 10, 2014, http://time.com/56997/japan-china-fighter-jet/.
49. *National Defense Program Guidelines for FY 2014 and Beyond*, Japan Ministry of National Defense, December 17, 2013, 3–4, http://www.mod.go.jp/j/approach/agenda/guideline/2014/pdf/20131217_e2.pdf.
50. *National Security Strategy* (of Japan), Japan Cabinet Secretariat, December 17, 2013, 11, http://www.cas.go.jp/jp/siryou/131217anzenhoshou/nss-e.pdf.
51. *National Defense Program Guidelines for FY 2014 and Beyond*, 7.
52. Harrison, *Korean Endgame: A Strategy for Reunification and U.S. Disengagement*, 331.
53. Harrison, 334.
54. Harrison, 338.
55. "Seoul, Moscow Agree on Upgraded Partnership, Gas Pipeline Involving N. Korea," *Yonhap News*, October 2, 2008. http://english.yonhapnews.co.kr/northkorea/2008/10/02/32/0401000000AEN20081001006400325F.HTML.
56. Seo, Ji-eun, "Park, Putin sign rail project MOU," *Korea JoongAng Daily*, November 14, 2013, http://koreajoongangdaily.joins.com/news/article/article.aspx?aid=2980442.
57. Scott Snyder describes various levels of "partnership" with China: "friendship and cooperative relationship" after normalization in 1992; "full-scale cooperative partnership" under Kim Dae-jung; "comprehensive cooperative partnership" under Rho Moo-hyun; and the further elevated "strategic partnership" under Lee Myung-bak. For further details, see Scott Snyder, "China-Korea Relations: Establishing a 'Strategic Cooperative Partnership'," *Comparative Connections, Pacific Forum/CSIS* (July 2008), 1.
58. Seung-joo Baek, "Han-mi Jeonryak Dongmaeng-gwa Hanmi Bangwi Hyubryuk Ganghwa (Strengthening the Repubic of Korea-U.S. Strategic Alliance and Defense Cooperation)" (paper presented at the Peace Foundation 22nd Forum: Hanmiil Ahnbo Hyubryeok Ganghwa-wa Dognbuga Gukje Gwngwe (Korea, U.S., and Japan Security Cooperation and International Relations in Northeast Asia), Seoul, Korea, June 24, 2008), 7.

59. "President Bush Participates in Joint Press Availability with President Lee Myung-Bak of the Republic of Korea," White House, April 19, 2008.
60. Alexander Vershbow, "Congratulatory Address," in *New Era: New Korea–U.S. Alliance*, Seoul, East Asia Institute, July 3, 2008.
61. "Joint Declaration in Commemoration of the 60th Anniversary of the Alliance between the Republic of Korea and the United States of America," the White House, May 7, 2013, http://www.whitehouse.gov/the-press-office/2013/05/07/joint-declaration-commemoration-60th-anniversary-alliance-between-republ.
62. Operational control (OPCON) is the authority of a commander at or below Combatant Command level to perform the command functions over subordinate forces, including organizing and employing forces to accomplish the mission.
63. Walter Sharp, "OPCON Transition in Korea," *Center for Strategic and International Studies*, December 2, 2013, 1.
64. Interview with Mike Keefe, U.S.–ROK CFC, Policy, July 27, 2006.
65. Sharp, 2.
66. *Mission of the ROK/U.S. Combined Forces Command* (USFK, July 19, 2008); available from http://www.usfk.mil/usfk/cfc.aspx.
67. Jr. Raymond P. Ayres, "Key Note Speech: Transfer of Wartime Command--Some Personal Thoughts," in *The Quest for a Unified Korea: Strategies for the Cultural and Inter-Agency Process*, ed. Jr. Bechtol, Bruce E. (Quantico: Marine Corps University, 2007), 2.
68. The 386 generation denotes those in their thirties (or forties) who were college age (or who actively demonstrated) during the height of the democracy movement in the 1980s, and were born in the 1960s.
69. U.S. Senate Armed Services Committee, *Statement of General B. B. Bell, Commander, United Nations Command; Commander, Republic of Korea–United States Combined Forces Command; and Commander, United States Forces Korea before the Senate Armed Services Committee*, March 11, 2008, 11.
70. *The Joint Communique: The 46th ROK-U.S. Security Consultative Meeting*, October 23, 2013, Washington, DC, 5, http://www.defense.gov/pubs/46th_SCM_Joint_Communique.pdf.
71. Hyeong Jung Park, *Looking Back and Looking Forward: North Korea, Northeast Asia and the ROK-U.S. Alliance* (Washington, DC: The Brookings Institution, December 2007), 14.
72. Bruce Klingner, "It's not right time to discuss OPCON transfer," in *Commentary*, Washington, DC, The Heritage Foundation, June 22, 2009. http://www.heritage.org/press/commentary/ed062209c.cfm.

73. James S. Marshall, "South Koreans' Guarded Views of China," ed. Office of Research, The U.S. State Department, August 8, 2008, 3.
74. Marshall, 2.
75. Marshall.
76. Jiyoon Kim, Karl Friedhoff, Chungku Kang, Euichol Lee, "South Korean Attitude on China: Public Opinion Studies Program," *The Asan Institute for Policy Studies*, July 2014, 16.
77. Yonson Ahn, *The Contested Heritage of Koguryo/Gaogouli and China-Korea Conflict*, January 11, 2008, http://www.japanfocus.org/-Yonson-Ahn/2631 (accessed September 29, 2009).
78. *N Korea makes World Heritage List*, July 1, 2004, http://news.bbc.co.uk/2/hi/asia-pacific/3856171.stm (October 2, 2009).
79. Ahn.
80. Ahn.
81. Jiyoon, Kim, et. al., *Asan Report: South Korean Attitudes on China*, The Asan Institute for Policy Studies, July 2014, 13–14.
82. Kim, 17.
83. Kim, 22.
84. Pollack and Lee, *Preparing for Korean Unification: Scenarios & Implications*, 77.
85. Green, *Japan's Reluctant Realism: Foreign Policy Challenges in an Era of Uncertain Power*, 112.
86. Contrary to the education system eliciting anti-Japanese feelings, the system does not focus on the same sentiments against North Korea, despite it starting the Korean War, or China, despite China's "volunteers" extending the Korean War by almost three years, or Russia, despite its major role in dividing the peninsula.
87. Cumings, *Korea's Place in the Sun: A Modern History*, 140.
88. *Dokdo and East Sea*, Republic of Korea Culture and Information Service, http://www.korea.net/Government/Current-Affairs/National-Affairs?affairId=83 (accessed October 4, 2009).
89. *The Issue of Takeshima*, Japan Ministry of Foreign Affairs, http://www.mofa.go.jp/region/asia-paci/takeshima/index.html (accessed August 23, 2009).
90. Oh, Seok-min, "S. Korea, U.S., Japan to sign info-sharing pact on N.K. nukes," *Yonhap News*, December 26, 2014, http://english.yonhapnews.co.kr/national/2014/12/26/77/0301000000AEN20141226002952315F.html.
91. "U.S. praises Korea, Japan for reaching breakthrough deal on wartime sexual slavery," *Korea Herald*, 29 December 2015, http://www.koreaherald.com/view.php?ud=20151229000236 (accessed February 10, 2016).

92. Pollack and Lee, *Preparing for Korean Unification: Scenarios & Implications*, 77.
93. Michael J. Finnegan, "PacNet #48—What Now? The Case for U.S.-ROK-PRC Coordination on North Korea," in *PacNet Newsletter*, Honolulu, Center for Strategic and International Studies Pacific Forum, September 12, 2008, 1.
94. Richard Halloran, "North Korea Conundrum," *Washington Times*, June 15, 2008, B4.
95. Victor Cha, "We Have No Plan," *Chosun Ilbo*, June 9, 2008.
96. "U.S. Offers Action Plan in Case of NK Collapse," *The Korea Times*, October 29, 2008, http://www.koreatimes.co.kr/www/news/nation/2008/10/113_33472.html.
97. "U.S. Offers Action Plan in Case of NK Collapse."
98. Juan Kang and Qiang Guo, "Allowing collapse of North Korea unacceptable: experts," *China Daily*, December 14, 2009, http://bbs.chinadaily.com.cn/viewthread.php?gid=2&tid=643479.
99. Kang and Guo.
100. Interview with a UN official in New York City, October 9, 2006.
101. *Office of Commander*, U.S.FK, http://www.usfk.mil/Leadership.aspx, (accessed December 28, 2009).
102. *Strategic Digest*, United Nations Command/U.S.-ROK CFC /USFK, Spring 2014, 28.
103. "United Nations Command-Rear Fact Sheet," United Nations Command, September 18, 2014, 2.
104. Interview with John Burzynski, UNCMAC, Seoul, July 31, 2006.
105. James Kelly, *Opening Remarks Before the Senate Foreign Relations Committee on the Six-Party Talks* (Washington, DC: March 2, 2004), 1.
106. Jayshree Bajoria and Carin Zissis, "The Six-Party Talks on North Korea's Nuclear Program," New York, Council on Foreign Relations, July 1, 2009, 2.
107. "North Korea claims nuclear test," *BBC News*, October 9, 2006, http://news.bbc.co.uk/2/hi/6032525.stm.
108. Christopher R. Hill, "Update on the Six Party Talks," Washington, DC, The Brookings Institution, February 22, 2007, 6–7.
109. "Background Note: North Korea."
110. Sang-hun Choe, "North Korea Destroys Tower at Nuclear Site," *The New York Times*, June 28, 2008. See also *North Korea Destroy Nuclear Plant - cooling tower (CNN footage)*, YouTube, June 27, 2008, http://www.youtube.com/watch?v=VxYeny9qwvU (accessed October 20, 2009).

111. *Security Council, acting unanimously, condemns in strongest terms Democratic People's Republic of Korea nuclear test, toughens sanctions, United Nations Security Council Resolution 1874* (New York: United Nations, June 12, 2009), 1.
112. Stephen Bosworth, *Briefing on Recent Travel to North Korea* (Washington, DC: U.S. Department of State, December 16, 2009), 1.
113. Nuland, Victoria, "U.S.-DPRK Bilateral Discussions," U.S. Department of State, February 29, 2012, http://www.state.gov/r/pa/prs/ps/2012/02/184869.htm.
114. Matthew Cordova, "A Whole of Government Approach to Stability," in *Dipnote*, Washington, DC, U.S. Department of State, June 10, 2009, http://blogs.state.gov/index.php/entries/government_approach_stability/.
115. "Stabilization and Reconstruction: Actions Are Needed to Develop a Planning and Coordination Framework and Establish the Civilian Reserve Corps," U.S. Government Accountability Office, November 2007, 3.
116. John Herbst, "Prepared Statement by Ambassador John Herbst, Coordinator for Reconstruction and Stabilization, U.S. Department of State, before the Subcommittee on Oversight and Investigations and Terrorism & Unconventional Threats and Capabilities," House Committee on Armed Services, February 26, 2008, 4.

CHAPTER 5

Preparing for and Responding to Collapse

Abstract This chapter reviews numerous challenges posed by a collapse and explores potential responses to mitigate the problems. Immediate issues include nuclear weapons loss, disorder and chaos, rescuing political camp prisoners, provision of food and basic needs, and mass migration. Medium- to long-term issues include unemployment, elites, poor infrastructure, military integration, social integration, and economic development. How these challenges are handled, and by whom, would affect stability on the peninsula and international relations in the region. It will take concerted effort to manage the aftermath of collapse.

A collapsed North Korea conjures up images of numerous challenges including social disorder, mass migration, and loss of control of nuclear weapons. How these challenges are handled, and by whom, would affect international relations and stability in the region.

Moo Bong Ryoo, an ROK army officer, describes possible courses of action for stability operations in North Korea after a collapse resulting from a cause other than war.[1] He assumes no internal or external conflict and the involvement of multinational forces, international entities, and NGOs. Because the South Korean constitution and public would prompt the ROK government into action, one course of action he considers is ROK army-led stability operations.[2] He says that with 560,000[3] active-duty and three million reserve personnel, the ROK army would have sufficient manpower to quickly deploy two divisions for disaster relief and community assistance. He believes that the transition to an

© The Editor(s) (if applicable) and The Author(s) 2016
Tara O, *The Collapse of North Korea*,
DOI 10.1057/978-1-137-59801-1_5

ROK civilian government would be faster and smoother as it would not require an interim government that might repeat the experience of the UN Protectorate situation at the end of World War II that ultimately resulted in the division of Korea.[4] He emphasizes that the disadvantages would be the high cost to the ROK government and the ROK army's limited peacekeeping experience. Since Ryoo's report, Korea has gained additional experience in peace operation. In the early 2000s, South Korea had about 450 engineers and medics deployed to various UN missions, which peaked at 760 in 2012, after a decrease during 2003–2007.[5] During 2004–2008, Korea sent a Zaytun Division of 3,500 personnel to conduct civil–military operations to northern Iraq, Kyrgyzstan, and Kazakhstan as part of the U.S.-led coalition.[6] Through the UN peacekeeping and coalition operations, the Korean military gained valuable experience that could be applied in a contingency operation.

A report from the Center for U.S.–Korea Policy also suggests that the South Korean army should prepare and lead the multinational and interagency stability and support operations in cooperation with the major powers.[7] The report stresses the importance of international endorsement, such as a UN Security Council mandate, for stability operations in the northern half of the peninsula. Another priority is providing strategic assurance to China that U.S.–ROK stabilization efforts would not undermine Chinese interests, and assuring Japan that it will not be marginalized.[8] After a collapse, the priorities would be restoring order, economic reconstruction, and social integration.

Nicholas Eberstadt contends that despite the fears of the challenges posed by unification, North Korea is more likely to implode than to muddle through. From his perspective, the sooner reunification occurs, the better.[9] Eberstadt asserts that the wholesale reconstruction of the industrial base of North Korea could reduce production costs, enhance workforce skills, and establish the basis for sustained economic growth.[10] This venture would have spillover effects for southern Korea as well as for Northeast Asia, contributing to prosperity in the region.

The loss of control of nuclear weapons and related materials, facilities, and personnel is a major concern for the U.S. and other powers in the region. Michael O'Hanlon examines the possible collapse of two nuclear-armed countries, North Korea and Pakistan, and the implications of an anarchical environment that would permit the purchase or confiscation of nuclear weapons by a terrorist group.[11] O'Hanlon implies that timely intelligence and actions are crucial, noting that weapons locations would be difficult to determine and that nuclear weapons could be moved within hours.[12]

Warnings of the importance of securing nuclear weapons and materials are echoed in various writings on unification scenarios, including Maxwell's "Catastrophic Collapse of North Korea," the Center for U.S.–Korea Policy's "North Korea Contingency Planning and U.S.–ROK Cooperation," and Stares and Wit's "Preparing for Sudden Change in North Korea."[13] These studies also emphasize the need for security and stability, humanitarian assistance, and economic development.

Pyongyang's collapse would have a number of serious consequences, especially for South Korea. North Korea has 1.2 million military personnel with the largest artillery arm in the world, enough to inflict mass casualties and severe damage to the greater Seoul metropolitan area.[14] North Korea has threatened to turn South Korea into a "sea of fire" multiple times.[15]

While the difficulties of collapse would be felt most heavily by those on the Korean Peninsula, regional powers would also be affected by the collapse and would likely help to resolve or mitigate the problems associated with a collapse scenario. This chapter examines the major challenges expected to emerge in the event of a North Korean collapse: the control of nuclear weapons, disorder in the immediate aftermath of collapse, provision of basic goods and services, mass migration, elite management, infrastructure, unemployment, social integration, military integration, economic development, reforestation and flood mitigation, and developing the DMZ. Some of these problems are likely to be immediate; others are longer term.

1   Control of Nuclear Weapons

North Korea's nuclear weapons program and its proliferation are key concerns to the five regional powers. North Korea conducted its first nuclear test in October 2006 followed by three more in 2009, 2013, and 2016. Estimates vary, but given that its 5 megawatt reactor can produce 5–7 kilograms of plutonium per year, North Korea may possess 14–23 nuclear weapons.[16] With the Six-Party Talks stalled and North Korea showing no intention of abandoning its nuclear weapons program, the control of nuclear weapons, materials, and related personnel would emerge as one of the top concerns after North Korea's collapse.

1.1 Nuclear Weapons Accountability

If North Korea is not denuclearized prior to its collapse, then the combined ROK–U.S. forces would have to safeguard and maintain control of the nuclear weapons, facilities, materials, and scientists upon reunification. The loss of control of nuclear weapons and materials poses a grave danger to the international community. The nuclear weapons and materials must be accounted for, the facilities must be secured, and the nuclear specialists must be rapidly protected and gainfully reemployed. It is critical to quickly identify what elements of North Korean society, if any, control the nuclear weapons and work with them to ensure accountability. There would be a number of actors involved in cooperation, including the ROK, the U.S., and China.

With an urgent need to safeguard nuclear weapons, the military may get involved. The U.S. special operations forces (SOF) with ROK's support, or ROK SOF, would be ideal for such a task. Trained in unconventional warfare and possessing unique skills, they would be able to employ speed, flexibility, and innovation in a counter-proliferation mission.[17] Robust intelligence support would be important for identifying relevant targets and planning and executing their missions.[18]

The details of SOF activities should not be divulged, but it is important to coordinate with China at the strategic level on counter-proliferation efforts. China does not want U.S. military forces near its border; it also does not want uncontrolled nuclear weapons and related materials smuggled inside its border, and so has an interest in insuring that responsible parties safeguard the weapons. Because uncoordinated activities could lead to misunderstanding, Beijing, Washington, and Seoul should coordinate on the nuclear issue prior to Pyongyang's collapse. North Korea shares a border with Russia, and Japan can be reached by a boat, so coordination with Russia and Japan would also be necessary.

In the medium to long term, if there is a request for U.S. support, the Department of Energy (DOE), rather than the Department of Defense (DOD), could be the lead agency to coordinate the effort on the U.S. side, working with Korean authorities. For instance, DOE, working with ROK counterparts and international agencies, could provide support to manage the weapons, facilities, and nuclear scientists. The DOE's strength is its expertise and experience with such programs as the Nunn-Lugar Cooperative Threat Reduction (CTR) Program, which helped the former Soviet states reduce, eliminate, and safeguard their nuclear stockpiles, facilities, and scientists.

1.2 Nunn-Lugar Act (Cooperative Threat Reduction Program)

The 1991 Cooperative Threat Reduction Program, sponsored by former Senators Sam Nunn and Richard Lugar, provides U.S. expertise and funding to help dismantle the vast stockpiles of nuclear, chemical, and biological weapons and their delivery systems in the former Soviet Union.[19] As of March 2013, the program had deactivated or destroyed 7,616 nuclear warheads, 914 intercontinental ballistic missiles (ICBMs), and thousands of other related materials.[20] The program facilitated the removal of all nuclear weapons from Ukraine, Kazakhstan, and Belarus, which had inherited a significant number of nuclear weapons after the Soviet breakup. In 2003, Congress approved the Nunn-Lugar Expansion Act, which allows the CTR program to operate outside the former Soviet states for nonproliferation measures. This expansion allowed the program to operate in Albania, and by 2007, chemical weapons in Albania were destroyed.

Beyond the efforts to eliminate WMD, the program also reaches out to nuclear scientists, employing 58,000 former weapons scientists in peaceful research projects using WMD-related facilities that were turned into research centers.[21] Congress authorized the Nunn-Lugar CTR program to receive financial support from foreign governments and other international institutions in 2010.[22]

The U.S. DOD would be able to spend up to one-tenth of the program's budget on unforeseen nonproliferation operations. The CTR would be a useful tool to control and manage nuclear, chemical, and biological weapons, related materials, and personnel inherited from North Korea.

2 Disorder in the Immediate Aftermath of Collapse

North Korean society, controlled by the Kim regime at every level, could fall into a state of disorder and chaos after collapse. People would feel anxious and uncertain, crime could increase, and mass migration could ensue. A quick response to restore order should be a major goal of planning.

2.1 System of Control

The Kim regime has a tight system of control using fear that reaches every level of society. Kim Il-sung created multiple and overlapping security organizations to investigate and monitor its citizens: the Ministry of People's Security (MPS), the Ministry of State Security (MSS), and the Military Security Command (MSC). They report through various chains, directly or indirectly, but ultimately to the leader. Not only do they watch and control people, but they also compete with each other, ensuring one does not become powerful to the point that it can challenge the Kim in power.

Virtually all North Koreans are required to belong to a political organization. The Korean Workers' Party (KWP) is the main important political and ideological organization, at the top of the network of party and state institutions where political, social, and economic policy is conceived and directed by a small elite group. The organization is elitist by nature, according to former Australian diplomat Adrian Buzo. It monopolizes state resources and

> is at the core of political culture marked by exclusion, centralization, strict accountability, hierarchy and discipline, while its style also reflects its ex-guerilla leadership—ruthless, Spartan, secretive, suspicious of intellectual activity, resourceful, predatory, and improvisatory.[23]

The KWP is active through an elaborate network of specialized and mass organizations, including the government, the military, and youth and women's organizations. Those with good *songbun* under 25 years until they graduate from college join the Kim Il-sung Socialist Youth League, which grooms future elites who later join the KWP.[24] Other organizations include *Sonyeondan*, the Children's Union, and *Inminban*, neighborhood groups of 30–50 families comprised primarily of housewives.[25] Such groups inculcate ideology and reverence for Kim Il-sung, Kim Jong-il, and now Kim Jong-un.

Through these mechanisms, the regime controls information flow and people's movement, speech, and behavior. The structure is hierarchical—orders flow from the top to the lowest levels in the township, where they are implemented. If the central government no longer functions, local-level governments may be reluctant to act. In the face of uncertainty, local governments could also fall. In anarchy, disorderliness may prevail. The lack of order would lead to further problems, such as mass migration and increased crime.

In a lawless situation, some loot since there is little risk of punishment. Other people will be gripped by fear and insecurity, which may lead them to depart from the area. It will be important to calm the public by persuading them that the situation is under control. In North Korea, the internet is nonexistent and not everyone has a television. To stem the potential migration, radio or loud speaker announcements in the markets and neighborhoods could reassure people that order exists. Such announcements, however, must be followed by deeds. Institutions at the local and provincial levels must be built with sufficient capability to restore order and inspire confidence within the populace.

2.2 Stability Operations

Until local capacity is built, restoration of order may fall on the ROK forces. The ROK constitution recognizes Koreans in North Korea as citizens of South Korea; therefore, South Korea has a constitutional requirement to protect and provide for them. Furthermore, it has moral and psychological responsibilities stemming from shared ethnicity, history, and culture. Despite the desire for gradual and peaceful unification, the South Korean public might demand that their government take action in a contingency. In a collapse/no war scenario, South Korea's active-duty military and reserve personnel could be deployed rapidly to each of the North's nine provinces and three special cities for stability operations, disaster relief, and community assistance.[26]

The UN is another possible actor. Since three UN Security Council members have strong interests on the peninsula, having the UN lead stability and reconstruction efforts may be more acceptable to the interested parties and provide international legitimacy. However, it would take longer to achieve UN consensus and organize peacekeeping forces large enough for stability operations. Using the UN Command, which already exists and is equipped with command and control capabilities and multinational integration, could provide more timely response.

China would be another player in case of a mass exodus of North Koreans into China following a collapse. China would likely employ the People's Liberation Army (PLA) and People's Armed Police (PAP) for managing the refugee flow. However, these entities have limited experience with mass refugees. China could cooperate with the UNHCR and relevant NGOs to better manage the situation.

2.3 Rescue Operation: Political Camp Prisoners

The North Korean regime considers the existence of its political prison camps a state secret and vehemently denies their existence. The regime is determined to destroy the evidence by issuing orders to kill the prisoners in case of a war or revolution. These gulags hold an estimated 200,000 people. If the orders are carried out, there would be a systematic massacre as war or a similar event unfolds. Careful planning must account for the prevention or amelioration of such a horror. Efforts to rescue these camp prisoners should be a high priority because time would be of the essence. A timely rescue operation is, therefore, crucial. Even before any contingency, steps could be taken that might reduce the chance of their massacre. Working through the UN Human Rights Commission, governments, and NGOs, greater pressure should be applied on Kim Jong-un and the prison guards alike for the consequences of such behavior. The commensurate punishment for issuing and carrying out any such orders should be announced. Since the Kim regime's aim is to destroy any proof of the existence of concentration camps, the prison guards should also be made aware that they are part of the "evidence" to be destroyed.

3 Providing for Basic Needs

3.1 Lack of Basic Goods and Services

Another problem of regime disintegration is the failure of institutions to provide food and services. If people cannot get basic goods and services, the likelihood of migration increases. The search for food and other basic needs could exacerbate the social order problem in the short term. Discontent arising from the scarcity of food and services could pose a long-term problem for the legitimacy of the new or transitional governing entity.

3.2 Basic Services Provision

North Koreans are no strangers to shortages of food and basic needs. In addition to food scarcity and famine, the lack of electricity is constant and unmistakable as depicted by the satellite imagery in Fig. 5.1, which shows the unlit upper half and the brightly lit lower half of the Korean Peninsula.

Fig. 5.1 Korea at Night: Dark North Korea, Bright South Korea (Satellite imagery of Korea at night, Image Caption ISS038-E-038300 (January 30, 2014). Image courtesy of the Earth Science and Remote Sensing Unit, NASA Johnson Space Center, http://eol.jsc.nasa.gov/SearchPhotos/photo.pl?mission=ISS038& roll=E&frame=38300 (accessed December 11, 2014) (Source: The Earth Science and Remote Sensing Unit, NASA Johnson Space Center)

Chronic shortages of heating materials have left the mountains bare of trees, as people cut them down for firewood, exchange it for food, or use the forestland to grow food. Deforestation considerably intensifies susceptibility to flood damage. After a catastrophic event, a shortage of water, especially potable water, would be a major problem. If governing institutions cannot deliver water, NGOs or international institutions may need to step in until local capacity is developed.

Health care is another basic need. Dr. Norbert Vollertsen, an NGO volunteer, reports a need for medicine and medical supplies throughout North Korea. For example, he witnessed a 30-minute surgery with a rusty knife performed on an emaciated teenager without anesthesia.[27] The hospital lacked medical supplies, such as antiseptic cleanser, and basic amenities, such as soap, running water, and light.

When there is low local capacity to provide for basic needs, assistance from donor countries, international institutions, or NGOs could fill the gap. Eventually, a functioning capacity will be needed. Measures to provide basic services and build governing institutional capabilities, especially at the local level, would help mitigate shortages while providing people with an incentive to stay and rebuild their lives. After reviewing NGOs' effectiveness in creating civil society, Mendelson and Glenn suggest that the best strategy is to integrate concrete projects with an inclusive decision-making process. The integrative approach builds local community and civil society, increasing participation and strengthening local capacity.[28]

The public will need to be informed that efforts to provide for basic needs are under way and how to access those goods and services. Again, announcements via radio, loud speakers, and posters may be necessary.

4   Migration

If one person in each North Korean household were to move to South Korea after reunification, more than three million people would migrate.[29] An immediate headlong rush from North Korea, as well as migration over the longer term, is a major concern for South Korea and China. The Germans experienced mass exodus from east to west when the Berlin Wall fell and other borders opened.

Indeed, three million may prove to be an underestimate. Already, the number of North Koreans defecting to South Korea has increased dramatically, to more than 28,000 by 2015.[30] According to the U.S. State Department's 2005 assessment, North Korean refugees in China number between 10,000 and 30,000; some NGOs estimate that the number could be as high as 300,000.[31] The numbers are difficult to estimate because refugees in China hide to avoid forced repatriation to North Korea where they would face imprisonment, torture, or execution, and women may be sold as brides or sex slaves in China.[32] Periodically, the Pyongyang regime tries to reign in defection. In May 2009, the Pyongyang regime gave orders that no North Korean resident may flee the country. They began harsher crackdowns, sending arrested defectors to concentration camps, where they are subject to lengthy forced labor and routine torture.[33] Shortly after Kim Jong-un assumed power, he clamped down on defection with more border guards, cameras, and even by luring back a small number of defectors for propaganda purposes.[34]

4.1 Short-term Migration

If there were a complete breakdown of institutions and public order, North Koreans would likely migrate en masse, primarily to China and South Korea, but also to Japan and Russia, and even to third countries. Those crossing the national borders are considered refugees. North Koreans crossing into South Korea would not be categorized as refugees, but as internally displaced persons, because they are considered South Korean citizens.

Initially, most North Korean emigrants may seek refuge in China because the Chinese border is easier to cross and the border to the south is heavily mined and dangerous, although there are two corridors in the DMZ. The 850 mile-long border between North Korea and China is relatively easy to cross and Korean–Chinese communities are found in the Yanbian Korean–Chinese autonomous district and the three Northeast states of Liaoning-sheng, Jilin-sheng, and Heilongjang-sheng.[35] China fears mass refugee movement into the country, and the People's Liberation Army and the People's Armed Police reportedly have plans to block the refugees.[36] China employs the PLA and PAP in times of natural disasters. These forces are not trained to deal with a large number of refugees, and if they were to develop such capabilities, it would likely be "rudimentary and even cruel" by world standards.[37] China may want to avoid intervention by international agencies and NGOs within its borders, but this would likely prolong and exacerbate the problem. Mismanagement of the refugees could damage China's international reputation. Therefore, permitting organizations like the UNHCR and others specialized in handling refugees to operate on its borders would help to alleviate the human crisis and to stabilize the region, as well as enhancing China's global image.

North Koreans would also want to enter South Korea. The heavily mined DMZ between South Korea and North Korea would make crossing the zone difficult, although there are roads linking both sides on the east and west corridors. With failed command and control, the action of the soldiers on the northern border would be unpredictable. Crossing the border anywhere other than by the two roads, therefore, would be dangerous. The South Korean government would also need to give clear instructions to their military on the border. While some may argue that the North–South border mines control migration, the mines would eventually need to be removed for Korea to unify. Mine removal is time-consuming and dangerous, but demining must be part of the plan.

An overall plan is crucial to manage the immediate mass migration. The South Korean government would need to devise a plan to manage the situation, perhaps with the help of NGOs and families. North Koreans migrating to South Korea are likely to search for families and relatives separated during the Korean War.

4.2   Medium- to Long-Term Migration

Even if security concerns are addressed and basic needs are met, the incentive to migrate will persist as long as income and social inequalities exist. In the medium to long term, North Koreans would no doubt be lured South by its economic and social conditions.

Mass migration would create significant social problems after unification. Once they arrive in South Korea, many North Korean defectors have difficulties adjusting to life in a completely different system. Northerners are not familiar with the South's economic, political, and cultural systems and customs. Communication is difficult because different words, especially foreign words, are widely used in South Korea. Some South Korean employers discriminate against North Koreans, making it hard for them to earn an income. Meanwhile, a good number seem to become dependent on government welfare.

South Koreans are mindful of the destabilizing potential of mass migration. They may face a lack of public services and competition for their children's education. The differences in psychosocial norms would pose a significant challenge to the social fabric. Unemployment and inflation may rise. Traffic and pollution would get worse. Housing would be inadequate in an already competitive market.

Migration can be halted or slowed by physical, motivational, and structural means. The physical would be a tangible barrier that prevents people from moving. Some have argued for temporarily retaining border control, including maintaining the DMZ. This option may have some South Korean support, but enforcement would be difficult, and human rights concerns may arise. As seen during the fall of the Berlin Wall, Koreans could also be swept with the nationalistic euphoria. A motivation-focused approach to migration control gives incentives for North Koreans to stay in place. In North Korea, housing currently belongs to the state; giving North Koreans home ownership might enhance their desire to stay where they reside. Broader land reform and redistribution is yet another issue, but is made even more complex by South Korean families potentially making historical land claims in the north.

Job creation is a key structural factor in ameliorating migration. After former communist states opened their economies, industries suffered from productivity loss due to inefficiency and reforms, which increased unemployment and underemployment. Public infrastructure is a sector that can absorb numerous unemployed people, and North Korea's infrastructure needs are enormous. Lacking are adequate roads, railroads, communications infrastructure, energy grids, water delivery systems, and other networks. The sheer size of these projects means this sector could provide jobs for a large number of North Koreans, including those demobilized from the North's 1.2 million military. Improved infrastructure would also attract businesses, which can spur additional employment, and enterprises can relocate to take advantage of low labor costs in northern Korea.

4.3   Education and Retraining

In a socialist system, people expect the government to provide goods and services. For North Koreans, who have little or no exposure to a capitalist system, education in market systems and skills training for future employment are crucial. Implementation should be immediate. If it takes too long, people may become disillusioned and decide to leave, creating additional problems.

5   Elites

During collapse, North Korean officials might worry that they would be under South Korea's authority and be punished, while ordinary North Koreans would eagerly await a new beginning after decades of anxiousness from persistent economic difficulties and systemic insecurity.[38] Given the atrocities and extensive human rights violations of the regime, those responsible must be accountable, including the top leader and a small circle of elites. Certainly, those most responsible should be brought to trial. This is part of the process of seeking justice as well as healing. To completely "de-Nazify" or "de-Bathify," however, probably adds complexity to the already difficult problem and lengthens the road to stability and development. Bureaucracies are critical to the functioning of any government, and some of the mid- to lower-level civil servants and other acceptable personnel should be integrated and given responsibilities. In the post–World War II Germany, de-Nazification did begin, but it was never fully completed because there were too many people involved and their technical and administrative expertise were crucial.[39] In post-war Japan, McArthur was instructed to rely "to the fullest extent practicable" on Japanese civil servants to facilitate the withdrawal of the U.S. forces in a timely manner.[40] This could also prevent the potential rise of armed opposition, which may use violence, creating an insecure environment, diverting resources away from other urgent issues, and interfering with the creation of a stable system. The Iraq experience showed that the "de-Bathification" did not heal the nation, but created an even more unstable and violent situation. This is not to say that there should be a blanket amnesty. Some investigations and re-education would be needed and alternate methods seeking reconciliation should be explored. The elites should also feel, as do ordinary citizens, that they have a stake in a new system and governance.

6 Infrastructure

For an economy to develop and function, public infrastructure is a prerequisite. A major disincentive for investment in eastern Germany after unification was its poor infrastructure, especially transportation and telecommunications networks.[41] The decrepit North Korean infrastructure hinders economic development. Building roads, internet infrastructure, and energy grids, for example, would require significant investment from private sources and multilateral development institutions. Building such infrastructure should be a priority to attract investments.

South Korea has an extensive and inexpensive public transportation system of subways, buses, and bullet trains connecting all parts of the country. The system could be a model for the northern half of the peninsula to build a modern, convenient, and affordable public transportation system.

Internet is practically nonexistent in North Korea because the Kim regime wants to keep out external information. In the short run, tethered balloons or satellite internet services may be needed, because they can be established quickly. In the long run, unencumbered by legacy infrastructure, the latest technology in internet infrastructure could give northern Korea one of the fastest internet services in the world.

Such activities will also have the benefit of creating large-scale engineering, construction, and technical jobs. The infrastructure needs of North

Korea are vast, so this sector can absorb a large portion of the unemployed, especially from military demobilization.

7 Unemployment (Medium- to Long-Term)

The greatest challenge for eastern Germany was reducing unemployment,[42] The east had an unemployment rate twice that of the west 15 years after German unification. Unemployment resulted from the outmoded and overstaffed industry that could not contend in a more competitive atmosphere. The 1:1 currency exchange rate equalized the wage structure between eastern and western Germany, but it exacerbated the unemployment problem in the east. With that exchange rate, the east could not offer lower wages to attract investment. Inadequate infrastructure further hindered investment in the region.

Dealing with the anticipated high unemployment will be critical to preventing mass migration and developing the economy. In a socialist economy, underemployment from working in unproductive state-owned enterprises (SOEs) is already a problem. The SOEs would be unsustainable in a collapsed system and the likely change to a capitalist system. Without the SOEs, formerly employed and underemployed people would become unemployed along with soldiers released from North Korea's huge military. A more positive way to view this issue is that North Korea would have an abundant supply of literate, low-cost, and disciplined workers, which would attract investors and could even trigger a growth spurt.[43]

The privatization of northern industries should be carefully planned and phased to avoid sudden and massive layoffs, especially if workers have no alternative employment prospects. On the other hand, privatization that is too slow could also hamper development; without privatization, investment may be hindered. At the microeconomic level, investment introduces new market-competitive products and processes. At the macroeconomic level, investment based on market principles rather than central resource allocation would be the means for sectoral and regional economic restructuring.[44] The establishment of appropriate laws to encourage investment and development would also be necessary.

In addition to privatization, currency conversion and exchange rate determination need careful consideration. Helmut Schmidt, the Chancellor of the former West Germany, emphasizes the importance of choosing the right exchange rate after unification, implying that setting a too-favorable exchange rate for the North in an attempt to reach immediate wage parity could discourage investment and exacerbate unemployment.[45] The speed of monetary integration also requires cautious deliberation. Once initiated, monetary integration is practically irreversible due to political problems. Delaying the currency union may be preferable to early integration.[46] One possibility is to free-float both currencies until stabilization policies are in place in northern Korea, at which time both sides could enter into a band of exchange rate.

Another option is to peg the value of northern currency to southern currency in the beginning, and introduce a new common currency when more favorable macroeconomic conditions are achieved. Delaying monetary integration can provide time to prepare for smoother transition.

8 Social Integration

Assimilation of North Koreans into the South Korean society would be especially challenging. Northerners have lived in a completely different system for over 60 years—three generations. The adjustment problems the North Korean defectors face in South Korea offer a glimpse of the social integration challenges after unification.

8.1 Defectors in South Korea

When defectors first arrive in South Korea after a harrowing journey, they feel hopeful about their future. After all, they speak the same language and share much of the same history. Upon arriving in South Korea, defectors receive two months of social adjustment training, counseling, and medical care at the Ministry of Unification's *Hanawon* (House of Unity) to help them prepare for life in capitalist South Korea. The government provides additional support through provisions of the 1997 Act on the Protection and Resettlement Support for the Residents Who Escaped from North Korea. Under this law, each North Korean adult receives about $36,000, of which about $7,400 is for a down payment toward a permanent apartment.[47]

Despite the support, however, North Korean defectors find it difficult to adjust their lives in South Korea. After a while, they realize that over six decades of division has created two entirely different cultures and systems. They find the language difficult to understand. South Koreans use a large number of English words and terms such as *budongsan* (real estate) and *boheom* (insurance), which are ubiquitous in capitalist societies, but these are foreign to North Koreans because these concepts do not exist in North Korea.[48] They also lack experience and knowledge of computers and other elements of modern capitalist society, which makes their work lives challenging. North Koreans also suffer from guilt about the families they left behind. They worry about the political consequences for their families, as North Korea treats defection as treason and can punish families accordingly. Defectors also face prejudice from some South Koreans who perceive them as socialists who are dependent, passive, lazy, and selfish.[49] Other South Koreans are simply too busy focusing on their own lives to show much interest. *Crossing*, a poignant movie released in 2008 about a North Korean defector and his efforts to bring his adolescent son out of North Korea, quickly moved out of the box office in South Korea despite the star cast and great reviews. While there may be other reasons for the film's unpopularity, it does raise questions about South Koreans' attitudes toward their northern brethren.

There certainly are successful defectors, such as Cho Myung-chul, the first North Korean defector to become a member of the South Korean National Assembly; Dr. Ahn Chan-il, the first defector to receive a PhD in South Korea; and Dr. Lee Ae-ran, the first female defector to receive a PhD in South Korea.[50] About 3% of the defectors arrive in South Korea with college or higher-level degrees from North Korea.[51] They also face the same difficulties that other defectors face, but they tend to adjust better to life in South Korea. Younger defectors also find adjusting to a new environment difficult. North Korea's education system, focused on the Kim family and its ideology, does not prepare them well for math, science, and other topics important in modern South Korea. Among the defector youth, there are a good number attending universities in South Korea, who are seen as future leaders in a unified Korea. For instance, The Future of the Korean Peninsula Foundation (*Hanbando Mirae Jaedan*) is an NGO that focuses on grooming such leaders in its Unification Leadership Academy.[52] In a post-unification scenario, the defectors, with an understanding of both societies, could indeed play an important role in bridging the two sides of the divided peninsula.

The current challenges faced by defectors are likely to be as great or greater for those who migrate south if North Korea collapses. At the same time, civil society as well as the defectors who are now living in South Korea could help address the integration challenges that are certain to rise after unification.

8.2 Education

South Korea should be preparing for an eventual merger. The difficult route to social integration faced by defectors highlights the need to educate South Koreans to show empathy and be more accommodating to North Koreans. Otherwise, the social division could contribute to discontent, leading to serious social problems. Educational institutions are a powerful way to inculcate basic facts and values in the next generation, affecting their attitudes and behavior. Since it takes a generation to achieve this, schools should start now to prepare the society for social integration and dealing with issues faced by defectors. Post unification, the major tasks for Korea's education system include providing Koreans from the north the "truth regarding capitalism, communism, democracy, and history, especially with respect to the former ROK and DPRK, the United States, and the range of international issues regarding North Korea."[53] North Koreans would need to unlearn the myth of the Kim family. Education should attempt to reverse the decades of damage inflicted on North Koreans regarding the exercise of initiative. Since the traditional South Korean education system would not include the older generation, one suggestion is to maintain the Korean Workers' Party practice of continuing education in the short term to develop individual skills and inspire constructive behavioral changes.[54]

9 Military Integration

North Korea has the world's fourth largest military with 1.2 million troops, nearly twice that of South Korea's 669,000. Integrating the two militaries formed under different political systems into one would be challenging. The transformation of the ideals of the military professionalism during the onset of a drastic political and social upheaval would require careful planning and implementation. Both militaries have seen the other side as enemies for decades. The political systems of the two militaries provide a completely different context. After the unification, at least some of the Korea People's Army (KPA) soldiers may remain at arms to serve the previously opponent state, as was the case in Germany. Avoiding social and economic marginalization of former KPA members would be important. Additionally, a sudden and drastic reduction of the military could have grave economic and social consequences, one of which is creating a large number of unemployed people. A careful approach is needed for both the integration and the reduction of the military.

The organizational structure of the military could also provide a more rapid and effective way to disseminate information and to educate and train military members to transition to civilian life in a changed environment. Downsizing and integration need to occur in controlled and phased stages to reduce the shock to the system.

Although on a much smaller scale, the German experience in integrating the militaries of the former West Germany and East Germany could provide some insight. Upon unification, the former East Germany's *Nationale Volksarmee* (NVA) was disbanded and its soldiers integrated into West Germany's army and now a unified Germany's *Bundeswehr*. On October 3, 1990, 90,000 NVA veterans became citizens and soldiers of the Federal Republic of Germany overnight.[55] To assure the neighbors of a peaceful demeanor in Germany, it also required a reduction of the forces from 600,000 to 370,000 by the end of 1994.[56] All NVA soldiers over 55 years of age, general-level officers, and females were immediately released from the military.[57] NVA officers above the lieutenant colonel rank were relieved of their duties. Out of over 110,000 NVA military personnel, 20,000 were initially accepted into *Bundeswehr*, and the rest released within two years, often with short notice and demotion.[58] According to the Unification Treaty (*Einigungsvertrag*), the *Bundeswehr* was to be reduced and 25% of the force was to be comprised of former NVA officers and enlisted troops by 1994. This created a large number of unemployed people, who lost their status and were marginalized economically and socially.

While categorizing those who can join the new military may be useful, the sudden discharge may not. A gradual approach with a program to help those in transition from the military to the civilian sector would be helpful. The U.S. military has such a program mandated by the Congress—the transition assistance program (TAP)—which provides information, resources, and assistance to transitioning personnel. Examining the TAP could provide some insight.

Studying the racial integration process of the U.S. military could also be helpful. While both North Koreans and South Koreans share the same ethnicity, the potential for discrimination cannot be overruled. A hybrid of South Korea's *Hanawon* program, which helps the newly arrived defectors to adjust to life in South Korea, and a program similar to the U.S. military's TAP can also be useful in assisting the military to transition to the other spheres of the society. The key is a gradual and methodical process involving entities beyond the Ministry of Defense to include other government entities and the civil society to avoid the disruptive effects of sudden reduction and integration.

10 Economic Development

10.1 Unification Cost and Financing

South Koreans fear the huge economic cost that has become synonymous with unification. A large number of South Koreans are not willing to assume the burden if it requires a huge sacrifice in their living standards. The unification cost estimates are in hundreds of billions to trillions of dollars, depending on the calculation model used. Calculations by Noland et al. show much lower estimates, even suggesting a net benefit of $541 billion in comparison to no unification.[59] However, this model assumes years of integration between South Korea and North Korea, which reduces the income gap between the two Koreas. Wolf and Akarmov estimate $50 billion to $667 billion, taking into account savings from the downsized North Korean military.[60] They claim that since North Korea's military expenditure is about 20–30% of its GDP, downsizing its military would yield savings. They also assume geography and physical barriers would restrict population movement. According to the 2013 South Korea's Ministry of Finance announcement, the unification cost could be about 7% of South Korea's GDP for a decade, which is roughly $1 trillion.[61] Yet another estimate places the cost much higher. Peter Beck of the Shorenstein Center calculates that increasing the North's income level to 80% of the South's would require $2 trillion to $5 trillion over 30 years.[62] Such a wide range of estimates reflects the difficulty of measuring the actual cost. The longer it takes to unify, the greater the gap between the South and North will become, because South Korea's economy is currently growing at a faster rate than the North's. It is clear, however, that the unification will require significant amounts of resources and planning.

How will the reunification cost be financed? Korea will have to consider various sources, domestic and foreign. Domestic funding sources are government surplus, tariffs, and new taxes. The government budget surplus is realistic only if there are more revenues than expenses. Even if this were the case, the surplus would be only a tiny fraction of requirements. Another source of revenue is new taxes. They could be corporate taxes, income taxes, value-added taxes, or a myriad of other possibilities. Careful balancing is required since overtaxing could discourage corporate investment and public savings accumulation, which are also necessary for developing the northern half of the peninsula.

An additional factor is the role of foreign capital. Many South Koreans assume that South Korea will bear all of the unification costs, which dampen the support for unification. South Korea has developed while receiving loans, grants, and foreign investments from abroad. The same concept could apply to North Korea. The sources of investment and development funds include Japan, the U.S., and the international community. It also includes IFIs, such as the World Bank and the ADB. The South Korean government's role would be to quickly develop an environment conducive to foreign direct investment and aid, which includes establishing proper laws.

Japan's capital would be crucial for financing Korea's unification cost. In 1965, when South Korea normalized relations with Japan, Japan provided $800 million (worth over $6 trillion in 2015 dollars)[63] in grants and concessional loans to South Korea.[64] The large Japanese contribution was seen as a way for Japan to rectify its history of harsh colonial rule and its link to the division of Korea.[65] Japan also views stability on the peninsula as important. Korea, however, should not rely on wartime guilt for Japan to provide financing. Korea should make efforts to develop warmer ties with Japan. Economic reconstruction of northern Korea is a realistic way to decrease instability on the peninsula, which is a constant concern for Japan as well as all the powers involved.

The U.S. could provide significant support for reunification and development. Both the public and private sectors could provide assistance and capital to Korea. The U.S. is also the key to approving or expediting IFI financial packages. Furthermore, investors value stability and the commitment to stability. The U.S. and the ROK–U.S. alliance could provide stability, and the commitment of the U.S. could help attract further foreign direct investment.

The support of the U.S. will be essential. During the U.S.–Soviet rivalry, South Korea was a strong U.S. ally on the frontier of the Cold War. As such, from 1945 to 1983, the U.S. provided $13.8 billion in assistance to South Korea, much of it in grants and concessional loans, with a large portion as military assistance.[66] The World Bank and the ADB, IFIs with strong U.S. influence, provided $5.3 billion (1945–1984) and $1.4 billion (1945–1981), respectively.[67] In the mid-1980s, South Korea was the third largest recipient of U.S. assistance on a per capita basis after Israel and Vietnam.[68] After the jump-start growth in the late 1970s and early 1980s,

South Korea advanced economically, politically, and militarily, and remains a staunch ally of the U.S. Given the impact of unification on Northeast Asian stability and its interest in the region, the U.S. could be expected to play a significant role, including using its influence on the IFIs to provide financing for the reunification.

10.2 North's Labor

While unification costs would be considerable, a unified Korea could produce a synergistic effect on the economy. South Korea's high wages encourage its companies to seek cheaper labor elsewhere, such as China. The wages for North Korean workers at the Gaesong Industrial Complex is about $70 per month, and with allowances and incentives, $130.[69] After the deductions made by the North Korean authorities, a worker takes home about $25 to $35, still much more than the average North Korean monthly salary outside the industrial park of $2 per month.[70] While not suggesting this amount after unification, North Korea offers low-cost labor as well as an educated and disciplined workforce, which is appealing to potential investors. Furthermore, North Korea has a greater percentage of younger population than South Korea, with 21.3% under the age of 15 compared to 16.8% in South Korea.[71] The higher percentage of youths means that retraining to adjust to the market system and new society would be handled through the conventional education system of elementary, middle, and high schools, rather than by specialized retraining geared toward the elderly population. North Korea's population growth rate estimate in 2014 of 0.53% is higher than South Korea's 0.16%.[72] The North Korean labor force, therefore, will grow at a faster pace.

10.3 North's Mineral Wealth

Another area of synergy is in the raw materials sector. Unlike resource-poor South Korea, which must import most of its mineral needs, North Korea is rich in raw materials, including coal, lead, tungsten, zinc, graphite, magnesite, iron ore, copper, gold, pyrites, salt, copper, and fluorspar.[73] North Korea has large quantities of strategic minerals, including those necessary for steel production.[74] A 2013 geological study by SRE Minerals Limited shows that North Korea could hold some 216 million tons of rare earths—minerals used in smartphones, high-definition televisions, and other consumer electronics.[75] Currently, China has 90% of the world's rare earth market, and South Korea and Japan are two main importers of the minerals.[76]

A unified Korea would have a greater diversity of mineral sources for consumption and growth.[77] In fact, a 2007 study by Goohoon Kwon cites these synergistic effects and the combined population of over 70 million in predicting that a unified Korea's GDP would surpass that of France, Germany, and possibly Japan in 30–40 years.[78] The study assumes gradual and peaceful integration of the two economies, rendering the forecast far less likely in a collapsed case. Nonetheless, the synergistic effect of combining the strengths of both sides deserves serious attention.

The need for a comprehensive rebuilding of the industrial base can yield unforeseen benefits. Reconstruction can form the basis for continued economic growth by reducing production costs, enhancing workforce skills, and significantly increasing productivity.[79] While South Korea is cautious about the unification cost, the benefits to Korea as a whole, at least economically, could be substantial.

11 Reforestation and Flood Mitigation

It takes a generation to restore trees to the mountains. Deforestation has been a problem in North Korea. Trees were destroyed during the war and logged for construction and industrialization. In recent times, trees have been cut for firewood to heat homes or to trade for food, and not replaced. A major consequence of deforestation is damage from floods, which occur annually during the monsoon season. Directly, floods destroy dwellings and cause deaths. Indirectly, floods reduce food supplies by damaging crops. As long as the mountains are barren, the cycle repeats, compounding the problems of flood damage and food shortages.

During heavy rains and floods, the contrast between North Korea and South Korea is stark. South Korea is about two-thirds mountainous and dispenses government resources for rescue operations. While South Korea also has flood problems, the damage is not nearly as severe as in North Korea. South Korea could have suffered worse damage if it did not have a nationwide reforestation project. South Korea began a massive reforestation campaign under President Park Chung-hee in the 1970s. The effort relied on neighborhood cooperatives, enlisting hundreds of thousands of volunteers, who planted 11 billon trees by 2008.[80] Three decades after the project began, South Korea's once barren mountains are lush with trees that control erosion and flood damage while providing hundreds of national parks for recreation and contributing to a greener environment.

Reforesting North Korea's mountains would yield similar benefits. One of Lee Myung-bak's campaign pledges was to help North Korea reforest its mountains. The Blue House spokesperson stated that South Korea would send seedlings to North Korea, although it did not materialize. Lee's main argument was business, but also environment. Once the Kyoto Protocol takes effect, South Korean companies can buy the right to emit carbon dioxide from North Korea.[81] Yet another potential advantage is jobs creation. As with infrastructure projects, a massive reforestation project could absorb many of the unemployed. Given the lengthy time it takes for trees to grow, the earlier the reforestation begins, the better.

12   Developing the DMZ

The heavily armed and mined DMZ bisecting the Korean Peninsula has been useful for maintaining the armistice that halted the armed conflict in 1953 by separating the two contesting sides. There have been skirmishes and serious incidents, such as when North Korean troops killed two U.S. army officers in the 1970s ax incident. For the most part, however, the DMZ sees little human activity and has become rich with flora and fauna, including over 1,100 plant species, 500 mammal species, hundreds of bird species, and 80 fish species.[82] Wildlife thrives in the area, especially endangered species. Red-crowned cranes, ring-tailed pheasants, and Siberian tigers have been spotted there.[83] Discussions are taking place to convert this zone into a "peace park" to preserve its substantial biodiversity and transform it into a symbol of peace and unity. This effort assumes there would be no armed conflict on the peninsula that would destroy the DMZ area. Preserving the DMZ as a natural habitat for wildlife may not take top priority after North Korea's collapse, as there would be more urgent needs. However, the biodiverse DMZ is a national treasure. Neglecting it at the beginning could have lasting consequences not only for the endangered species, but for national development as well. Korea does not top the list of tourist destinations in Asia when there are other options such as China, Japan, and Thailand. The bio-rich DMZ could provide ecotourism opportunities that could help with economic development and create employment while preserving the environment.

In summary, the collapse of North Korea would present a number of serious challenges and opportunities to both the people on the peninsula and the major powers with interests in the area. This chapter describes the most serious and predictable problems that might arise, given the current situation in North Korea. While some of these challenges are likely to play out over the medium and long term, others would emerge immediately and require a quick response from South Korea and the international community to minimize human suffering and forestall further problems and disorder.

Notes

1. Moo Bong Ryoo, "The ROK Army's Role When North Korea Collapses without a War with the ROK," Fort Leavenworth, School of Advanced Military Studies, U.S. Army Command and General Staff College, February 1, 2001, 41.
2. Ryoo, 42.
3. The active-duty ROK military personnel figure is from the time of Moo Bong Ryoo's writing. See Table 6 for the latest figure.
4. Ryoo, 42.
5. Shin-wha Lee and Joon Sung Park, "Peacekeeping Contribution Profile: South Korea," *Providing for Peacekeeping*, updated June 2014, http://www.providingforpeacekeeping.org/2015/03/30/peacekeeping-contributor-profile-south-korea/ (accessed July 15, 2015).
6. Lee and Park.
7. "North Korea Contingency Planning and U.S.-ROK Cooperation," in *A Project of the Asia Foundation*, Seoul, Center for U.S.–Korea Policy, September 2009, 9.
8. "North Korea Contingency Planning," 10.
9. Nicholas Eberstadt, "Hastening Korean Reunification," *Foreign Affairs* 76, no. 2 (1997): 79.
10. Eberstadt, 83.
11. Michael O'Hanlon, "Dealing with the Collapse of a Nuclear-Armed State: The Cases of North Korea and Pakistan," in *The Princeton Project on National Security Papers*, Princeton, The Woodrow Wilson School of Public and International Affairs, Princeton University, 2009, 1.
12. O'Hanlon, 3.
13. For further details, see David S. Maxwell, "Catastrophic Collapse of North Korea: Implications for the United States Military," in *The DPRK Briefing Book: Policy Area: Scenarios*, San Francisco, The Nautilus Institute, 1996; "North Korea Contingency Planning and U.S.-ROK Cooperation," in *A Project of the Asia Foundation*, Seoul, Center for U.S.–Korea Policy, September 2009; and Paul B. Stares and Joel S. Wit, "Preparing for

Sudden Change in North Korea: The Effectiveness of Concessional Assistance," Washington, DC, U.S. Agency for International Development, 1985.
14. Kathleen T. Rhem, "North Korean Military 'Very Credible Conventional Force'," *American Forces Press Service*, November 18, 2003, http://www.defenselink.mil/news/Nov2003/n11182003_200311181.html.
15. North Korea has threatened to turn South Korea into a "sea of fire" on numerous occasions. For instance, see "North Korea threatens 'sea of fire' if attacked" *BBC News*, January 22, 1999, http://news.bbc.co.uk/2/hi/asia-pacific/260067.stm. "U.S. military bases will become a 'sea of fire' if war breaks out on the Korean peninsula," *World Net Daily*, February 5, 2005, http://www.wnd.com/news/article.asp?ARTICLE_ID=42733.
16. Jonathan Pollack, "North Korea's Nuclear Weapons Program to 2015," in *NBR Special Report No. 13 North Korea and Iran: Nuclear Futures and Regional Responses*, ed. Tim Cook, The National Bureau of Asian Research, May 2007, 13.
17. "Joint Publication 3–05 Doctrine for Joint Special Operations," ed. Joint Staff, U.S. Department of Defense, December 17, 2003, I-2.
18. "Joint Publication 3–05 Doctrine for Joint Special Operations," IV-1.
19. Discussions with John Merrill, U.S. Department of State. It was Merrill who suggested the idea of applying Nunn-Lugar Cooperative Threat Reduction program for North Korea during 2001–2, Washington, DC.
20. The program expired in June 2013 after Putin rejected Obama's proposal to extend the program. See Bresolin, Justin, "Fact Sheet: The Nunn-Lugar Cooperative Threat Reduction Program," The Center for Arms Control and Non-Proliferation," June 2014, http://armscontrolcenter.org/publications/factsheets/fact_sheet_the_cooperative_threat_reduction_program/ (accessed December 20, 2014).
21. "The Nunn-Lugar Cooperative Threat Reduction Program: Lugar celebrates opening of largest Nunn-Lugar WMD destruction project," Office of U.S. Senator Richard G. Lugar, 2009.
22. *Nunn-Lugar Reforms Included in Defense Budget Bill*, Nuclear Threat Initiative, October 16, 2009, http://gsn.nti.org/gsn/nw_20091016_8437.php (accessed December 14, 2009). 2009–2010 111th Congress, "H.R. 2647 National Defense Act for fiscal Year 2010," U.S. Congress, 2010.
23. Buzo, *The Guerilla Dynasty: Politics and Leadership in North Korea*, 28.
24. Interview with L.J. Singleton, North Korea specialist, June 25, 2015.
25. Lankov, *North of the DMX: Essay on Daily Life in North Korea*, 174 and 203.
26. Ryoo, "The ROK Army's Role When North Korea Collapses without a War with the ROK," 42.

27. Norbert Vollertsen, *Michin Goseseo Ssuen Ilgi (Diary of a Mad Place)* (Seoul: Jogwang Chulpahn Insoe Jushik Hoesa, 2001), 33–34.
28. Sarah E. Mendelson and John K. Glenn, eds., *The Power and Limits of NGOs: A Critical Look at Building Democracy in Eastern Europe and Eurasia* (New York: Columbia University Press, 2002), 208.
29. Jeong-ju Na, "3 Million NK Refugees Expected in Crisis: BOK," *The Korea Times*, January 26, 2007, http://times.hankooki.com/1page/200701/kt2007012618090610160.htm.
30. "Bookhan Ital Joomin Jeognchaek (North Korean Defectors Policy)," ROK Ministry of Unification, August 2015, http://www.unikorea.go.kr/content.do?cmsid=1518 (accessed August 5, 2015).
31. "2005 Annual Report," Congressional-Executive Commission on China, October 11, 2006, 114.
32. *L.I.N.K. (Liberty in North Korea)*, DoSomething.org, March 22, 2008, http://www.dosomething.org/project/link-liberty-north-korea (accessed December 2, 2009).
33. "N. Korea in Brutal Crackdown on Defectors," *Chosun Ilbo*, September 1, 2009, http://english.chosun.com/site/data/html_dir/2009/09/01/2009090100232.html.
34. Gale, Alastair, "North Korea Clamps Down on Defections," *The Wall Street Journal*, August 20, 2013, http://www.wsj.com/articles/SB10001424127887324747104579024322751521350.
35. Jack Rendler, "The Last Worst Place on Earth: Human Rights in North Korea," in *Planning for a Peaceful Korea*, ed. Henry D. Sokolski, Carlisle, Strategic Studies Institute, U.S. Army War College, February 2001, 119.
36. McVadon, "China's Goals and Strategies for the Korean Peninsula," 140.
37. McVadon, 141.
38. Jae-Jean Suh, "Bookhan-ui Geubbyeon Sahtae-shi Sahwe Moonhwa Boomoon-ui Dae-eung-chaek," (Responses to Sociocultural Aspects during North Korean Contingency), in *Bookhan-ui Geubbyeon Sahtae-wa Uri-ui Dae-eung (Contingency Plan for North Korea's Crisis)*, Gwan-yong Park, ed, 21st Century National Development Institute, Paju, Korea: Hanwool, 2007, 143.
39. Dewey A. Browder, "State Building in Post-World War II Germany" in Colloquium on Stability Operations and State Building: Continuities and Contingencies, Dewey A. Browder and Greg Kauffman, Strategic Studies Institute, October 2008, 62–3.
40. Peter F. Schaefer, "Post War Nation Building" in Colloquium on Stability Operations and State Building: Continuities and Contingencies, Dewey A. Browder and Greg Kauffman, Strategic Studies Institute, October 2008, 98.
41. Noland, *Avoiding the Apocalypse*, 293.

42. Bernd Grässler, "Germany's Slow Economic Reunification: Some believe it will take another 15 years to reach economic parity," *Deutsche Welle*, September 29, 2005.
43. Goohoon Kwon, "A Unified Korea? Reassessing North Korea Risks (Part I)," in *Global Economic Paper No. 188*, New York, Goldman Sachs, September 21, 2009, 9.
44. Noland, *Avoiding the Apocalypse*, 291.
45. Helmut Schmidt, *Chairman's Report on the High-Level Expert Group Meeting: The Lessons of the German Unification Process for Korea* (Paris: InterAction Council, February 17–18, 1993), 9.
46. Goohoon Kwon, "Experience with Monetary Integration and Lessons for Korean Unification," in *IMF Working Paper*, Washington, DC, International Monetary Fund, May 1997, 8.
47. Byung-ho Chung, "Between Defector and Migrant: Identities and Strategies of North Koreans in South Korea," *Korean Studies* 32 (2008): 10.
48. Chung, 16.
49. Jae-jean Shu, "North Korean Defectors: Their Adaptation and Resettlement," *East Asian Review* 14, no. 3 (Autumn 2002): 81.
50. "Interview: Cho Myung-chul, S. Korea's first N. Korean exile legislator," *New Focus International*, October 4, 2012, http://newfocusintl.com/cho-myung-chul/ and "North Korean defectors emerge from periphery," *The Korea Herald*, April 18, 2012, http://www.koreaherald.com/view.php?ud=20120418000968.
51. Tara O, "The Integration of North Korean Defectors in South Korea: Problems and Prospects," *International Journal of Korean Studies*, XV, No. 2, Fall/Winter 2011, 160.
52. The author delivered a couple of lectures to the defector students participating in the Unification Leadership Academy at the *Hanbando Mirae Jaedan* in 2012 and 2013. For more information, see http://www.korea-future.com/intro/industries/asia.php.
53. Paul F. Chamberlain, "Cultural Dimensions of Korean Reunification: Building a Unified Society," *International Journal on World Peace* XXI, no. 3 (September 3, 2004): 18.
54. Chamberlain, 19.
55. Smith, Patricia J., Ed., *After the Wall: Eastern Germany Since 1989*. (Boulder: Westview Press, 1998), 259.
56. Smith.
57. Bickford, Andrew. "Soldiers, Citizens, and the State: East German Army Officers in Post-Unification Germany," *Comparative Studies in Society and History*, Vol. 51, No. 2, (April 2009), 261.
58. Bickford, 262.
59. Noland, *Avoiding the Apocalypse*, 308.

60. Wolf and Akramov, *North Korean Paradoxes: Circumstances, Costs, and Consequences of Korean Unification*, 39.
61. Shearf, Daniel, "South Korea Committee to Prepare for Reunification with North."
62. Beck, "Contemplating Korean Reunification," http://online.wsj.com/article/SB10001424052748704340304574635180086832934.html.
63. The inflation-adjusted figure is calculated using the calculator from Savings.org, http://www.savings.org, accessed September 22, 2015.
64. Bradley O. Babson, "Designing Public Sector Capital Mobilization Strategies for the DPRK," in *A New International Engagement Framework for North Korea? Contending Perspectives*, ed. Nicholas Eberstadt and Young-sun Lee (Washington, DC: Korea Economic Institute of America, 2004), 244.
65. Tadashi Kimiya, *Economic Assistance to North Korea: A Positive Engagement as the Road to Stability*, 2001, http://www.asahi.com/english/asianet/report/eng_2001_05.html (accessed November 23, 2009).
66. David I. Steinberg, "Foreign Aid and the Development of the Republic of Korea: The Effectiveness of Concessional Assistance," Washington, DC, U.S. Agency for International Development, 1985, 4.
67. Steinberg, 4.
68. Steinberg, 5.
69. "S. Korea reviewing NK move over Kaesong workers' wages," December 9, 2014, *The Korea Herald*, http://www.koreaherald.com/view.php?ud=20141209000796.
70. Andrei Lankov, "Gaesong Industrial Complex Faces Serious Threat," *The Korea Times*, May 15, 2009, http://www.koreatimes.co.kr/www/news/nation/2009/10/120_44994.html.
71. *CIA World Factbook*.
72. CIA.
73. *CIA World Factbook*, North Korea: Natural Resources, updated June 20, 2014, https://www.cia.gov/library/publications/the-world-factbook/geos/kn.html (accessed January 20, 2015).
74. Kwon, "A Unified Korea? Reassessing North Korea Risks (Part I)," 10.
75. Shearf, Daniel, "North Korea's Rare Earths Could Be Game Changer," *Voice of America*, January 17, 2014, http://www.voanews.com/content/north-korea-rare-earths-game-changer/1832018.html (accessed January 24, 2015).
76. Shearf.
77. South Korean reserves are the sum of confirmed and estimated reserves (2007); North Korean data are potential reserves only; bn: billion.
78. Kwon, 1.
79. Eberstadt, "Hastening Korean Reunification," 83.

80. Mohit Joshi, "South Korea looks to reforest North Korea, South-East Asia," *TopNews.in*, August 13, 2009, http://www.topnews.in/south-korea-looks-reforest-north-korea-southeast-asia-2201245.
81. Yon-se Kim, "S. Korea to Help N. Korea Plant More Trees," *Korea Times*, March 5, 2008, http://www.koreatimes.co.kr/www/news/nation/2008/03/116_20185.html.
82. *About the DMZ Forum* (The DMZ Forum for Peace and Nature Conservation, October 5, 2009); available from http://www.dmzforum.org/aboutus/about_dmzforum.php.
83. Robert Willoughby, *North Korea: The Bradt Travel Guide* (Bucks: Bradt Travel Guide, Ltd., 2003), 142.

CHAPTER 6

Summary

Abstract The North Korean regime cannot execute one of the most important functions of a government—feeding its people—which damages its legitimacy. It is unlikely to implement substantive reform and open up its economy, because such actions could invite new ideas that would challenge the regime itself. This unsustainable posture could lead to a collapse. After reviewing various unification scenarios, the author identified indicators and triggers of collapse. A collapse would be a momentous event that could drastically change the geopolitical realities in a region where some of the world's major powers' interests converge. These powers need to cooperate and prepare for such an event, because the challenges would be too great to ignore.

North Korea displays the characteristics of a failed state. Kim Jong-il's and now Kim Jong-un's insistence on *Juche* ideology and their continued emphasis on nuclear weapons development and the military, with the ultimate aim of regime survival rather than providing basic needs to its people, has led to a failed economic system with disastrous and tragic results. A million people died from starvation in the mid-1990s.[1] Tens of thousands, perhaps hundreds of thousands, have left North Korea for China in search of food and a better life.[2] Their hopes are often shattered as they are sold into human trafficking or deported back to North Korea, where they are marked as traitors for crossing the border and face harsh punishment, including death. Yet the government insists on complete loyalty to and sacrifices for the Kim family. North Korea's reliance on Chinese, South Korean, and international aid makes the regime's insistence on *Juche* ideology incongruent with reality. The *Songun* and *Byungjin* direct resources away from basic human needs toward the military and weapons development. Even with acute food and energy shortages, Pyongyang has conducted nuclear and missiles tests, placing higher priority on nuclear weapons and military capability.

Ironically, North Korea commands the world's attention for two reasons: nuclear weapons and hunger. This paradox makes the situation in the peninsula uneasy. North Korea may soon receive global attention due to a contingency. The regime is unlikely to make the most profound changes necessary for stability—implementing substantive reform and opening up the economy—because such actions could invite new ideas that would challenge the regime itself.

1   Unification Scenarios

How would the two Koreas unify? The three scenarios discussed in this study give a glimpse of the range of possibilities. The gradual and peaceful "soft landing" takes a long-term approach to unification. Many in South Korea, hoping to avoid instability and the high cost of unification, prefer this outcome, although this preference is slowly changing.

The "hard-landing" scenario is war, and unification as a by-product of war. Whether begun by a desperate Kim regime or escalation of minor incursion, the initial stage would be devastating. It is assumed that the ROK–U.S. combined military would eventually achieve victory resulting in unification under the South Korean government and system. As victors, South Korea and the USA would have a justified presence in North Korea, but China would be alarmed by the U.S. military presence. To prevent misunderstandings and conflict, there needs to be a mechanism for consultation.

The case that was particularly widely discussed after the German unification was the collapse and absorption scenario. In the early 1990s, the prevailing view was that North Korea too would collapse, and South Korea would absorb North Korea, German style. Although North Korea's endurance is surprising, the possibility of a North Korean regime collapse seems to grow from its unwillingness or inability to implement genuine changes to fix its dysfunctional economy and the outside information challenging the regime's version of truth, endangering the Kim family's legitimacy.

2   Collapse Indicators and Triggers

What, then, might lead North Korea to collapse? Chapter 3 explores six indicators and three triggers. The indicators are the economic system, external assistance, information, leadership power consolidation, the elites, and defectors. The triggers are elite disaffection, famine and migration, and mass opposition.

2.1   Economic System

For North Korea, reform is necessary, but it carries the danger of destabilizing the regime. Reform opens doors to information flow, increasing the possibility of discontent among the populace when they discover the vast gap between reality and what they have been told by their government. Discontent could lead to the downfall of the regime as it loses support. North Korea has instituted measures to introduce markets, but has also taken steps back when the government seemed to lose control. Since regime survival is the top priority, reform takes a back seat, which weakens the system. The balancing act is precarious and the brittle system could crack and the regime could collapse.

2.2   External Assistance for Sustenance

North Korea's weakness, ironically, affects its immediate neighbors' policies. Neither China nor South Korea wants to see North Korea collapse. Because the other states in the region have become more developed and rely on each other for their prosperity, they share a vested interest in the stability of the peninsula. This is especially true of China and South Korea. Regime collapse would bring instability to the peninsula with people streaming across the borders into China and South Korea. To avert this possibility, Beijing has been providing the majority of North Korea's fuel and food needs and encouraging Pyongyang to reform. Many in South Korea, sobered by the cost of German unification, also do not want the North's collapse. Seoul's aid to Pyongyang has drastically been cut recently, but during the Sunshine Policy period, Seoul provided billions of dollars in food, fertilizer, and other assistance, crucial for the Kim regime's survival.

2.3 Information Control

North Koreans live in the dark not only due to lack of energy, but also due to the iron-clad control of information by the Kim regime. There are signs, however, that information is leaking into North Korea. Increasing numbers of people travel to China for food and work. Many of them return with stories of life in China, which seems wealthy compared to that of North Korea, and of South Korea, which is even wealthier. Black and gray markets sell South Korean dramas, which are reportedly popular among North Koreans. The inter-Korean Gaesong Industrial Complex business projects delivered not only hard currency but also outside information to North Koreans.

2.4 Leadership Succession and Power Consolidation

Kim Jong-un acceded to power after Kim Jong-il's death in December 2011. The succession and power consolidation process are watched closely because a power struggle could lead to the loss of control, which could then lead to a collapse. Many believed that Jang Song-taek, Kim Jong-un's uncle, would play a powerful behind-the-scenes role, and it appeared he did, until his purge and execution in December 2013. Purges, promotions, and other personnel changes are still ongoing. While some state that Kim Jong-un is fully in charge others believe there may be other sotto voce powers. The Kim family regime's power status is an important indicator of a potential collapse.

2.5 Elite Disaffection and Factionalism

One succession scenario envisions a power struggle. Is there a split among the elites, the military, the party, and government officials who receive perquisites and pledge loyalty in return? Are they unified, or are there factions? It would be imperative to define and identify the elites, categorize them into different groups, and monitor their actions carefully during and after the succession. Knowledge of the various groups would provide helpful clues about internal struggle and the possibility of a collapse.

2.6 Defectors

The North Korean defection rate has risen dramatically.[3] More than 28,000 North Korean defectors arrived in South Korea by 2015. As many as 300,000 North Koreans live in China, the destination country for most North Koreans due to its relatively porous border.[4] Defectors and refugees normally cross the North Korean–Chinese border and live there for years before departing for South Korea, often through a third country. Their lives do not seem to improve much in China as they fear being caught by the Chinese police and sent back to North Korea, where severe punishment awaits. A high number of women are sold into the sex industry or as brides in the country where the "one child" policy and a social preference for sons have skewed the male to female ratio. Despite these hardships, they continue to leave North Korea at an increasing rate. Defection is a reflection and an indicator of North Korea's broken system.

The indicators show a trend reflecting the deteriorating situation that may lead North Korea to collapse. Certain events, such as succession, another famine, and mass opposition, may tip the scale and trigger a collapse.

3 The Roles of the Regional Powers

The Korean Peninsula is a pivotal junction in Northeast Asia where the interests of the world's major powers—the USA, China, Japan, and Russia—converge. These powers are brought together for geopolitical reasons, and their interests have great influence on Korean affairs. Historically, all four major powers sought influence over the Korean Peninsula. Korea has served as the invasion route from Mongolia to China to Japan, from Japan to China, and from Japan to Russia. Japan's colonization of Korea in 1910 and Korea's tributary relationship with China are important factors in Korea's history. The Korean War of 1950–53 represented not only a contest between South Korea and North Korea, but also one between the USA and the Soviet Union as part of the Cold War.

3.1 National Interests

The USA, China, Japan, and Russia consider the Korean Peninsula important to their strategic interests. South Korea is a strong democratic ally for the USA on the Asian mainland with a market economy tightly woven into the international system of trade and finance, and linked to the USA through a security alliance. A united Korea that is nuclear weapons–free, democratic, and capitalistic would serve the U.S. interest even better.

China prefers a friendly state on its border. Beijing views an unstable North Korea and the likely flood of cross-border migrants as a major concern, and continues to provide food and fuel to North Korea, despite its disapproval of Pyongyang's continued development of nuclear weapons. Meanwhile, it has normalized relations with South Korea and has strong economic trade and investment relations with Seoul.

Japan has unresolved historical and territorial issues with South Korea that prevent the development of stronger ties. Japan's concern over citizens abducted by North Korea is another issue not likely to be resolved soon. Japan would want a unified Korea that is nuclear-free, friendly, and open to Japan.

Russia has lost its influence in Northeast Asia, but would want to restore its lost status in the region and around the globe. Its vast energy reserves and the TSR could become important for developing a unified Korea and linking it to the European market.

3.2   Regional Cooperation

Seventy years after the division, the major powers' strategic considerations, including security, territorial sovereignty, and regional influence, are still important. However, the region has changed considerably, with greater economic interactions that contribute to the prosperity of all the neighboring countries except North Korea. Furthermore, South Korea has changed dramatically. South Korea, backed by its U.S. ally, has become an advanced industrialized democracy with a strong military. Even the Soviet Union and China, traditional sponsors of North Korea, have established diplomatic relations with South Korea. South Korea has also demonstrated soft power through *Hallyu*, the Korea Wave of modern films and music popular throughout Asia.

If North Korea collapses, South Korea has the capability and the will to play a leading role in managing the aftermath and embarking on the developmental and integration process. However, South Korea will need support from neighboring countries and the international community. Developing coordination mechanisms would be crucial to avoid misunderstandings and focus on development efforts. Seoul needs to plan and prepare for the collapse of Pyongyang, as it would greatly impact South Korea's national interests.

3.3 Nuclear Weapons and Regional Relations

Concerns about nuclear weapons led to the Six-Party Talks on the denuclearization of North Korea among the USA, China, Japan, Russia, South Korea, and North Korea. The Six-Party Talks did not denuclearize North Korea and are currently stalled. North Korea's nuclear weapons pose a threat to South Korea, Japan, and the USA as North Korea has short- and long-range delivery systems; however, North Korea already possesses massive conventional weapons that can inflict severe damage to nearby countries. Thus, the main dangers of North Korea's nuclear weapons are proliferation and weapons security.

If North Korea's nuclear weapons fall into the hands of terrorists, it would pose a threat to the vital interests of the USA and other countries. Additionally, Japan may feel the need to develop its own nuclear capability if threatened by a nuclear-armed North Korea. China and South Korea would then feel threatened by Japan, and China might increase its nuclear arsenal and devote even greater resources to military capability development while South Korea might want to develop its own nuclear weapons capability. Immediately following a collapse, the priority should be to locate and safeguard nuclear weapons, materials, facilities, and personnel to prevent proliferation. The USA, China, and South Korea could have prior consultation to minimize misunderstanding, especially if U.S. forces are involved, and to increase nuclear weapons safeguards, particularly against the possibility of weapons being smuggled across the border with China.

4 Preparing for and Responding to Collapse

Chapter 5 expands the collapse scenarios presented in Chap. 2. A collapse would unleash numerous challenges. As the regime loses control, there would be chaos and anarchy. Food, fuel, and other basic goods and services, already deficient, would become scarcer and could trigger mass migration into China or South Korea. Swept by the euphoria of unification, it is easy to imagine a throng of North Koreans heading for South Korea, directly or indirectly. In the long term, more would likely want to move to the wealthier South as the gravitational pull of Seoul would be irresistible. Southward mass migration in search of a better life and higher wages could occur even after order is restored in the North. South Koreans are worried about the potential economic and social problems of such a mass-scale migration.

4.1 Control of Nuclear Weapons

Accountability for nuclear weapons, materials, facilities, and specialists is the weakest when authority is confused or lacking. South Korea, the USA with ROK support, or a combined ROK–U.S. team should quickly account for and control these items and personnel. Consulting China beforehand is important to reduce the chance that they might misinterpret the role of the U.S. military and to increase the effectiveness of securing nuclear weapons. After positive control, the authorities could work to reduce, destroy, or safeguard nuclear weapons and personnel through mechanisms like the Nunn-Lugar Cooperative Threat Reduction Program.[5] The U.S. Congress has permitted the program to operate outside the former Soviet states through the Nunn-Lugar Expansion Act, providing a useful tool for dealing with the situation that might emerge in Korea.

4.2 Disorder in the Immediate Aftermath of Collapse

Disorder would describe the scene immediately following collapse. In the case where North Korea's strict and hierarchical system of control might break down, looting and increased crimes would be concerns. The lawlessness and fear could also trigger a mass migration from North Korea. It is assumed that the South Korean government would play a significant role, but international institutions and NGOs could also provide support. Authority and order must be established early and maintained.

4.3 Providing for Basic Needs

Along with quick restoration of order, basic goods and services must be also provided for. Lack of food and services could encourage mass migration and cause social problems. Again, the South Korean government, international community, and NGOs could provide these provisions initially, with the goal of establishing local capacity in the long term.

4.4 Migration

As stated above, the breakdown of order and the inability to provide for basic needs could trigger mass migration. In the initial stages of collapse, China could work with international organizations and NGOs to manage the refugee crisis, and South Korea, working with NGOs and families, could focus on safe and managed border crossing.

In the medium to long term, creating opportunities and incentives in northern Korea will help address the migration problem. To encourage North Koreans to return home after migrating or to stay in place, longer-term solutions are needed. Viable employment along with home and landownership could encourage people to stay. It would take time to generate employment, but the conditions conducive in absorbing development aid and foreign investment must be created.

4.5 Elites

The North Korean regime has conducted systematic violations of human rights and the elites sustained such a system. Accountability is most likely demanded and will be important as part of national healing. However, replicating "de-Bathification" is not advisable, because of the sheer number, the need for their bureaucratic skills, and not creating a disenfranchised group of people, who can actively oppose the efforts to create stability. An alternate method to integrate them would help establish stability that is quicker and more durable.

4.6 Infrastructure

North Korea would need a major infrastructure development in communications, transportation, energy, and other areas as a precondition for attracting additional investments. Additionally, these massive projects would create jobs that could absorb those projected to join the ranks of the unemployed after military demobilization. Employment opportunities on infrastructure projects would also help mitigate migration.

4.7 Unemployment

Government policies on privatization and currency conversion could help reduce unemployment, but careful analysis and planning are required. In considering policy options, it is important to highlight labor competitiveness as a factor attracting direct investments. Projects that could help develop North Korea while creating employment include infrastructure, reforestation, and DMZ development.

4.8 Social Integration

Economic integration would be daunting, but social integration would be just as challenging, if not more so. North and South Koreans share a common ethnic heritage, language, and culture, raising expectations that northerners will adjust quickly to the South Korean way of life. The experience of defectors shows that this expectation is simplistic and unrealistic. Many of the 28,000 North Korean defectors resettled in South Korea have difficulty adjusting, their dreams of a prosperous and fulfilling life shattered by the cultural, linguistic, political, and economic differences that have emerged in the seven decades of division. Studying some of the success stories could help develop policies and ways ahead, some of which could begin implementation prior to the collapse to develop a condition more conducive for social integration.

4.9 Military Integration

Calls for peace dividend after unification may lead to hasty downsizing, but such measures could have negative economic and social impact. More than a million becoming unemployed overnight would be a disaster. The military structure also provides a certain level of order and would be conducive for educating and training military personnel to adjust to new lives in changed surroundings. Lessons could be learned from studying the German military integration after its unification, the U.S. military's racial integration, and the U.S. military's transition assistance program. Some of the lessons may be helpful in gradually reducing the force and integrating the two militaries.

4.10 Economic Development

The economic cost of unification is estimated at hundreds of billions of dollars. Shouldering the cost would be an immediate problem for South Korea. It is important to broaden the funding sources, as South Korean taxes and investments would not be enough. IFIs, with strong support from the USA, could provide significant funding. Japan could also play a significant role. Financial resources could be directed to developing infrastructure and creating conditions to encourage further direct investment.

In the long term, the synergy between South and North Korea could propel a unified Korea into one of the top economies in the world.

South Korea has the capital and technology while North Korea has a younger, low-cost labor force and a significantly greater amount of natural resources. The combination would enhance productivity and increase national wealth.

4.11 Other Efforts

North Korea chronically suffers from floods, which are exacerbated by cutting trees and leaving the mountains bare. Subsequent flooding affects the harvest, reducing the food supply. A major reforestation project would also help mitigate flood damages, while creating employment. Reforestation has proven successful in South Korea in addressing such problems during its developmental period. Another opportunity is to develop the DMZ, taking advantage of flora and fauna unspoiled for over 60 years. Employment from a potential echo-tourism would also help the development efforts.

5   Conclusion

The challenges of North Korea's collapse and the accompanying unification with South Korea will be colossal. It would require commitment, planning, and cooperation among the affected parties, particularly South Korea, China, and the USA, as well as Japan and Russia, with South Korea in the lead. The regional powers should prepare for North Korea's collapse by developing plans to address the challenges. A focus on short-term interests during the unification process could destabilize the region. Although the region is marked by disputes and rivalries, the regional powers could cooperate to promote successful unification, an outcome that will contribute to regional security and prosperity.

Notes

1. Haggard and Noland, *Famine in North Korea: Markets, Aid, and Reform*, 1.
2. The number ranges from 20,000 (Chinese government estimate) to 400,000 (NGO estimate). See Yoonok Chang, Stephan Haggard, and Marcus Noland, "Migration Experiences of North Korean Refugees: Survey Evidence from China," in *Working Paper Series WP 08-4*, Washington, DC, Peterson Institute for International Economics, March 2008, 1.

3. "Tongil Baekseo 2005 (Unification White Paper 2005)," 171.
4. Ko, Chung, and Oh, "North Korean Defectors: Their Life and Well-Being after Defection," 68.
5. *The Nunn-Lugar Scorecard: Destroying Weapons and Materials of Mass Destruction through Cooperation.*

Appendix 1

Unification and South Korea

This study assumes that South Korea would play a major role in the event that North Korea collapses. South Korean government and nongovernmental organizations (NGOs) would likely seek to create institutions and systems similar to those of South Korea. Accordingly, this study assumes that a unified Korea would be a market economy and a democracy.

Unification and Reunification

The terms "unification" and "reunification" are used interchangeably in this study. The Korean term "tong-il" means unification. Although "re" in reunification exists in Korean, Koreans do not use it. Disuse of "re" does not indicate that Koreans do not mean re-merger. Korea had been a unified country for centuries until the division of the last six decades. Therefore, the term "reunification" is also appropriate.

Korean Names and Spelling

Korean names and spellings follow the latest South Korean government convention in this study. For instance, in this research, the former South Korean president's name is spelled "Park Chung-hee." Previously "Park Chung Hee" was also used. The use of hyphenation and lower case after the hyphenation in "Chung-hee" is the new convention. If the latter style

(Chung Hee) is used, then the person published documents using that style, and that style is usually found in the endnotes or bibliography. Kim is the last name and is placed first, consistent with Korean practice. For instance, Kim Jong-il's last name is Kim and is placed before Jong-il. Kim Jong-un is also spelled Kim Jong-eun; the latter is based on the South Korean government's new convention. If the name appears to be Korean, but the last name is placed at the end, then it implies the person is a Korean-American using the "American" way of displaying surname after the first name, or has published using the American convention of placing last name at the end.

Additionally, some place-name spellings are different. The old method uses Kaesong, Keumgang, Inchon, and Pusan, for example. The new way uses Gaesong, Geumgang, Incheon, and Busan, respectively.

In this study, the author uses Songun (pronounced Seon-goon) for military first policy, rather than using the latest protocol on corresponding vowels and consonants in Korean to English, because "Songun" has been used more widely. This is not to be confused with *Songbun* (*Seongboon* using the Korean government system), which is similar in meaning as the caste system.

Various Ways to Express "Korea"

In general, South Korea and North Korea are used. Sometimes, their official names, Republic of Korea (ROK) and Democratic People's Republic of Korea (DPRK), respectively, are employed. Occasionally, depending on the context, "Korea" is used to refer to the formerly unified Korea prior to the division, or as an identity for both Koreas as a whole.

Bibliography

111th Congress, 2009–2010. H.R. 2647 National Defense Act for fiscal year 2010. U.S. Congress, 2010.
2005 Annual Report. Congressional-Executive Commission on China, 11 October 2006.
A Dozen Senior N. Korean officials defect. *The Chosun Ilbo*, 2 July 2015, http://english.chosun.com/site/data/html_dir/2015/07/02/2015070201795.html. Accessed 6 July 2015.
About the DMZ Forum. The DMZ Forum for peace and nature conservation, http://www.dmzforum.org/aboutus/about_dmzforum.php. Accessed 5 Oct 2009.
Ahn, Yonson. 2008. The contested heritage of Koguryo/Gaogouli and China-Korea conflict. *Japan Focus*, January 11, http://www.japanfocus.org/-Yonson-Ahn/2631. Accessed 29 Sept 2009.
Alternative NGO report on the Committee on Economic, Social and Cultural Rights of the second periodic report of democratic People's Republic of Korea. Seoul: The Good Friends, November 2003.
Annual report to Congress: Military power of the Peopl's Republic of China 2006. ed. by Office of the Secretary of Defense, Washington, DC, U.S. Department of Defense, 2006.
Arrouas, Michelle. Japanese fighter jet scrambles against China have hit a record high. *Time*, 10 April 2014, http://time.com/56997/japan-china-fighter-jet/
Atkinson, Rick. Germany's integration lab; Soldiers of East, West successfully join forces. *The Washington Post (Pre-1997 full text)*, 12 May 1994, a01. http://search.proquest.com/docview/307758188?accountid=167280
Ayres, Jr. Raymond P. 2007. Key note speech: Transfer of wartime command—Some personal thoughts. In *The quest for a unified Korea: Strategies for the*

cultural and inter-agency process, ed. Jr. Bechtol, Bruce E. Quantico: Marine Corps University.

Babson, Bradley O. 2004. Designing public sector capital mobilization strategies for the DPRK. In *A new international engagement framework for North Korea? Contending perspectives*, ed. Nicholas Eberstadt and Young-sun Lee. Washington, DC: Korea Economic Institute of America.

Baek, Seung-joo. Han-mi Jeonryak Dongmaeng-gwa Hanmi Bangwi Hyubryuk Ganghwa (Strengthening the Repubic of Korea-U.S. strategic alliance and defense cooperation). Paper presented at the Peace Foundation 22nd Forum: Hanmiil Ahnbo Hyubryeok Ganghwa-wa Dognbuga Gukje Gwngwe (Korea, U.S. and Japan Security Cooperation and International Relations in Northeast Asia), Seoul, 24 June 2008.

Baek, Seung-joo. Interview, Korea Institute for Defense Analysis (KIDA), Seoul, July 13, 2006.

Baiyi, Wu. 2006. China on the Korean Peninsula: Interests and roles. *The Korean Journal of Security Affairs* 11(1): 61–81.

Bajona, Claustre, and Tianshu Chu. 2004. *China's WTO accession and its effect on state-owned enterprises*, East–West Center working papers. Hawaii: East–West Center.

Bajoria, Jayshree, and Carin Zissis. 2009. The six-party talks on North Korea's nuclear program. New York: Council on Foreign Relations.

Bechtol Jr., Bruce E. 2007. *Red rogue: The persistent challenge of North Korea*. Washington, DC: Potomac Books.

Bechtol, Jr. Bruce E. 2008. Understanding the North Korea threat to the security of the Korean Peninsula and East Asia: Declined or evolved? In *Korea at the crossroads: Challenges and prospects; IKS international conference*. Seoul: The Institute of Korean Studies.

Beck, Peter. Contemplating Korean reunification. *The Wall Street Journal*, 4 January 2010.

Beck, Peter. Interview, International Crisis Group, Seoul, 23 June 2006.

Becker, Jasper. 2005. *Rogue regime: Kim Jong Il and the looming threat of North Korea*. Oxford: Oxford University Press.

Bickford, Andrew. 2009. Soldiers, citizens, and the state: East German Army officers in post-unification Germany. *Comparative Studies in Society and History* 51(2): 260–287.

Blumenthal, Dan, and Aaron Friedberg. 2009. An American strategy for Asia. In *A report of the Asia strategy working group*. Washington, DC: American Enterprise Institute.

Bookhan Ital Joomin Jeognchaek (North Korean defectors policy). *ROK Ministry of Unification*, October 2014, http://www.unikorea.go.kr/content.do?cmsid=1518. Accessed 21 Dec 2014.

Bookhan Sookchung-ui Yeogsa (The history of North Korean purges). *Daehanmingook Geun Hyeondaisa Series* (Korea's Recent Events), 29

December 2013, http://koreastory.kr/bbs/board.php?bo_table=issue&wr_id=56&page=1. Accessed 6 July 2015.

Bosworth, Stephen. 2009. *Briefing on recent travel to North Korea*. Washington, DC: U.S. Department of State.

Bradner, Stephen. Interview, Special Adviser, U.S. Forces Korea, Seoul, 31 July 2006.

Bradner, Stephen. North Korea's strategy. In *Competitive strategies*. Arlington: NPEC/Institute for National Security Studies, Army War College, 12–14 June 2000, updated 1 August 2000.

Breen, Michael. Interview, President, Insight Communications Consultants and author of *Kim Jong Il: North Korea's dear leader*, Seoul, 3 July 2006.

Bresolin, Justin. Fact sheet: The Nunn-Lugar Cooperative Threat Reduction Program. The Center for Arms Control and Non-Proliferation, June 2014, http://armscontrolcenter.org/publications/factsheets/fact_sheet_the_cooperative_threat_reduction_program/. Accessed 20 Dec 2014.

Brookes, Peter. Interview, Senior Fellow, National Security Affairs and Chung Ju-yung Fellow for Policy Studies, Asian Studies Center, Heritage Foundation, Washington, DC, 26 September 2006.

Browder, Dewey A., et al. 2008. State building in post-World War II Germany. In *Colloquium on stability operations and state building: Continuities and contingencies*, ed. Dewey A. Browder and Greg Kauffman. Carlisle: Strategic Studies Institute.

Burghart, Sabine, and Rudiger Frank. 2008. Inter-Korean cooperation 2000–2008: Commercial and non-commercial transactions and human exchanges. In *Vienna working papers on East Asian economy and society*, vol. 1, no. 1, ed. Rudiger Frank. Vienna: University of Vienna.

Burzinsky, John. Interview, United Nations Military Armistice Command, Seoul, 31 July 2006.

Buzo, Adrian. 1999. *The guerilla dynasty: Politics and leadership in North Korea*. New York: I.B. Tauris & Company Limited.

Cha, Victor. Meeting, Director for Asia, National Security Council, Washington, DC, 25 September 2006.

Cha, Victor. We have no plan. *Chosun Ilbo*, 9 June 2008.

Chamberlain, Paul F. 2004. Cultural dimensions of Korean reunification: Building a unified society. *International Journal on World Peace* XXI(3): 3–42.

Chang, Jae-soon, and Joint Press Corps. Park calls Korean unification 'jackpot' for neighbors too. *Yonhap News*, 22 January 2014, http://english.yonhapnews.co.kr/northkorea/2014/01/22/96/0401000000AEN20140122009200315F.html

Chang, Yoonok, Stephan Haggard, and Marcus Noland. 2008. *Migration experiences of North Korean refugees: Survey evidence from China*, Working paper series WP 08-4. Washington, DC: Peterson Institute for International Economics.

China-ROK joint statement. Beijing: People's Republic of China Ministry of Foreign Affairs, 28 May 2008.

China hints at substantial economic aid to N. Korea. *Chosun Ilbo*, 30 September 2009.

Chinese president's speech celebrating first spacewalk published. *Sina English*, 8 November 2008.

Choe, Sang-hun. North Korea destroys tower at nuclear site. *The New York Times*, 28 June 2008.

Choi, Brent. Interview, Journalist/North Korea specialist, Joong-Ang Ilbo, Seoul, 20 July 2006.

Choi, Song-Min. Buk Musanseo Boahnwon-Jangsakkeun Jipdan Nantoogeuk... Sasangja Sushipmyeong (Security personnel-merchants groups scuffle in Musan, North Korea), *DailyNK*, 29 June 2015, http://www.dailynk.com/korean/read.php?cataId=nk04500&num=106436. Accessed 2 July 2015.

Chu, Henry. China snarls North Korean reform. *Los Angeles Times*, 5 October 2002.

Chun, Susan. Radio gives hope to North and South Koreans. *CNN*, 27 February 2008.

Chung, Byung-ho. 2008. Between defector and migrant: Identities and strategies of North Koreans in South Korea. *Korean Studies* 32: 1–27.

Chung, Chong-wook. Meeting, Visiting Professor, Graduate School of International Studies, Seoul National University and former National Security Adviser to the Republic of Korea's former President Kim young-sam, 7 August 2006.

Chung, Kyung-yung. Interview, Senior Researcher, Research Institute on National Security Affairs (RINSA), Korea National Defense University, Seoul, 27 June 2006.

CIA World Factbook. Central Intelligence Agency, 2014.

Cloud, David S. Defense Secretary Ashton Carter warns Beijing on South China Sea Island-building. *Los Angeles Times*, 29 May 2015, http://www.latimes.com/nation/la-na-ashton-carter-china-20150529-story.html. Accessed 9 July 2015.

Collins, Robert. Interview, Strategy and policy, Combined Forces Command, Seoul, 26 July 2006.

Cordova, Matthew. 2009. A whole of government approach to stability. In *Dipnote*. Washington, DC: U.S. Department of State.

Country profile: North Korea. Washington, DC: Library of Congress, July 2007.

Craft, Lucy. TV dramas from South saturates black market in North Korea, bringing hope, and risk. *CBS News*, 10 December 2013, http://www.cbsnews.com/news/north-koreas-dangerous-addiction-to-daytime-tv/

Cumings, Bruce. 1997. *Korea's place in the sun: A modern history*. New York: W. W. Norton & Company.

Defense of Japan 2014, Japan Ministry of Defense, 2014.
Dokdo and East Sea. 2009. Republic of Korea Culture and Information Service, http://korea.net/. Accessed 4 Oct 2009.
Dujarric, Robert. Meeting, Visiting Fellow, Japan Institute of International Affairs and Hitachi Fellow, Council on Foreign Relations, Tokyo, 9 August 2006.
Dujarric, Robert (ed.). 1998. *Korea: Security pivot in Northeast Asia*. Indianapolis: Hudson Institute.
Dujarric, Robert. 2000. *Korean unification and after: The challenge for U.S. strategy*. Indianapolis: Hudson Institute.
East Asia maps, U.S. Central Intelligence Agency, Washington, DC, 2011, courtesy of the University of Texas Libraries, The University of Texas at Austin, http://www.lib.utexas.edu/maps/middle_east_and_asia/asia_east_pol_2011.jpg. Accessed 6 Oct 2015.
Eberstadt, Nicholas. 1997. Hastening Korean reunification. *Foreign Affairs* 76(2): 77–92.
'Fake photo' revives Kim rumours. 2008. *BBC News*, http://news.bbc.co.uk/2/hi/asia-pacific/7715458.stm. Accessed 23 Sept 2009.
Ferguson, Joseph P. 2003. Russia's role on the Korean Peninsula and great power relations in Northeast Asia: Ramifications for the U.S.-ROK alliance. *NBR Analysis*.
Finnegan, Michael J. Interview, Department of Defense, Washington, DC, 21 September 2006.
Finnegan, Michael J. 2008. PacNet #48 – What now? The case for U.S.-ROK-PRC coordination on North Korea. In *PacNet Newsletter*. Honolulu: Center for Strategic and International Studies Pacific Forum.
Flake, L. Gordon. Interview, Executive Director, Mansfield Foundation, Washington, DC, 19 September 2006.
Gaesong Gongdan Saengsanaek Mit Bukhan Geunroja Hyeonghwang (Gaesong industrial complex production and North Korean workers's current status), Ministry of Unification, data as of September 2014, http://www.unikorea.go.kr/content.do?cmsid=1515. Accessed 5 Nov 2014.
Gale, Alastair. North Korea clamps down on defections. *The Wall Street Journal*, 20 August 2013, http://www.wsj.com/articles/SB10001424127887324747104579024322751521350
Gause, Ken E. 2012. *Coercion, control, surveillance and punishment: An examination of the North Korean police state*. Washington, DC: Committee for Human Rights in North Korea.
GDP per capita (Current US$). *The World Bank*, http://data.worldbank.org/indicator/NY.GDP.PCAP.CD. Accessed 4 Dec 2014.
Global firepower, http://www.globalfirepower.com. Accessed 14 Nov 2014.
Governments of South Korea and North Korea. 2000. June 15 South–North Joint Declaration.

Gransbach, Stephen. Interview, Deputy Chief, Strategy and policy, U.S. Forces Korea, Seoul, 26 July 2006.

Grässler, Bernd. Germany's slow economic reunification: Some believe it will take another 15 years to reach economic parity. *Deutsche Welle*, 29 September 2005.

Green, Michael J. 2003. *Japan's reluctant realism: Foreign policy challenges in an era of uncertain power, a Council on Foreign Relations book*. New York: Palgrave.

Gregg, Donald P. Interview, former U.S. ambassador to the Republic of Korea, New York, 30 May 2006.

Gregg, Donald P. Park Chung Hee: Despite a dictatorial streak, South Korea's long-serving president converted an economic basket case into an industrial powerhouse. *Time* 154, no. 7/8, 23–30 August 1999.

Gross domestic product estimates for North Korea in 2013, Bank of Korea, 28 June 2014, 5, http://www.bok.or.kr/autonomy.search?home=eng

H.R. 5443 (110th): United States-Republic of Korea Defense Cooperation Improvement Act of 2008, govtrack.us, February 2008, https://www.govtrack.us/congress/bills/110/hr5443 and Library of Congress, October 2, 2008, https://www.congress.gov/bill/110th-congress/house-bill/5443/text

Haggard, Stephan, and Marcus Noland. 2007a. *Famine in North Korea: Markets, aid, and reform*. New York: Columbia University Press.

Haggard, Stephan, and Marcus Noland. 2007b. *North Korea's external economic relations*, Working paper series. Washington, DC: Peterson Institute for International Economics.

Halloran, Richard. North Korea conundrum. *Washington Times*, 15 June 2008.

Han, Sung-joo. Meeting, former Republic of Korea Minister of Foreign Affairs and Trade and former ambassador to the U.S., 26 September 2006.

Han, Yong-sup. Interview, Director Research Institute on National Security Affairs (RINSA), Korea National Defense University, Seoul, 27 June 2006.

Harden, Blaine. North Korea's Kim Jong Il chooses youngest son as heir. *The Washington Post*, 3 June 2009.

Harlan, Chico. New Japanese defense plan emphasizes China threat. *The Washington Post*, 13 December 2010, http://www.washingtonpost.com/wp-dyn/content/article/2010/12/12/AR2010121203857.html. Accessed 1 June 2011.

Harrison, Selig S. 2002. *Korean endgame: A strategy for reunification and U.S. disengagement*. Princeton: Century Foundation, Princeton University Press.

Herbst, John. Prepared statement by Ambassador John Herbst, Coordinator for Reconstruction and Stabilization, U.S. Department of State, before the Subcommittee on Oversight and Investigations and Terrorism & Unconventional Threats and Capabilities. House Committee on Armed Services, 26 February 2008.

Herman, Steve. North Korea cuts key military hotline with South. *Voice of America*, 27 March 2013, http://www.voanews.com/content/north-korea-severs-military-hotline-with-south/1629434.html. Accessed 28 Oct 2014.

Hill, Christopher R. 2007. *Update on the six party talks*. Washington, DC: The Brookings Institution.

Hobbes, Thomas. 1988. *The Leviathan*. Buffalo: Prometheus Books.

Humphrey, Peter. 2008/2009. Korean reunification: How it will happen. *American Intelligence Journal* 26(2): 68–74.

Hunger and human rights: The politics of famine. Washington, DC: U.S. Committee for Human Rights in North Korea, 2 November 2007.

Hunter, Helen-Louise. 1999. *Kim Il-song's North Korea*. Westport: Praeger.

Hwang, Jaeho. 2014. The ROK's China policy under Park Geun-hye: A new model of ROK-PRC relations. *International Journal of Korean Unification Studies* 23(1): 104.

Hwang, Jang Yup. North Korea's Southern policy and Inter-Korean relations. *Testimonies of North Korean Defectors*, fas.org, January 1999.

Hwang, Jang Yup. Preparations for war in North Korea. *Testimonies of North Korean Defectors*, fas.org, January 1999.

Hyundai Heavy, South Korean shipyards plan debt sales. *Infomarine*, 13 March 2009.

Import/export by country. *Korea Customs Service*, 2015, http://www.customs.go.kr/kcshome/trade/TradeCountryList.do?layoutMenuNo=21031. Accessed 2 Feb 2016.

Inoguchi, Takashima (ed.). 2002. *Japan's Asian policy: Revival and response*. Tokyo: Palgrave Macmillan.

Inter-Korean investment lowest since 2000. In *NK Brief*. Seoul: The Institute for Far Eastern Studies, 9 December 2009.

Interview: Cho Myung-chul, S. Korea's first N. Korean exile legislator. *New Focus International*, 4 October 2012, http://newfocusintl.com/cho-myung-chul/

Is Korea prepared for superpower China? *Chosun Ilbo*, 3 October 2009.

Jang, Song-hyon. Interview, President, Royal Asiatic Society, Seoul, 19 July 2006.

Jang, Hwan-bin, and Sung-woo Kwon. Interview, Hyundai-Asan, Seoul, 2006.

Jiyoon, Kim et al. 2014. *Asan report: South Korean attitudes on China*, 13–14. Seoul, Korea: The Asan Institute for Policy Studies.

Joint Communiqué: The 40th U.S.-ROK Consultative Meeting. United States-Republic of Korea, 17 October 2008.

Joint Declaration in commemoration of the 60th anniversary of the alliance between the Republic of Korea and the United States of America. *The White House*, 7 May 2013, http://www.whitehouse.gov/the-press-office/2013/05/07/joint-declaration-commemoration-60th-anniversary-alliance-between-republ

Joint Publication 3–05 Doctrine for Joint Special Operations, ed. Joint Staff, U.S. Department of Defense, 17 December 2003.

Jooyo Gookbyeol Soochool Ib-ag (Import export by priority trading partners). *Korean Statistical Information Service,* 15 December 2014, http://kosis.kr/bukhan/statisticsList/statisticsList_01List.jsp#SubCont

Joshi, Mohit. South Korea looks to reforest North Korea, South-East Asia. *TopNews.in,* 13 August 2009.

Jun, Bong-geun. Interview, Institute of Foreign Affairs and National Security (IFANS), Seoul, 24 July 2006.

Jun, Bong-geun. 2008. *Scenarios of North Korea's power shift: After Kim Jong-il's 'Reported Illness',* Policy brief, no. 2008-7. Seoul: Institute of Foreign Affairs and National Security.

Jung, Sung-ki. S. Korea, US chart contingency plans on N. Korea. *Korea Times,* 22 April 2009.

Kang, Juan, and Qiang Guo. Allowing collapse of North Korea unacceptable: experts. *China Daily,* 14 December 2009.

Kaplan, Robert D. When North Korea falls. *The Atlantic,* October 2006, http://www.theatlantic.com/magazine/archive/2006/10/when-north-korea-falls/305228/

Kartman, Charles. Interview, former Executive Director, Korean Peninsula Energy Development Organization (KEDO) and former special envoy for the Korean peace talks, New York, 30 April 2007.

Kawashima, Yutaka. 2003. *Japanese foreign policy at the crossroads: Challenges and options for the twenty-first century.* Washington, DC: Brookings Institution Press.

Keefe, Mike. Interview, Policy Analyst, Strategy and policy, U.S.-Republic of Korea Combined Forces Command, Seoul, 26 July 2006.

Kelly, James. 2004. *Opening remarks before the Senate Foreign Relations Committee on the six-party talks.* Washington, DC: US State Department.

Kemp, Peter. Interview, Deputy Secretary, UN Command Armistice Commission, Seoul, 31 July 2006.

Kim, Chang-su. Interview, Director, U.S. Studies, Korea Institute for Defense Analysis (KIDA), 13 July 2006.

Kim, Chong-hui. Interview, former special adviser to the Republic of Korea's former President Rho Tae-woo, Seoul, 28 June 2006.

Kim, Christine. Korean unification may cost South 7% of GDP: ministry. *Reuters,* 1 January 2013, http://www.reuters.com/article/2013/01/01/us-korea-north-unification-idUSBRE90004F20130101. Accessed 1 Nov 2014.

Kim, Hee-sang. Meeting, former National Security Adviser to the Republic of Korea's former President Rho Moo-hyun, 7 August 2006.

Kim, Heung-Kyu. China's position on Korean unification and ROK-PRC relations. *Korea Research Institute for Strategy,* no date (posted on 1 January

2014), http://www.brookings.edu/~/media/events/2014/1/21-korean-peninsula-unification/kim-heung-kyu-paper.pdf. Accessed 13 July 2015.

Kim, Hyun-uk. Meeting, President, The Peace Forum for Foreign Policy and National Security and former Chairman, Committee on Unification, Foreign Affairs and Trade, National Assembly, 6 July 2006.

Kim, Il Sung. 1996. Chosun Minju ju-ui Inmin Gonghwaguk Jeongbu-ui Dangmyun Gwaeob-e Daehayeo (Regarding the tasks facing the government of Democratic People's Republic of Korea); A speech at the Supreme People's Council on 23 October 1962. In *Ryunbangje Joguk Tongil Bangahn-e (Confederation as an approach to the unification of the motherland)*. Pyongyang: Chosun Rodongdang Chulpahnsah (North Korean Workers' Party Publisher).

Kim, InSung, and Karin Lee. 2009. *Mt. Kumgang and inter-Korean relations.* Washington, DC: National Committee on North Korea.

Kim, Jae-bum. Interview, Distinguished Professor of Diplomacy, Yonsei University and former Ambassador, Republic of Korea Ministry of Foreign Affairs and Trade, Seoul, 4 July 2006.

Kim, Jong-il. 1992. *On the fundamentals of revolutionary party building: A treatise written on the occasion of the 47th anniversary of the foundation of the Workers' Party of Korea, October 10, 1992.* Pyongyang: Foreign Language Publishing House.

Kim, Jong-il. 1993. *Let us prepare the young people thoroughly as reliable successors to the revolutionary cause of Juche.* Pyongyang: Foreign Language Publishing House.

Kim, Jong-rho. Interview, Director, International Cooperation Team, Ministry of Unification, Republic of Korea, Seoul, 12 July 2006.

Kim, Nam-ho. 2001. *Mahn-nahm.* Pyongyang: Pyongyang Publications.

Kim, Sam. N. Korea test-fires missiles, draws line ahead of talks: Analysts. *Yonhap News Agency*, 12 October 2009.

Kim, Samuel S. 2002. China, Japan, and Russia in inter-Korean relations. In *Korea briefing 2000–2001: First steps toward reconciliation and reunification*, ed. Kongdan Oh and Ralph C. Hassig, 109–148. New York: Asia Society, M.E Sharpe.

Kim, So Yeol. Byungjin lives a Kim seeks guns and butter. *DailyNK*, 1 April 2013, http://www.dailynk.com/english/read.php?cataId=nk01700&num=10453

Kim, Yon-se. S. Korea to help N. Korea plant more trees. *Korea Times*, 5 March 2008.

Kim, Yun-chul, and Soon-sung Park (eds.). 2002. *Bukhan Gyungje Gaehyuk Yungu (The study of North Korean economic reform)*. Seoul: Humanista.

Kirk, Donald. Kim Jong Un: North Korea's next leader? *The Christian Science Monitor*, 2 June 2009.

Kirk, Donald. US redeployments to Iraq rattle South Korean alliance. *The Christian Science Monitor*, 20 May 2004.

Klingner, Bruce. 2008. *Supporting our South Korean ally and enhancing defense cooperation*, Asia and the Pacific issues. Washington, DC: The Heritage Foundation.

Klingner, Bruce. 2009. It's not right time to discuss OPCON transfer. In *Commentary*. Washington, DC: The Heritage Foundation.

Ko, Sung-ho, Ki-seon Chung, and Yoo-seok Oh. 2004. North Korean defectors: Their life and well-being after defection. *Asian Perspective* 28(2): 65–99.

Korea-U.S. Free Trade Agreement, ed. Office of the United States Trade Representative, Executive Office of the President, 29 July 2009.

Korea Institute for International Economic Policy. 2003/04. *2003/04 Bukhan Gyungje Baeksuh (2003/04 White paper on North Korean economy)*. Seoul: KIEP.

Kretchum, Nat and Jane Kim. A quite opening: North Koreans in a changing media environment. *Intermedia*, May 2012, p. 8.

Kwon, Goohoon. 1997. *Experience with monetary integration and lessons for Korean unification*, IMF working paper. Washington, DC: International Monetary Fund.

Kwon, Goohoon. 2009. *A unified Korea? Reassessing North Korea risks (Part I)*, Global economic paper, no. 188. New York: Goldman Sachs.

L.I.N.K. (Liberty in North Korea). 2008. DoSomething.org, http://www.dosomething.org/project/link-liberty-north-korea. Accessed 2 Dec 2009.

Lankov, Andrei. Changes in view of outside world by North Koreans. *Yonhap News*, 5 November 2009.

Lankov, Andrei. Gaesong industrial complex faces serious threat. *The Korea Times*, 15 May 2009.

Lankov, Andrei. Interview, North Korea specialist and professor, Seoul, 20 June 2006.

Lankov, Andrei. 2007. *North of the DMZ: Essay on daily life in North Korea*. Jefferson: McFarland and Company.

Lee, Chang-hyung. Interview, Research Fellow, Korea Institute for Defense Analysis (KIDA), Seoul, 13 July 2006.

Lee, Chang-Kyun, Jinhee Bonny, and Young Yoon Choi. 2007. *North Korea cracks down on Korean wave of illicit TV*. Washington, DC: Radio Free Asia.

Lee, Hyun-chool. National Assembly Library, Republic of Korea, 19 July 2006.

Lee, Seung J. Interview, Assistant Secretary for Liaison, UN Command Military Armistice Commission, Seoul, 31 July 2006.

Lee, Shin-wha, and Joon Sung Park, "Peacekeeping contribution profile: South Korea," *Providing for Peacekeeping*, updated June 2014, http://www.providingforpeacekeeping.org/2015/03/30/peacekeeping-contributor-profile-south-korea/. Accessed 15 July 2015.

Levin, Norman D., and Yong-Sup Han. 2002. *Sunshine in Korea: The South Korean debate over policies toward North Korea*. Santa Monica: RAND.

Macintyre, Donald. Interview, International Crisis Group, Seoul, 3 July 2006.
MacTaggart, Lee. Interview, Economics Officer, U.S. Embassy, Seoul, 28 June 2006.
Major foreign holders of treasury securities. U.S. Treasury Department, http://www.treasury.gov/resource-center/data-chart-center/tic/Documents/mfh.txt. Accessed 10 January 2015.
Marshall, James S. South Koreans' guarded views of China, ed. Office of Research, The U.S. State Department, 8 August 2008.
Martin, Alexander. Abe re-elected Japan's Prime Minister. *The Wall Street Journal*, 24December2014,http://www.wsj.com/articles/abe-re-elected-japans-prime-minister-1419401541
Maxwell, David S. 1996. Catastrophic collapse of North Korea: Implications for the United States military. In *The DPRK briefing book: Policy area: Scenarios*. San Francisco: The Nautilus Institute.
Mazzetti, Mark, and Sang-hun Choe. North Korea's leader is seriously ill, U.S. Intelligence Officials say. *The New York Times*, 9 September 2008, A15.
McPherson, Kurt. Meeting, U.S. Air Attache, U.S. Embassy, Seoul, 23 June 2006.
McVadon, Eric A. 2001. China's goals and strategies for the Korean Peninsula. In *Planning for a peaceful Korea*, ed. Henry D. Sokolski, 215–226. Carlisle: Strategic Studies Institute, U.S. Army War College.
Memorandum of agreement between the government of the Republic of Korea and the government of the United States of America regarding the agreed recommendation for implementation of the agreement between the Republic of Korea and the United States of America on the relocation of the United States Forces from the Seoul metropolitan area (Yongsan relocation plan). Edited by U.S.-ROK Status of Forces Agreement Joint Committee Ad Hoc Subcommittee for the Yongsan Relocation Plan. Seoul: Governments of the United States and the Republic of Korea, 26 October 2004.
Mendelson, Sarah E., and John K. Glenn (eds.). 2002. *The power and limits of NGOs: A critical look at building democracy in Eastern Europe and Eurasia*. New York: Columbia University Press.
Merrill, John. Discussions, U.S. Department of State, 2001–2, Washington, DC.
Michell, Tony. Interview, President, Korea associates business consultancy, Seoul, 28 July 2006.
Military and security developments involving the Democratic People's Republic of Korea, Office of the Secretary of Defense annual report to Congress, 4 February 2014.
Military Expenditure 1988–2013. Stockholm International Peace Research Institute (SIPRI), www.sipri.org. Accessed 25 Dec 2014.
Mission of the ROK/US Combined Forces Command, 19 July 2008. United States Forces Korea, http://www.usfk.mil/usfk/cfc.aspx. Accessed 14 Dec 2009.

Mission Statement. 1998–2009. Radio free Asia, http://www.rfa.org/english/about/mission.html. Accessed 17 Dec 2009.

Mitchell, Derek. 2002–03. A blueprint for U.S. policy toward a unified Korea. *The Washington Quarterly* 26(1): 123–137.

Mitchell, Derek J. 2002. *A blueprint for U.S. policy toward a unified Korea*, CSIS working group report. Washington, DC: Center for Strategic and International Studies.

Mitchell, Derek. Meeting, Senior Fellow, International Security Program, Center for Security and International Studies (CSIS), Washington, DC, 28 September 2006.

Monoghan, Angela. China surpasses U.S. as the world's largest trading nation. *The Guardian*, 10 January 2014, http://www.theguardian.com/business/2014/jan/10/china-surpasses-us-world-largest-trading-nation

Moon, Jung-in. Interview, Republic of Korea Ministry of National Defense, Seoul, 20 July 2006.

Moon, Sang-gyun. Interview, Republic of Korea Ministry of National Defense, Seoul, 20 July 2006.

Moon, Sung Hwee. Public currency announcement broadcast. *DailyNK*, 1 December 2009, http://www.dailynk.com/english/read.php?cataId=nk01500&num=5722. Accessed 28 Dec 2009.

Morrison, Wayne M., and Marc Labonte. 2008. *China's holdings of U.S. securities: Implications for the U.S. economy*, CRS report to Congress. Washington, DC: Congressional Research Service.

Myers, B.R. Interview, North Korea specialist and professor, Seoul, 26 June 2006.

Myers, B.R. 2010. *The cleanest race*. New York: Melville House.

N. Korea backtracks as currency reform sparks riots. *Chosun Ilbo*, 15 December 2009.

N. Korea confirms execution of army chief. *The Chosun Ilbo*, 15 June 2015, http://english.chosun.com/site/data/html_dir/2015/06/15/2015061501311.html. Accessed 3 July 2015.

N. Korea in brutal crackdown on defectors. *Chosun Ilbo*, 1 September 2009.

N Korea makes World Heritage list. *BBC News*, 1 July 2004, http://news.bbc.co.uk/2/hi/asia-pacific/3856171.stm. Accessed 2 Oct 2009.

N. Korea names new defense chief. *Chosun Ilbo*, 16 June 2015, http://english.chosun.com/site/data/html_dir/2015/06/16/2015061601225.html. Accessed 6 July 2015.

Na, Jeong-ju. 3 million NK refugees expected in crisis: BOK. *The Korea Times*, 26 January 2007.

Nam Bookhan-ui Jooyo Geongje Jipyo Bigyo (Comparison of key economic indicators between South Korea and North Korea. Bank of Korea, http://www.bok.or.kr/broadcast.action?menuNaviId=2236. Accessed 6 Oct 2015.

National Accounts Main Aggregates Database. United Nations Statistics Division, September 2008.

National Defense Program Guidelines for FY 2014 and Beyond, Japan Ministry of National Defense, 17 December 2013.
National Security Strategy (of Japan), Japan Cabinet Secretariat, 17 December 2013.
Noland, Marcus. 2000. *Avoiding the apocalypse*. Washington, DC: Institute for International Economics.
Noland, Marcus. 2005. North Korea in transition. *The Korean Journal of Defense Analysis* XVII(1): 7–32.
Noland, Marcus. Interview, Senior Fellow, International Institute of Economics, Washington, DC, 27 September 2006.
North Korea claims nuclear test. *BBC News*, 9 October 2006.
North Korea in the 21st century – At the crossroads of nuclear armament or open reform. *North Korea A to Z*, Korea Broadcasting Service, http://world.kbs.co.kr/english/event/nkorea_nuclear/general_02e.htm. Accessed 15 Nov 2009.
North Korea contingency planning and U.S.-ROK cooperation. 2009. *A project of the Asia Foundation*. Seoul: Center for U.S.-Korea Policy.
North Korea destroy nuclear plant – Cooling tower. *CNN* footage, 27 June 2008.
North Korea hunger. In *AlertNet*, Thomson Reuters Foundation, 7 October 2008.
North Korea spends about a third of income on military: group, *Reuters Canada*, 18 January 2011, http://ca.reuters.com/article/topNews/idCATRE70H1BW20110118. Accessed 5 July 2015.
North Korea statistics: Export import by countries, (Jooyo Gookbyeol Soochool Ib Ak), *Korean Statistical Information Service*, http://kosis.kr/bukhan/statisticsList/statisticsList_01List.jsp#SubCont. Accessed 7 Dec 2014.
North Korea threatens 'sea of fire' if attacked. *BBC News*, 22 January 1999.
North Korean defectors emerge from periphery. *The Korea Herald*, 18 April 2012, http://www.koreaherald.com/view.php?ud=20120418000968
Nuland, Victoria. U.S.-DPRK bilateral discussions. U.S. Department of State, 29 February 2012, http://www.state.gov/r/pa/prs/ps/2012/02/184869.htm
Nunn-Lugar reforms included in defense budget bill. *Global Security Newswire*, 16 October 2009. Nuclear Threat Initiative, http://gsn.nti.org/gsn/nw_20091016_8437.php. Accessed 14 Dec 2009.
O Tara. 2011. The integration of North Korean defectors in South Korea: Problems and prospects. *International Journal of Korean Studies* XV(2): 151–169.
O Tara. 2013. Human rights policies toward North Korea. *Korea Review* 3(1): 3–6.
O'Hanlon, Michael. 2009. Dealing with the collapse of a nuclear-armed state: The cases of North Korea and Pakistan. In *The Princeton project on national security papers*. Princeton: Woodrow Wilson School of Public and International Affairs, Princeton University.

Obama, Barack, and Park Geun-hye. Joint declaration in commemoration of the 60th anniversary of the alliance between the Republic of Korea and the United States of America. *The White House*, 7 May 2013.

Obama has misgivings about Korea-U.S. FTA. *Chosun Ilbo*, 15 February 2008.

Obama signs defense policy bill. *Washington Times*, 28 October 2009, http://www.washingtontimes.com/news/2009/oct/28/obama-signs-defense-policy-bill/?page=all

Oberdorfer, Don. Interview, Chairman, U.S.-Korea Institute, School of Advanced International Studies, Johns Hopkins University, Washington, DC, 21 September 2006.

Oberdorfer, Don. 2001. *The two Koreas: A contemporary history*. Indianapolis: Basic Books.

Office of Commander. *USFK Command and Staff*, United States Forces Korea, http://www.usfk.mil/usfk/officeofthecdr.aspx. Accessed 28 Dec 2009.

Official documents confirm Kim Jong Un as next ruler of North Korea. *The Mainichi Daily News*, 8 September 2009.

Oh, Choong-seok. Interview, Office of South–North Dialogue, Ministry of Unification, Seoul, 10 July 2006.

Oh, Kongdan. Meeting, Research Staff Member, Institute of Defense Analyses, Washington, DC, 28 September 2006.

Oh, Kongdan. 2007. North Korea: The nadir of freedom. In *Living without freedom: A history institute for teachers*. Philadelphia: Foreign Policy Research Institute.

Oh, Kongdan, and Ralph C. Hassig. 2000. *North Korea: Through the looking glass*. Washington, DC: Brookings Institution Press.

Oh, Kongdan, and Ralph C. Hassig (eds.). 2002. *Korea briefing 2000–2001: First steps toward reconciliation and reunification, Korea briefing*. Armonk: M.E. Sharpe; The Asia Society.

Oh, Seok-min. S. Korea, U.S., Japan to sign info-sharing pact on N.K. nukes. *Yonhap News*, 26 December 2014, http://english.yonhapnews.co.kr/national/2014/12/26/77/0301000000AEN20141226002952315F.html

Opinion Analysis: Inter-Korean Summit: Roh and Kim playing to a largely skeptical South Korean Public, ed. Office of Research, U.S. State Department, 2007.

Opinion Analysis: ROK On-Line Panel Welcomes a "Changing" America, ed. Office of Research, U.S. State Department, 2008.

Opinion Analysis: South Koreans react with concern to DPRK, ed. Office of Research, U.S. State Department, 2009.

Over 2,800 N. Korean defectors come to South in 2008. *Yonhap News Agency*, 27 September 2009.

Over 40% of N. Korean brass replaced by purges. *The Chosun Ilbo*, 15 July 2015, http://english.chosun.com/site/data/html_dir/2015/07/15/2015071500951.html

Park, Hyeong Jung. 2007a. *Looking back and looking forward: North Korea, Northeast Asia and the ROK-U.S. Alliance.* Washington, DC: The Brookings Institutions.

Park, Hyeong Jung. 2007b. *Looking back and looking forward: North Korea, Northeast Asia and the ROK-U.S. alliance.* Washington, DC: The Brookings Institution.

Park, Sang-sub, and Jae-sung Jun (eds.). 2003. *Geundae Gukje Jilsuh-wa Hanbando (Recent International Order and the Korean Peninsula).* Seoul: Uelyoo Publications.

Park, Seung-je. Interview, Asia Strategy Institute, Seoul, 21 June 2006.

Park, Young-ho. Interview, Korea Institute for National Unification (KINU), Seoul, 27 June 2006.

Peace and prosperity: White paper on Korean unification 2005, ed. Republic of Korea Ministry of Unification, 2005.

Plumber, Brad. America's staggering defense budget in charts. *The Washington Post*, 7 January 2013, http://www.washingtonpost.com/blogs/wonkblog/wp/2013/01/07/everything-chuck-hagel-needs-to-know-about-the-defense-budget-in-charts/

Pollack, Jonathan. 2007. North Korea's nuclear weapons program to 2015. In *North Korea and Iran: Nuclear futures and regional responses*, NBR special report, no. 13, ed. Tim Cook. Seattle: The National Bureau of Asian Research.

Pollack, Jonathan D., and Young-Koo Cha. 1995. *A new alliance for the next century: The future of U.S.-Korean security cooperation.* Santa Monica: RAND.

Pollack, Jonathan D., and Chung-Min Lee. 1999. *Preparing for Korean unification: Scenarios & implications.* Santa Monica: RAND.

President Bush participates in joint press availability with President Lee Myung-Bak of the Republic of Korea. *White House*, 19 April 2008.

Pritchard, Charles "Jack". Interview, President, Korea Economic Institute, Washington, DC, 9 September 2006.

Rendler, Jack. 2001. The last worst place on Earth: Human rights in North Korea. In *Planning for a peaceful Korea*, ed. Henry D. Sokolski. Carlisle: Strategic Studies Institute, U.S. Army War College.

Report of the detailed findings of the Commission of Inquiry on Human Rights in the DPRK, the UN Human Rights Council, 7 February 2014.

Republic of Korea Ministry of Unification. 2001. Peace and cooperation: White paper on Korean unification 2001.

Republic of Korea Ministry of Unification. 2003. Promoting peace and cooperation: Five years of the Kim Dae-jung administration.

Republic of Korea Ministry of Unification. 2006. "North Korea facts and figures." Figures and graphs: Number of South Korean visitors to North Korea, number of North Korean visitors to South Korea, inter-Korean contacts, number of confirmation of fates, reunions, assistance to North Korea, Korean defectors, Seoul.

Revere, Evans. Interview, Principal Deputy Assistant Secretary and Acting Assistant Secretary of State for East Asian and Pacific Affairs, New York, 22 May 2006.

Rhee, Sang-Woo. 2014. *Bukhan Jeongchi Byeoncheon Shinjeongchejeui Jinhwa gwajeong (Evolution of North Korean theocracy)*. Seoul: Doseo Chulpan Oreum.

Rhem, Kathleen T. North Korean military 'very credible conventional force'. *American Forces Press Service*, 18 November 2003.

Rousseau, Jean Jacques. 1950. *The social contract and discourses*. Trans. G. D. H. Cole. New York: E.P. Dutton and Company.

Rumsfeld, Donald H. 2004. *Global posture: Testimony as prepared for delivery by Secretary of Defense Donald H. Rumsfeld, Senate Armed Service Committee*. Washington, DC: U.S. Department of Defense.

Ryoo, Moo Bong. 2001. The ROK Army's role when North Korea collapses without a war with the ROK. Fort Leavenworth: School of Advanced Military Studies, U.S. Army Command and General Staff College.

Ryu, Kihl-jae. Interview, Dean of Academic Affairs, Associate Professor of Political Science, University of North Korean Studies, Seoul, 22 June 2006.

S. Korea reviewing NK move over Kaesong workers' wages. *The Korea Herald*, 9 December 2014, http://www.koreaherald.com/view.php?ud=20141209000796

Satellite imagery of Korea at night, Image Caption ISS038-E-038300 (30 Jan. 2014). Image courtesy of the Earth Science and Remote Sensing Unit, NASA Johnson Space Center, http://eol.jsc.nasa.gov/SearchPhotos/photo.pl?mission=ISS038&roll=E&frame=38300. Accessed 11 Dec 2014.

Savings.org calculator, http://www.savings.org. Accessed 22 Sept 2015.

Schaefer, Peter F., et al. 2008. Post war nation building. In *Colloquium on stability operations and state building: Continuities and contingencies*, ed. Dewey A. Browder and Greg Kauffman. Carlisle: Strategic Studies Institute.

Schmidt, Helmut. 1993. *Chairman's report on the high-level expert group meeting: The lessons of the German unification process for Korea*. Paris: InterAction Council.

Schott, Jeffrey J. 2007. *The Korea-US free trade agreement: A summary assessment*, Policy brief. Washington, DC: Peterson Institute for International Economics.

Scobell, Andrew. 2008. *Projecting Pyongyang: The future of North Korea's Kim Jong Il regime*. Carlisle: Strategic Studies Institute.

Security Council, acting unanimously, condemns in strongest terms Democratic People's Republic of Korea nuclear test, toughens sanctions. United Nations Security Council Resolution 1874. New York: United Nations, 12 June 2009.

Security Council strongly condemns DPR Korea's satellite launch attempt. *UN News Centre*, 16 April 2012, http://www.un.org/apps/news/story.asp?NewsID=41784&Cr=Democratic&Cr1=Korea&Kw1=#.VG0JdPnF98Y. Accessed 5 Nov 2014.

Seo, Ji-eun. Park, Putin sign rail project MOU. *Korea JoongAng Daily*, 14 November 2013, http://koreajoongangdaily.joins.com/news/article/article.aspx?aid=2980442

Seoul, Moscow agree on upgraded partnership, Gas pipeline involving N. Korea. *Yonhap News*, 2 October 2008.

Severe drought hits DPRK. *Korean Central News Agency of DPRK*, 16 June 2015, http://www.kcna.co.jp/index-e.htm

Shades of red: China's debate over North Korea. In *Asia Report No. 179*. Seoul: International Crisis Group, 2 November 2009.

Shearf, Daniel. North Korea's rare earths could be game changer. *Voice of America*, 17 January 2014, http://www.voanews.com/content/north-korea-rare-earths-game-changer/1832018.html. Accessed 24 Jan 2015.

Shearf, Daniel. South Korea committee to prepare for reunification with North. *Voice of America*, 25 February 2014, http://www.voanews.com/content/south-korea-forming-committee-to-prepare-for-reunifcation-with-north-korea/1858571.html. Accessed 1 Nov 2014.

Shin, Eun Seo. 'Ungu 7 Inbang' Buk U Dong Cheuk Jinanhae Jasal (The suicide of U Dong Cheuk, 1 of '7 key figures surrounding the funeral car,' Last year). *TV Chosun*, 6 December 2013, http://news.chosun.com/site/data/html_dir/2013/12/06/2013120603492.html?Dep0=twitter&d=2013120603492. Accessed 2 July 2015.

Shin, Hyon-hee. Seoul to pull out of Gaesong Park. *The Korea Herald*, 10 February 2016, http://m.koreaherald.com/view.php?ud=20160210000364&ntn=0#jyk. Accesed 11 Feb 2016.

Shin, Young-sub. 1998. *Nambukhan Gyungje Tonghab-ui Sungyul Gwaje (The process of South Korea-North Korea economic union)*. Seoul: Joongang Media Books.

Shu, Jae-jean. 2002. North Korean defectors: Their adaptation and resettlement. *East Asian Review* 14(3): 67–86.

Sigal, Leon. Interview, Director, Northeast Asia Cooperative Security Project, Social Science Research Council, New York, 23 May 2006.

Singleton, L.J. North Korea specialist at U.S.-ROK Combined Forces Command, interview, 25 June 2015.

Sinuiju designated as H.K.-type special zone: First market economy experience in DPRK. *The People's Korea*, 28 September 2002.

SIPRI Military Expenditure Database, Stockholm International Peace Research Institute, http://www.sipri.org/research/armaments/milex/milex_database. Accessed 11 Oct 2014.

Slack, Megan. President Obama meets with President Park of South Korea. *The White House Blog*, 7 May 2013, http://www.whitehouse.gov/blog/2013/05/07/president-obama-meets-president-park-south-korea

Smith, Patricia J. (ed.). 1998. *After the wall: Eastern Germany since 1989*. Boulder: Westview Press.

Snyder, Scott. China-Korea relations: Establishing a "Strategic cooperative partnership". *Comparative Connections, Pacific Forum/CSIS* (July 2008).

Snyder, Scott. 2009. *Lee Myung-bak's foreign policy: A 250-day assessment*. Seoul: Korea Institute for Defense Analyses.

Snyder, Scott. North Korea currency reform: What happened and what will happen to its economy? Paper presented at *2010 Global Forum on North Korea Economy*, Korea Economic Daily and Hyundai Research Institute, Seoul, 31 March 2010, 4.

Snyder, Scott, and Joel Wit. 2007. *China views: Breaking the stalemate on the Korean Peninsula*, USIP special report, no. 183. Washington, DC: United States Institute of Peace.

South Korea's POSCO expands energy work. *United Press International*, 14 October 2009.

South Korea: Trade statistics, *GlobalEDGE*, 2013, http://globaledge.msu.edu/countries/south-korea/tradestat. Accessed 3 Dec 2014.

Stabilization and reconstruction: Actions are needed to develop a planning and coordination framework and establish the Civilian Reserve Corps. U.S. Government Accountability Office, November 2007.

Stares, Paul B., and Joel S. Wit. 2009. *Preparing for sudden change in North Korea*, Council special report, no. 42. New York: Council on Foreign Relations.

Steinberg, David I. 1985. *Foreign aid and the development of the Republic of Korea: The effectiveness of concessional assistance*. 93, Washington, DC: U.S. Agency for International Development.

Strategic Digest, United Nations Command/U.S.-ROK Combined Forces Command/U.S. Forces Korea, Spring 2014.

South Koreans grow wary of unification. *Washington Post*, 17 October 2011, http://www.washingtonpost.com/world/south-korean-youth-grow-wary-of-unification/2011/10/14/gIQA3ujmqL_story.html. Accessed 28 Oct 2014.

Sudogwon Ingu Jibjoong Hyunhwang (Current population of metropolitan capital area). Narajipyo, 2009.

Suh, Jae Jean. 2007. Bookhan-ui Geubbyeon Sahtae-shi Sahwe Moonhwa Boomoon-ui Dae-eung-chaek (Responses to socio-cultural aspects during North Korean contingency). In *Bookhan-ui Geubbyeon Sahtae-wa Uri-ui Dae-eung (Contingency plan for North Korea's crisis)*, ed. Gwan-yong Park, 21st Century National Development Institute. Paju: Hanwool.

Suh, Jae Jean. The Lee Myung-bak Government's North Korea policy: A Study on its historical and theoretical foundation. *Korea Institute for National Unification*, May 2009.

Sung Hwee Moon. Public currency announcement broadcast. *DailyNK*, 1 December 2009, http://wwwldailynk.com/english/read.php?cataId=nk01500&num=5722. Accessed 1 Nov 2014.

Sutter, Robert. PacNet #38 "Xi Jinping's foreign policy: image versus reality – Some adjustment required. *Pacific Forum CSIS*, 7 July 2015
Sweeny, Joe. Meeting. Assistant Army Attache, U.S. Embassy, Seoul, 23 July 2006.
Switzer, Warren. Interview, Strategy and Policy Division, U.S. Forces Korea, Seoul, 26 July 2006.
Szechenyi, Nicholas, Victor Cha, Bonny S. Glaser, Michael J. Green, and Christopher K. Johnson. China's air defense identification zone: Impact on regional security. *Center for Strategic and International Studies*, 26 November 2013, http://csis.org/publication/chinas-air-defense-identification-zone-impact-regional-security. Accessed 9 July 2015.
Takita, Kenji. 2006. Japan's response to the peace process on the Korean Peninsula. *The Korean Journal of Security Affairs* 11(1): 49.
Tara, O. 2007. Building a peace regime on the Korean Peninsula and in Northeast Asia. *Korea and World Affairs* 31(4): 417–433.
Tharp, Stephen. Interview, Public Affairs, U.S. Forces Korea, Seoul, 26 July 2006.
The issue of Takeshima. Japan Ministry of Foreign Affairs, http://www.mofa.go.jp/region/asia-paci/takeshima/index.html. Accessed 23 Aug 2009.
The Joint Communique: The 46th ROK-U.S. Security Consultative Meeting. Washington, DC: United States-Republic of Korea, 23 October 2013, 5.
The New Korea: U.S. Forces Korea Strategic Digest. Seoul: U.S. Forces Korea, June 2009.
The Nunn-Lugar Cooperative Threat Reduction Program: Lugar celebrates opening of largest Nunn-Lugar WMD destruction project. Office of U.S. Senator Richard G. Lugar, 2009.
The Nunn-Lugar scorecard: Destroying weapons and materials of mass destruction through cooperation. 2009. *Nunn-Lugar Program*, Office of the U.S. Senator Richard G. Lugar, http://lugar.senate.gov/nunnlugar/scorecard.html. Accessed 14 Dec 2009.
The road to a happy unification. *Korea Institute for National Unification*, (broschure), circa 2014, file: http://www.kinu.or.kr/eng/pub/pub_02_01.jsp?page=1&num=190&mode=view&field=&text=&order=&dir=&bid=DATA05&ses=, 10. Accessed 30 June 2015.
Tongil Baekseo 2005 (Unification White Paper 2005), ed. Tongilbu (Republic of Korea Ministry of Unification), 2005.
Tongil Baeksuh (Unification White Paper 1995). Tongilwon (Republic of Korea Office of Unification, predecessor to the Ministry of Unification), 1995.
Top trading partners – Surplus, deficit, total trade. In *Foreign Trade Statistics*, U.S. Census Bureau, U.S. Department of Commerce, 2009.
U.S. military bases will become a 'sea of fire' if war breaks out on the Korean Peninsula. *World Net Daily*, 5 February 2005.
U.S. military facilities: Korea. Globalsecurity.org, http://www.globalsecurity.org/military/facility/korea-updates-2.htm. Accessed 30 Aug 2009.

U.S. praises Korea, Japan for reaching breakthrough deal on wartime sexual slavery. *Korea Herald*, 29 December 2015, http://www.koreaherald.com/view.php?ud=20151229000236. Accessed 10 Feb 2016.
U.S. Senate Armed Services Committee. *Statement of general B. B. Bell, Commander, United Nations Command; Commander, Republic of Korea-United States Combined Forces Command; and Commander, United States Forces Korea before the Senate Armed Services Committee*, 11 March 2008.
US-China trade statistics and China's world trade statistics. The U.S.-China Business Council, http://www.uschina.org/statistics/tradetable.html. Accessed 10 Oct 2009).
US lawmakers pass 680-billion-dollar defense budget bill. *AFP*, 8 October 2009.
US offers action plan in case of NK collapse. *The Korea Times*, 29 October 2008.
United Nations Command-Rear Fact Sheet. United Nations Command, 18 September 2009.
Vershbow, Alexander. 2008. Congratulatory address. In *New era: New Korea-US alliance*. Seoul: East Asia Institute.
Vershbow, Alexander. Meeting, U.S. Ambassador to the Republic of Korea, Seoul, 26 July 2006.
Vollertsen, Norbert. 2001. *Michin Goseseo Ssuen Ilgi (Diary of a mad place)*. Seoul: Jogwang Chulpahn Insoe Jushik Hoesa.
Walter Sharp. OPCON transition in Korea. *Center for Strategic and International Studies*, 2 December 2013.
"Weapons of mass destruction: KN-02 short range ballistic missile" in global security, http://www.globalsecurity.org/wmd/world/dprk/kn-2.htm. Accessed 31 May 2011
'Widespread anger' as N. Korea limits currency exchange. *Chosun Ilbo*, 3 December 2009.
Willoughby, Robert. 2003. *North Korea: The Bradt travel guide*. Bucks: Bradt Travel Guide.
Wolf Jr., Charles, and Kamil Akramov. 2005. *North Korean paradoxes: Circumstances, costs, and consequences of Korean unification*. Santa Monica: RAND.
'Women power' gathers against N. Korean currency shock. *Chosun Ilbo*, 8 December 2009.
World development indicators: Size of the economy. *2014 World View*, World Bank, http://wdi.worldbank.org/table/1.1. Accessed 10 Nov 2014.
Yoon, Deok-ryol. Interview, Department of International Macroeconomis and Finance, Korea Institute for International Economic Policy, Seoul, 2 August 2006.
Yoon, Young-gwan, and Young-ja Bae (eds.). 2003. *Segehwa-wa Hanguk (Globalization and South Korea)*. Seoul: Uelyoo Publications.

Youn, Miryang. Interview, Woodrow Wilson International Center for Scholars, Washington, DC, 20 September 2006.
YouTube, http://www.youtube.com/watch?v=VxYeny9qwvU. Accessed 20 Oct 2009.
Yun, Joseph. Interview, Minister-Counselor, Political Affairs and Acting Deputy Chief of Mission, U.S. Embassy, Seoul, 28 June 2006.
Zhijian, Zhang. Chinese ambassador to Finland. China's economic and commercial relations with the neighbouring Northeast Asian countries. People's Republic of China Embassy in Finland, 14 May 2004, http://www.fmprc.gov.cn/ce/cefi/eng/zfgx/dsjh/t106157.htm. Accessed 28 Sept 2009.

Index

A
abduction, 62
aid, 2, 5, 10, 11, 25, 27–9, 41n24, 49n6, 49n8, 49n11, 52, 60, 65, 80–2, 113, 121n66, 124, 131, 133n1
air defense identification zone (ADIZ), 57, 73, 74, 86n19
airspace, 63
alliance
    Japan-U.S., 51
    Korea-U.S./ROK-U.S., 89n60, 89n71
    transformation, 53, 55, 69
    transition, 69
anarchy, 98, 129
annexation/annexing, 61
armistice, 70, 71, 79, 116
artillery, 12, 14, 57, 95
ASEAN Regional Forum (ARF), 68
Asian Development Bank, 83
assertive, 57, 60, 74, 75
assistance, 11, 14, 23–5, 27–9, 35, 52, 56, 60, 65, 67, 81, 82, 93, 95, 99, 102, 111, 113, 118n13, 121n65, 121n66, 125, 132
Association of Southeast Asian Nations (ASEAN), 68

B
Banco Delta Asia, 80
basic needs, 1, 6, 24–7, 83, 93, 100–2, 104, 123, 130
battlefield, 71
Berlin Wall, 1, 17, 102, 104
bilateral issues
    Korea-China, 72–5
    Korea-Japan, 75–7
    Korea-Russia, 64
    Korea-U.S., 68–72
biodiverse / biodiversity, 116
black market. *See* economy
border, 13, 14, 16, 26, 28, 30, 35, 38, 39, 43n60, 47, 52, 57–9, 64, 66, 67, 73, 81, 82, 96, 102–4, 123, 125, 127–9, 131
Bosworth, Stephen, 81, 92n112
Bundeswehr, 111
Byungjin, 4, 5, 6n6, 16, 29, 124

C

capital, 10, 18, 21n27, 61, 68, 75, 113, 121n64, 133
capitalist, 105, 107–9
Central and East Europe, 3
chaos, 11, 19, 38, 58, 71, 77, 79, 81, 93, 97, 129
Cheonan, 10, 13
China, 1, 2, 5, 6, 12–14, 16, 21n31, 25–8, 30, 35, 38, 39, 41n24, 45–65, 67, 68, 72–5, 77–84, 85n3, 85n4, 85n9, 86n16, 86n18–86n20, 86n22–86n25, 87n29, 88n57, 90n86, 94, 96, 99, 102, 103, 114, 116, 119n36, 123–30, 133
civilian control, 70
civil society, 47, 102, 109, 112
claim, 31, 61, 72–4, 76, 91n107, 105, 112
coalition, 94
coercion, 6n2, 6n4, 61
Cold War, 60, 64, 65, 68, 69, 113, 127
collapse
  indicators, 23–39, 125–7
  of North Korea, 5, 15, 78, 109, 117n, 125, 128, 135
  planning, 45, 46, 95
  preparing for, 93–117
  regime, 3, 5, 15, 16, 24, 35, 124, 125
  triggers, 23–39, 125–7
colonization/colonial, 61, 68, 76, 113, 127
Combined Forces Command (CFC). *See* U.S.-ROK Combined Forces Command
command
  chain of, 71
  structure, 71
  unity of, 70, 71
commander, 70, 71, 79, 89n62, 89n69, 101

Commonwealth, 8
communist bloc, 30
concentration camps. *See* prison camps
conflict, 9, 12–14, 16, 19, 33, 49, 56, 69, 90n77, 93, 116, 124
constitution/constitutional, 62, 93, 99
contact, 10, 31, 51, 53, 68
contingency, 2, 3, 23, 34, 39, 46, 67, 77, 78, 85n1, 94, 95, 99, 100, 117n7, 117n13, 119n38, 124. *See also* collapse
contingency/contingencies, 2, 3, 23, 34, 39, 46, 63, 67, 68, 77, 78, 85n1, 94, 95, 99, 100, 117n7, 117n8, 117n13, 119n38, 124
cooperation, 2, 6, 9–10, 12, 14, 17, 20n9, 20n12, 41n26, 41n27, 45, 47, 51, 53–4, 56, 59, 68–9, 76–84, 88n58, 94–6, 117n6, 117n7, 117n13, 128, 133, 134n5
Cooperative Threat Reduction (CTR), 96, 97, 118n19–118n21, 130
coordination, 2, 82, 83, 91n93, 92n115, 96, 128
Corridors, 10, 103
cost
  human, 60
  unification, 2, 7, 8, 17–19, 112–15
Crimea, 61
crisis, 18, 36, 38, 77, 103, 119n29, 119n38, 131
Crossing, 35, 38, 47, 103, 109, 123, 131
cult of personality, 3
culture, 9, 10, 47, 76, 84, 90n88, 98, 99, 108, 132
currency exchange, 107

D

dagger, 61
de-Bathify/de-Bathification, 105, 106, 131

declaration, 9, 14, 20n10, 57, 74, 80, 86n14, 89n61
defectors, 20n16, 21n29, 30, 35–6, 43n57, 43n59, 102, 102n49–102n51, 104, 108–11, 119n30, 119n33, 125–7, 132, 134n4
deforestation, 101, 115
demilitarized zone (DMZ), 10
demining, 103
demobilization/demobilize, 18, 83, 105, 107, 131
democracy, 15, 54, 59, 66, 68, 69, 71, 89n68, 110, 119n28, 128, 135
Democratic People's Republic of Korea (DPRK) / North Korea, 1, 20n8, 40n7, 49, 92n111, 136
demonstration effect, 30
de-Nazify/de-Nazification, 105, 106
denuclearization, 11, 58, 80, 129
Department of Defense, 49, 88n46, 96, 118n17
Department of Energy, 96
deter/deterrence, 12, 14, 19, 63
development, 2, 5, 6, 9, 13, 17, 28, 29, 34, 47, 49, 56–8, 61, 62, 66–9, 74, 75, 82–4, 93, 95, 105–7, 112–16, 118n13, 119n38, 121n66, 124, 128, 129, 131–3
Diaoyu, 57, 63. *See also* Senkaku
diplomatic/diplomacy, 51, 59, 60, 62, 64, 65, 72, 80, 128
disaster, 2, 69, 83, 93, 99, 103, 132
disorder, 6, 93, 95, 97–100, 117, 130
disputes, 62, 63, 84, 133
division, 3, 11, 22n40, 27, 61, 65, 93, 94, 108, 110, 113, 128, 132, 135, 136
Dokdo, 76, 90n88. *See also* Takeshima
Domestic, 4, 5, 18, 48, 62, 64, 81, 112, 296

E
East and Central Europe, 29
East China Sea, 57, 60, 63, 74
East Sea, 21n24, 76, 90n88. *See also* Sea of Japan
economic relations, 41n23, 47, 50–3, 67
economy
 black market, 1
 central plan / central planning, 1
 distribution, 1, 24
 dysfunctional, 1, 124
 failed, 15, 52, 123
 model, 51, 66
 open up, 1, 123
 reform, 1, 25, 26, 35, 51
eco-tourism, 116
education, 10, 11, 32, 34, 60, 67, 75, 90n86, 104–6, 109, 110, 114
Einigungsvertrag, 111
elites, 24, 31, 35, 39, 93, 98, 105, 106, 125, 126, 131
embargo, 81
endangered species, 116
energy, 25, 27, 28, 52, 56, 69, 80–4, 87n42, 96, 105, 106, 124, 126, 128, 131
environment, 9, 44n75, 55, 63, 65, 69, 77, 82, 83, 94, 106, 109, 111, 113, 116
escalation, 13, 81, 124
ethnic, 68, 73, 75, 132
exchanges, 7, 9–11, 16, 17, 29, 41n27, 52, 59, 60, 63, 67
export, 28, 50–2, 55, 61, 85n5, 85n6, 87n32

F
families, 10, 32, 66, 98, 104, 105, 109, 131
famine, 4, 24, 25, 36, 38, 39, 40n6, 40n8, 100, 125, 127, 133n1. *See also* great famine

federation, 8, 65
finance, 18, 27, 112, 127
floods, 4, 25, 37, 57, 95, 101, 115–16, 133
flora and fauna, 116, 133
fog and friction of war, 71
food
   aid, 5, 25, 81, 82
   shortages, 4, 16, 25, 27, 37–9, 115
foreign aid / assistance, 27, 121n66
foreign direct investment, 28, 67, 76, 113
Free Trade Agreement (FTA), 56, 67
   Korea-U.S. (KORUS), 56

G

Gaesong Industrial Complex (GIC), 10, 30, 31, 42n36, 53, 114, 121n70, 126
General Agreement on Tariffs and Trade (GATT), 50
geographic / geography, 60, 67, 75, 112
geopolitical landscape / geopolitics, 1, 2, 45–84
German/Germany, 17, 18, 48, 50, 55, 106, 107, 110, 111, 115, 119n39, 120n42, 120n55, 120n57
   East, 17, 38, 111, 120n57
   West, 17, 18, 38, 107, 111
Geumgang, 10, 11, 30, 31, 53, 60, 136
global posture, 69
Goguryeo, 73, 74
Gorbachev, 65
gray zones, 63
great famine, 24
Gross Domestic Product (GDP)/ Gross National Income (GNI), 13, 17, 18, 48
gulags. *See* prison camps

H

Hallyu, 30, 66, 128
Hanawon, 108, 111
hard currency, 25, 52, 60, 126
hard power, 72
health care, 101
hegemony, 58
Heilongjiang, 73
History, 18, 42n43, 43n62, 45, 47, 61, 62, 73–6, 90n87, 99, 108, 110, 113, 120n57, 127
Hong Kong, 51, 52
hostile / hostilities, 10, 32, 53, 61, 64, 77
humanitarian, 11, 16, 25, 29, 56, 62, 80, 83, 95
human rights, 3, 6n2, 33, 40n13, 42n42, 42n45, 56, 69, 100, 104, 105, 119n35, 131

I

identity, 60, 73, 76, 136
Ieodo, 57. *See also* Suyan Jiao
Import, 28, 51, 52, 85n5, 85n6, 87n32, 114
independence, 24, 59, 66, 70, 75
indicators. *See* collapse
inflation, 18, 26, 104, 121n63
influence, 31, 49, 54, 56–9, 63–5, 67, 75, 77, 82, 113, 114, 127, 128
information
   control of, 30, 126
   external, 1, 106
   flow, 98, 125
   monopoly of, 3
infrastructure
   communication, 105
   internet, 106
   transportation, 106, 131
Inminban, 98
inspection/inspectors, 80, 81

instability, 1, 2, 4, 14, 27, 36, 45, 53, 57, 62, 72, 77, 78, 113, 124, 125
Interagency Management System (IMS), 83, 84
interdependence, 53, 77
internally displaced persons, 103
International Atomic Energy Agency (IAEA), 80, 81
International Financial Institution (IFI), 67, 113
International Monetary Fund (IMF), 18, 120n46
Interoperability, 70, 72
investment / investors, 8, 25, 26, 28, 29, 41n28–41n30, 45, 46, 49, 50, 65, 67, 68, 75–7, 82, 83, 106–8, 113, 114, 128, 131, 132
Iraq, 83, 94, 106
Irredentism, 73, 75
Island, 10, 11, 13, 57, 60, 61, 63, 65, 76, 86n20

J

Jackpot, 46, 85n2
Jang Song-taek, 34, 36, 126
Japan, 1, 2, 5, 6, 12, 21n24, 45, 47–64, 67, 68, 74–7, 79, 83, 84, 85n9, 87n34, 88n49, 88n50, 88n58, 90n89–90n91, 94, 96, 103, 106, 113, 115, 116, 127–9, 132, 133
JCS. *See* Joint Chiefs of Staff
Jilin, 73, 103
Joint Chiefs of Staff (JCS), 70
Juche, 4, 5, 16, 123, 124

K

Kasong Industrial Complex. *See* Gaesong Industrial Complex
Kazakhstan, 94, 97

Khasan, 66
Kim Dae-jung, 9, 20n12, 29, 41n26, 88n57
Kim Il-sung, 3, 5, 9, 33, 37, 64, 65, 97, 98
Kim Jong-il, 3, 9, 10, 14–16, 25, 33, 34, 37, 38, 43n54, 98, 123, 126, 136
Kim Jong-un, 3, 5, 13, 24, 32–8, 43n60, 98, 100, 102, 123, 126, 136
Kingdom, 23, 73
Korea Command (KORCOM). *See* U.S. Korea Command
Korean People's Army (KPA), 36, 110
Korean War, 32, 54, 58, 60, 64, 65, 90n86, 104, 127
Korean Wave. *See* Hallyu
Korean Workers' Party (KWP), 3, 20n8, 98, 110
Kumgang. *See* Geumgang
Kyrgyzstan, 94

L

Land Partnership Program (LPP), 55
land reform, 104
leap day agreement, 81
Lee Myeong-bak, 2
legacy, 68, 73, 106
legitimacy, 2–5, 27, 29, 30, 37, 72, 81, 99, 100, 123, 125
Liaoning, 73, 103
loud speaker, 13, 99, 102

M

Macau, 80
Manchuria, 58, 61, 64, 73
marginalization / marginalize, 64, 94, 110, 111
maritime, 61, 63, 64, 66

Maritime Territories, 64
Market, 4, 6n5, 24–6, 38, 39, 40n15, 47, 68, 69, 104, 105, 107, 114, 115, 127, 128, 135
mass exodus. *See* migration
McArthur, 106
Medvedev, Dmitry, 66
migration
   mass, 1, 2, 6, 15, 17, 23, 36, 38, 93, 95, 97, 98, 104, 107, 129, 130
   refugees, 102, 103
   military, 4, 5, 10, 12–15, 18, 19, 21n25, 22n39, 24, 25, 29, 32, 34, 35, 37, 47, 49, 50, 55, 56, 58, 60, 62, 63, 65–70, 72–4, 76, 78, 79, 83, 87n46, 93–6, 98, 99, 103, 105, 107, 110–13, 117n1, 117n3, 117n13–15, 123, 124, 126, 128–32, 136
Military Committee Meeting, 78
military first policy, 136
military integration, 93, 95, 110–12, 132
Military Security Command (MSC), 98
Mines, 10, 13, 103
Ministry of National Defense, 70, 88n49
Ministry of People's Security (MPS), 98
Ministry of State Security (MSS), 37, 98
miscommunication, 57
Missile, 2, 5, 11–13, 21n23, 21n24, 25, 27–9, 53, 60–3, 65, 76, 80, 81, 97, 124
mistrust, 72
misunderstanding, 78, 79, 82, 83, 96, 124, 128, 129
monetary integration, 108120n46
Mongols, 61
monitor, 84, 98, 126
multinational, 93, 94, 99

N

National Defense Program Guideline, 63, 88n49, 88n51
Nationale Volksarmee, 111
national interest, 1, 2, 6, 47, 49, 53–68, 77, 84, 127–8
nationalism / nationalistic, 62, 63, 75, 76, 104
National People's Army (NVA), 111
National Security Strategy, 63, 88n50
natural gas, 65
negotiation, 51, 61, 79–81
9/1, 69. *See also* September 11
non-governmental organization (NGO), 35, 40n7, 101, 109, 133n2, 135
Nonproliferation Treaty, 80
normalize / normalization, 51, 60–2, 65, 67, 68, 88n57, 113, 128
North Atlantic Treaty Organization (NATO), 69
Northeast Asia, 5, 45, 46, 50, 51, 53, 54, 63, 64, 77, 85n4, 88n58, 89n71, 94, 114, 127, 128
Northeast project, 73, 75
North Korea, 1, 7, 23, 45, 93, 123
North Korean system
   autocratic / autocracy, 3
   theocratic / theocracy, 3, 6n1
   totalitarian /totalitarianism, 3
nuclear
   card, 81–2
   device, 81
   facility, 94
   material, 94
   program, 62, 80, 91n106
   scientist, 96, 97
   standoff, 81
   umbrella, 57
   underground, 81
   weapons control, 35
   weapons loss, 6

INDEX 165

Nunn-Lugar Act. *See* Cooperative Threat Reduction

O
Obama, Barack, 56
Obstacles, 68
Oil, 14, 28, 61, 65, 76
Olympics, 74
OPCON. *See* operational control
operational control (OPCON), 54, 69–72, 89n62
operations
 civil-military, 94
 military, 70, 72, 94
 multilateral, 71
 stability, 99
 support, 94
opposition, 27, 33, 36, 38–9, 72, 106, 125, 127

P
Park Chung-hee, 61, 115, 135
Park Geun-hye, 2, 11, 46, 59, 66, 69, 72, 74, 86n14, 87n30
parliament, 62
partnership, 55, 56, 59, 68, 88n55, 88n57
party, 3, 4, 15, 16, 20n8, 22n36, 24, 27, 32–5, 37, 41n31, 57, 59, 79–81, 91n105, 91n106, 91n108, 95, 98, 110, 126, 129
peace, 20n9, 20n12, 21n31, 41n26, 50, 53, 56, 58, 59, 67, 69, 70, 72, 87n43, 87n46, 88n58, 94, 116, 120n53, 122n82, 132
peacekeeping, 94, 99, 117n5
peacetime, 63
People's Armed Forces (PAF), 34, 37
People's Liberation Army (PLA), 99, 103

planning of collapse. *See* collapse
presence, 14, 31, 47, 69, 72, 80, 82, 84, 124
prison camps
 existence, 32, 100
 rescue operation, 100
production / productivity, 18, 24, 26, 42n36, 80, 94, 105, 114, 115, 133
proliferation, 57, 81, 95, 96, 129
prosperity/prosperous, 2, 5, 6, 30, 53, 60, 69, 77, 84, 94, 125, 128, 132, 133
provincial, 83, 99
provocation, 13, 29, 53, 57, 58, 60, 80
Public Distribution System (PDS), 4, 24, 26, 38
Putin, Vladmir, 66

R
radio, 4, 30, 39, 40n12, 42n34, 42n35, 99, 102
Railway
 Trans-Korea Railway (TKR), 66
 Trans-Siberian Railway (TSR), 66
Rajin, 66
raw material, 52, 114
reciprocity, 10, 11, 60
reconstruction, 45, 49, 67, 69, 83, 84, 92n115, 92n116, 94, 99, 113, 115
reforestation, 95, 115–16, 131, 133
reform. *See* economy
reform inability, 4
reform refusal, 53
refugees, 35, 57, 74, 82, 99, 102, 103, 119n29, 127, 133
regime, 1–5, 8–16, 19, 23–7, 29–33, 35–9, 40n1, 43n55, 51, 53, 59, 60, 78, 97, 98, 100, 102, 105, 106, 123–6, 129, 131

remittances, 68
reparation, 21n29, 23, 34, 61, 76, 77
Republic of Korea (ROK)/South Korea, 2
resource, 4, 33, 34, 53, 55, 61, 71, 76, 87n42, 98, 106, 107, 111, 112, 114, 115, 121n73, 124, 129, 132, 133
reunification, 5, 20n5, 21n22, 22n45, 22n46, 60, 62, 83, 88n52, 94, 96, 102, 112–14, 117n9, 120n42, 120n53, 121n61, 121n79, 135. *See also* unification/reunification
Rho Moo-hyun, 29, 59, 70, 71, 78, 88n57
Rho Tae-woo, 8, 65
rocket, 12, 13, 28, 80
Russia, 1, 2, 5, 6, 14, 25, 45–50, 53–5, 60–2, 64–7, 77, 78, 81, 82, 84, 90n86, 96, 103, 127–9, 133
Russo-Japanese War, 61, 64

S

satellite, 01, 28, 41n25, 80, 81, 100, 106
Schmidt, Helmut, 107, 120n45
sea lanes, 61
sea of fire, 95, 118n15
Sea of Japan, 63, 76
security, 3, 5, 6n7, 21n24, 21n26, 28, 32, 33, 37, 39, 41n25, 43n54, 44n72, 49, 51, 55–63, 67–72, 78, 79, 81, 82, 84, 86n19, 86n24, 87n43, 88n50, 88n58, 89n70, 92n111, 94, 95, 98, 99, 104, 117n11, 127–9, 133
security guarantee, 5, 60
Senkaku, 57, 60, 63. *See also* Diaoyu
Seoul, 8, 10, 12, 14, 19n4, 20n7, 20n11, 20n14, 21n26, 29, 40n7, 41n19, 41n28, 43n54, 46, 51, 53, 59, 61, 63–6, 68–70, 73, 74, 76–8, 85n7, 85n12, 86n28, 88n55, 91n104, 96, 117n7, 125, 128, 129
September 11, 69
Seven Phases of Collapse, 24
Singapore, 51
Six-Party Talks, 57, 79–81, 91n105, 95, 129
social integration, 93–5, 108, 110, 132
soft power, 66, 67, 128
songbun
 class system, 31–6
 core, 33, 35
 family background, 3
 hostile, 32
 loyalty, 3, 31, 33
 wavering, 32
songun, 4, 5, 16, 25, 29, 124, 136. *See also* military first policy
Sonyeondan, 98
South China Sea, 57, 74, 86n20
South Korea, 1, 7, 25, 45, 93, 124
South Korean drama, 4, 126
sovereignty, 49, 71, 75, 128
Soviet Union, 3, 5, 12, 15, 25, 29, 35, 56, 60, 64, 65, 97, 127, 128
space, 56, 63, 86n17, 101
Special Operations Forces (SOF), 82, 96
Spratley Islands, 57
stability, 2, 6, 13, 14, 28, 36, 47, 49, 52–4, 57–9, 62, 67, 72, 82–4, 92n114, 93–5, 99, 105, 113, 114, 119n39, 121n65, 124, 125, 131
stabilization, 23, 45, 49, 82–4, 92n115, 94, 108
staff, 36, 37, 70, 79, 117n1, 118n17
state-owned enterprises (SOEs), 85n3, 107

state security apparatus
 Military Security Command (MSC), 98
 Ministry of People's Security (MPS), 98
 Ministry of State Security (MSS), 37, 98
State Sponsors of Terrorism, 80
Status of Forces Agreement, 79, 85n12
strategic minerals, 114
strategic / strategy, 3, 5, 12, 49, 58, 59, 65, 68, 69, 76, 78, 86n19, 88n57, 88n58, 89n63, 91n93, 91n102, 94, 96, 114, 119n35, 119n39, 127, 128
succession, 1, 24, 33–5, 37, 39, 126, 127
Sunshine Policy, 5, 9, 10, 12, 25, 29, 45, 66, 125
survival, 3, 27, 29, 61, 123, 125
suspicion, 58
Suyan Jiao, 57. *See also* Ieodo

T
Taiwan, 52, 55, 57, 59, 60, 68, 75
Takeshima, 76, 90n89. *See also* Dokdo
technology, 28, 61, 66, 67, 73, 74, 81, 106, 133
tensions, 8, 9, 12, 63, 72
territorial, 49, 53, 60–4, 75, 76, 84, 128
terrorism, 56, 62, 69, 80, 92n116
threat, 21n26, 27, 51, 54, 63, 69, 72–4, 81, 96, 97, 118n19–22, 121n70, 129, 130
386 generation, 71, 89n68
Tibet, 74, 75
totalitarian, 3, 64
track II, 78

trade
 global, 54
 partners, 28, 63
 relations, 25, 52, 59
Trading with the Enemy Act, 80
Transition Assistance Program (TAP), 111, 132
tributary, 75, 127
triggers. *See* collapse
troops, 13, 14, 47, 58, 65, 75, 77, 82, 110, 111, 116

U
UN Command, 78, 79, 99
UN Command's Military Armistice Commission (UNCMAC), 79
Unemployment, 93, 95, 104, 105, 107–8, 131
UNESCO, 73, 74
UN High Commissioner for Refugees (UNHCR), 82
unification/reunification. *See also* unification scenarios
 absorption, 15–16
 collapse, 15–16
 confederation, 8–12
 cost, 17–19
 peaceful and gradual, 7
 war, 12–14
unification scenarios
 collapse, 15–16
 peaceful and gradual, 7
 war, 12–14
Unification Treaty. *See* Einigungsvertrag
Unified Command Plan, 71
UN Protectorate, 94
UN Security Council Resolution, 79, 81
U.S. Forces Korea (USFK), 49, 71, 89n69

U.S. Korea Command (KORCOM), 71
U.S.-ROK Combined Forces
  Command (CFC), 12
U.S. State Department's Office of the
  Coordinator for Reconstruction
  and Stabilization (S/CRS), 83
U.S. Treasury Department, 55, 80
U.S. Treasury Securities, 54, 55

V
Vershbow, Alexander, 69, 89n60
vicious circle of poverty, 54
volunteers, 60, 65, 90n86, 115

W
War, 6n7, 8, 10, 12–17, 19, 21n29,
  32, 35, 38, 45, 47, 49, 50, 54,
  58, 60, 61, 64–72, 74, 76,
  90n86, 93, 94, 99, 100, 104,
  106, 113, 115, 117n1, 118n15,
  118n26, 119n35, 119n39,
  119n40, 124, 127

warfighting command, 70–2
weapons of mass destruction (WMD),
  12, 21n24. *See also* nuclear
  weapons
White Paper, 20n9, 43n57, 60, 61,
  134n3
whole of government, 83, 84, 92n114
wildlife, 116
World Bank, 48, 83, 86n15, 113
world heritage, 73, 74, 90n78
World War II, 50, 61, 64, 74, 76, 94,
  106, 119n39

Y
Yanbian, 103
Yeonpyeongdo, 10
Yongsan Relocation Program (YRP),
  55

Z
Zaytun Division, 94

CPI Antony Rowe
Chippenham, UK
2016-12-27 13:28